S0-BWR-372

RENEWALS 458-4574

WITHDRAWN
UTSA LIBRARIES

The Sea and Medieval English Literature

Studies in Medieval Romance

ISSN 1479–9308

Series Editors
Corinne Saunders
Roger Dalrymple

This series aims to provide a forum for critical studies of the medieval romance, a genre which plays a crucial role in literary history, clearly reveals medieval secular concerns, and raises complex questions regarding social structures, human relationships, and the psyche. Its scope extends from the early middle ages into the Renaissance period, and although its main focus is on English literature, comparative studies are welcomed.

Proposals or queries should be sent in the first instance to one of the addresses given below; all submissions will receive prompt and informed consideration.

Dr Corinne Saunders, Department of English, University of Durham, Durham, DH1 3AY

Boydell & Brewer Limited, PO Box 9, Woodbridge, Suffolk, IP12 3DF

Volumes already published

The Sea and Medieval English Literature

SEBASTIAN I. SOBECKI

D. S. BREWER

© Sebastian I. Sobecki 2008

All Rights Reserved. Except as permitted under current legislation
no part of this work may be photocopied, stored in a retrieval system,
published, performed in public, adapted, broadcast,
transmitted, recorded or reproduced in any form or by any means,
without the prior permission of the copyright owner

The right of Sebastian I. Sobecki to be identified as
the author of this work has been asserted in accordance with
sections 77 and 78 of the Copyright, Designs and Patents Act 1988

First published 2008
D. S. Brewer, Cambridge

ISBN 978–1–84384–137–1

**Library
University of Texas
at San Antonio**

D. S. Brewer is an imprint of Boydell & Brewer Ltd
PO Box 9, Woodbridge, Suffolk IP12 3DF, UK
and of Boydell & Brewer Inc.
668 Mount Hope Ave, Rochester, NY 14604, USA
website: www.boydellandbrewer.com

A CIP catalogue record for this book is available
from the British Library

This publication is printed on acid-free paper

Printed in Great Britain by
Antony Rowe Ltd, Chippenham, Wiltshire

dla Alicji

Bèl dous companh, tan sui en ric sojorn
Qu'eu non vòlgra mais fos alba ni jorn.

Contents

Illustrations

Acknowledgements

My list of thanks must begin with Chris Page, who was there when the idea was hatched and who supervised it when it snowballed into a PhD thesis. I owe my gratitude to many scholars and friends for their encouragement and generous time: James Simpson, Helen Cooper, David Wallace, Ad Putter, Charles Moseley, Andrew Johnston, Alfred Hiatt, Richard Axton, Maik Goth, Jill Mann, Richard Beadle, Edda Frankot, Luuk Houwen, Margaret Bridges, Christopher Cannon, Nicholas Jacobs, Angel Pascual-Ramsay, David Jackson, Ian Robson, Otto Zwierlein, Craig Thorrold, Andrew Doe, Mark Pitter, Ilker Özhan, Dieter Schmudlach, Martin Warnke, Paul Halpern, Jonathan Dent, the manuscript's anonymous reader and my editor at Boydell & Brewer, Caroline Palmer, for turning a possibility into tangible reality.

This book grew out of a Cambridge dissertation, and I am very thankful to St John's College for having elected me to a generous Benefactors' Scholarship with the help of which the thesis had been written. My gratitude also extends to the Board of Graduate Studies for a Research Maintenance Grant, and to the University for electing me to a Jebb Scholarship and an Isaac Newton European Research Scholarship in the course of my graduate studies.

I would further like to thank the following: the British Library, the Bibliotheca Ambrosiana, the Landschaftsmuseum Obermain Kulmbach, the Stadtarchiv Kulmbach and the Universitätsbibliothek at Heidelberg for permission to reproduce some of their treasures; Kluwer Academic Publishers for allowing me to reuse my article 'From the *Désert Liquide* to the Sea of Romance: Benedeit's *Le Voyage de Saint Brandan* and the Irish *Immrama*' (*Neophilologus* 87:2 (2003), 193–207, with kind permission of Springer Science and Business Media), and Taylor & Francis (http://www.tandf.co.uk/journals) for permission to reprint my article 'Littorial Encounters: The Shore as Cultural Interface in *King Horn*' from *Al-Masaq: Islam and the Medieval Mediterranean* 18:1 (2006), 79–86.

But above all, I will remain indebted to my wife Alicja for her love, forbearance and sharp insight, which exposed many a feeble argument.

Abbreviations

CCCM   Corpus Christianorum, Continuatio Mediaevalis (Turnhout, 1966–)

CCSL   Corpus Christianorum Series Latina (Turnhout, 1947–)

CSEL   Corpus Scriptorum Ecclesiasticorum Latinorum (Vienna, 1866–)

ELN   *English Language Notes*

EETS   Early English Text Society (various locations, 1864–)

GCS   Die Griechischen Christlichen Schriftsteller der ersten drei Jahrhunderte (various locations, 1897–)

IMEV   *Index of Middle English Verse*, eds C. Brown and R. H. Robbins (New York, 1943)

JEGP   *Journal of English and Germanic Philology*

KJV   The Bible – King James Version (Authorised Version) (Cambridge, 1995)

LCB   Loeb Classical Library (Cambridge, MA, 1911–)

MED   *The Middle English Dictionary*, eds Hans Kurath and Sherman M. Kuhn, 19 vols (Ann Arbor, MI, 1956–2001)

MLN   *Modern Language Notes*

PL   *Patrologia Latina*, ed. J.-P. Migne, 221 vols (Paris, 1844–64)

PMLA   *Publications of the Modern Language Association of America*

OED   *Oxford English Dictionary* (second edn, Oxford, 1989)

Rot. Parl.   *Rotuli Parlamentorum, 1278–1503*, gen. ed. J. Strachey, 6 vols (London, 1767–83)

TEAMS   *The Consortium for the Teaching of the Middle Ages* (Kalamazoo, MI, 1990–)

All citations from the Bible refer to the Vulgate and all translations are taken from the Douay Rheims version. I have relied on the following editions: *Biblia Sacra iuxta vulgatam versionem*, ed. Robert Weber, rev. by Roger Gryson (fourth edn, Stuttgart, 1994; originally published 1969) and *The Holy Bible – Douay Rheims Version*, rev. by Richard Challoner (1749–52) (Rockford, IL, 1971).

This news made Xerxes furious. He ordered his men to give the Hellespont three hundred lashes and to sink a pair of shackles into the sea. I once heard that he also dispatched men to brand the Hellespont as well. Be that as it may, he did tell the men he had thrashing the sea to revile it in terms you would never hear from a Greek. 'Bitter water,' they said, 'this is your punishment for wronging your master when he did no wrong to you.'

> Herodotus (fifth century BC), *The Histories*, trans. Robin Waterfield
> (Oxford, 1998) Book 7, 35

But what are the birds of the sky to us, what to us are the stars of the heavens? For we are the wretched fish of the sea, we are the sands of the seashore, we are pounded by the waves of earthly life like the sands, we are swept away in the tides of worldly incertitude.

> *The Letter of Goswin of Mainz to His Student Walcher* (*c.* 1065),
> Chapter 15, translated in C. Stephen Jaeger, *The Envy of Angels:*
> *Cathedral Schools and Social Ideals in Medieval Europe,*
> *950–1200* (Philadelphia, 1994), p. 358

And as they came, the shypborde faste I hente,
And thoughte to lepe; and even with that I woke,
Caughte penne and ynke, and wroth this lytell boke.

> John Skelton (*c.* 1460–1529), *The Bowge of Courte*, lines 530–2

Introduction

Wherto schulde thou passe the see?
Hyt is bettur at home to bee.

Guy of Warwick (fifteenth century), lines 881–2

Englishness, Myth and Connectivity

Barely four weeks in office, on 4 June 1940, Winston Churchill went before the House of Commons to perform one of his most defining rhetorical feats. On the previous day the evacuation at Dunkirk had effectively been completed but the new Prime Minister did not deem this a cause for celebration: with France teetering on the brink of collapse and the prospect of Hitler's invasion of Britain seeming only a matter of time, Churchill chose to dispel any illusions Britons might be harbouring at this stage. As his speech unfolded, he reminded his audience that wars are not won by evacuations and, more importantly, that Britain's struggle for survival was imminent. Yet the closing words of his address remove themselves from the ineluctable reality of a war going badly and, instead, weave a vision of a mythical victory built on defiance, providence and the mobilisation of the inner sanctum of British identity, insularity:

> We shall defend our Island, whatever the cost may be. We shall fight on the beaches, we shall fight on the landing-grounds, we shall fight in the fields and in the streets, we shall fight in the hills; we shall never surrender; and even if, which I do not for a moment believe, this Island or a large part of it were subjugated and starving, then our Empire beyond the seas, armed and guarded by the British Fleet, would carry on the struggle, until, in God's good time, the New World, with all its power and might, steps forth to the rescue and liberation of the Old.[1]

Only nine days later the German army captured Paris, accelerating France's defeat. Churchill was once more forced to address the threat of an invasion, and in his speech of 17 June he again taps into Britain's insularity: 'We shall defend our Island home, and with the British Empire we shall fight on unconquerable until the curse of Hitler is lifted from the brows of mankind.'[2] As his published recollections of World War II indicate, Churchill

---

1   Winston Churchill, *The Second World War*, 6 vols (London, 1985; first published 1949), vol. 2, p. 104.
2   Churchill, *The Second World War*, vol. 2, p. 191.

1

frequently referred throughout this period to some pressing need or quality of 'our Island': 'the defence of our Island', 'our Island strength', 'our Island history', 'our Island fortunes', 'our Island people', and even the jingoistic 'our Island race'.[3] And when trying to convey what he perceived to be a people's preparedness to take on a terrifying enemy, he conjured up an almost metaphysical 'white glow, overpowering, sublime, which ran through our Island from end to end'.[4]

I have cited these passages from Churchill's own memoirs, *The Second World War*, counting on the support of his idiosyncratic orthography since Churchill, unlike many modern scholars, chooses to capitalise 'Island' (as well as 'Empire'). What Churchill invokes on all these occasions is a latent, residual understanding of British identity as insular, as cut off from its geo-political context by the sea, as an island in the ocean. This aspect of Brit-ishness is defensive in motivation, concentrating emotions on the image of a people perched on a frail raft surrounded on all sides by a hostile sea.[5] Consequently, Churchill does not omit the shore as the Island's natural and now also moral frontier when he talks of taking the fight against the invaders to the 'beaches' and to the 'landing-grounds'. 'Our Island' is not a symbol for the shrinking British Empire here but a synecdoche for Britishness: Britain may be more than the Island but the Island is culturally in and of Britain.

There are no such appeals to Britain's geo-political insularity in William Pitt the Younger's speeches during the Napoleonic invasion scares of 1798 and 1803. This can be partly explained by formal circumstances: parliamen-tary protocol at the time did not provide for a highly affective modality and speeches in the Commons had not yet acquired the public significance they would assume in the age of radiowaves and mass media. More importantly, perhaps, Napoleon's forces may not have seemed sufficiently overwhelming and menacing a threat to Britain at the time. For an appeal to 'our Island' it needed a much more fundamental threat, a threat that would imperil the very culture of the Island itself: newspaper columns and radio broadcasts had helped turn the danger of Hitler's invasion into something much more real, tangible and existential.

A twelfth- or thirteenth-century writer may have recognised Churchill's 'our Island' as an allegorical ship with 'londisse' people bound together by 'kynde', adrift in a hostile ocean and equipped with only the most necessary of victuals. Someone writing in sixteenth-century England, however, might not only be more likely to identify 'our Island' with Britain but also be more inclined to identify him- or herself as one of its English dwellers, who find

---

3   For the references, see Churchill, *The Second World War*, vol. 1, pp. 199 and 430; vol. 3, p. 539; and vol. 2, pp. 142, 204 and 248. In his *History of the English Speaking Peoples* Churchill uses this phrase to denote the inhabitants of Britain before the Norman Conquest (see Kathleen Wilson, *The Island Race: Englishness, Empire and Gender in the Eighteenth Century* (London and New York, 2003), p. 54.

4   Churchill, *The Second World War*, vol. 2, p. 88.

5   It is therefore hardly surprising that, with Britain's rising fortunes in the war, 'our Island' appears progressively less frequently during the course of the six volumes of Churchill's war memoirs.

themselves encircled by the sea. It is not that an inhabitant of sixteenth-century England might be more familiar with the claim of the Crown to rule the entire island – after all, more than one Welsh or Scottish war had been fought in the hope of realising Geoffrey of Monmouth's *totius insulae monarchia*. What proved much more effective in importing an awareness of insularity into Englishness was the realisation, arrived at sometime after the loss of the country's possessions on the Continent during the close of the Hundred Years War, that that which geographically and culturally *defines* Britain and a large part of England is above all the sea.

Perhaps the first to express this geo-political definition of Englishness as being 'of our Island' are two very different fifteenth-century texts: the political poem *The Libelle of Englyshe Polycye* (1436/7) and John Capgrave's *Liber de illustribus Henricis* (1453). Both works can be credited with introducing into a political and specifically English context the *intransmeabili undique circulo* [uncrossable ring of sea] of Gildas (*c.* 504–70) when they speak of England as being surrounded by the sea which forms a natural wall around its coasts.[6] This wall, the *Libelle of Englyshe Polycye* argues unremittingly, ought to be defended at all cost: 'Kepe than the see abought in speciall, / Whiche of England is the rounde wall' (lines 1,092–3).[7] The anonymous writer of this poem may have found himself putting forward an unfashionable yet visionary policy during the crisis triggered by Burgundy's forsaking of its alliance with England, but the transformation of Gildas's uncrossable ring around Britain into an English military structure proved relevant enough for John Capgrave to seize on seventeen years later. Capgrave's bric-a-brac chronicle of kings and emperors named 'Henry', written in the last year of the Hundred Years War, chides Henry VI for neglecting the *murus Angliae* and lambasts England's failure to keep its seas. Capgrave's use of Latin allows him to summon those historiographers who followed Gildas: 'It was said by the ancients that the sea is like England's wall; and, since the enemies are pressing at the gates, what do you think they will do with unexpected neighbours?'[8] The circumstance of a Latin text translating the idea of the sea as the wall of England from an earlier English text only serves to underline the origin of 'our Island' as a vernacular concept, a point reflected in the observation that of the three languages in use in England, only English was exclusive to the island.

A century later, Shakespeare could incorporate the idea into John of Gaunt's description of Britain as a privileged island fortress that has repelled the Armada of 1588:

---

6 The passages in question are discussed in detail on pp. 73–3 (Gildas talks of Britain, not England).
7 George Warner, ed., *The Libelle of Englyshe Polycye – A Poem on the Use of Sea Power, 1436* (Oxford, 1926).
8 My translation. For the Latin text and a discussion of this passage, see pp. 158–9.

> This fortress built by Nature for herself
> Against infection and the hand of war,
> This happy breed of men, this little world,
> This precious stone set in the silver sea
> Which serves it in the office of a wall
> Or as a moat defensive to a house.[9]

Before the character of John of Gaunt could speak of Britain (alias England) as 'this precious stone set in the silver sea', texts such as the *Libelle of Englyshe Polycye* and Capgrave's *Liber de illustribus Henricis* had to contribute to shedding the idea of land defined through law, that is, not on the basis of its natural geographical boundaries but in line with the forms of jurisdiction exercised by its kings and inhabitants.[10] In other words, these fifteenth-century texts use the sea to define their idea of England.

I would therefore like to argue that the literary history of the sea in English literature becomes a part of the vernacular discourse of Englishness. What is more, such a literary history can throw open fresh perspectives on the emergence of insularity in the context of 'being English'. My narrative will intersect at various nodes with the history of Englishness from the Norman Conquest to the close of pre-modernity, and it is one of my intentions to offer a network of close readings and contextualisations of these and other intersections to show how English writers employ the sea to generate literary meaning and negotiate two broad cultural fields, those of myth and connectivity. Between the Norman Conquest and the end of the Hundred Years War, English writers' use of the sea betrays their anxieties about their own forming identity. In their texts the sea oscillates between being rejected, feared, braved and allegorised until it is finally accepted and utilised as a determining constituent of Englishness. This process is neither linear nor incremental; it is jagged, at times erratic, replete with counter-readings, misreadings and abandoned possibilities, yet it is a discourse that cannot be divorced from the formation of England's budding self.

'The sea', writes Jonathan Raban, 'is one of the most "universal" symbols in literature; it is certainly the most protean. It changes in response to shifts of sensibility as dramatically as it does to shifts of wind and the phases of the moon.'[11] In many ways, Raban's characterisation of the sea is not open to question. For the fisherman it is life-giving and yet a dangerous foe to be

---

[9] William Shakespeare, *Richard II*, ed. Andrew Gurr, The New Cambridge Shakespeare (Cambridge, 1990), Act 2, Scene 1, lines 43–8. Norman Longmate cites this passage in his aptly named popular history *Defending the Island from Caesar to the Armada* (London, 1989; repr. 2001). Longmate opens and closes his book with the respective phrases 'in the beginning was the sea' and 'in the end, as in the beginning, what mattered was the sea' (pp. 3 and 499).

[10] In *The Grounds of English Literature* (Oxford, 2004), Christopher Cannon reads Laʒamon's *Brut* as outlining this older, legal definition of land ('The Law of the Land: Laʒamon's *Brut*', pp. 50–81).

[11] Jonathan Raban, ed., *Oxford Book of the Sea* (Oxford, 1992), p. 3.

reckoned with. For Tristan, the sea is a powerful token of his physical and social separation from Yseult but he also remembers it as the place in which their fatal love was sealed. It becomes Custance's prison, a pilgrimage territory for Brendan and the cruel, great leveller for the historiographers of naval battles.

What is the sea? To answer a question of this magnitude in a single sentence, a pre-modern reader only had to reach for Isidore of Seville's (*c.* 560–636) *Etymologies*, a book written to provide plain definitions and histories – for the two were one and the same – of everything worth knowing. As a scrupulous student of creation, Isidore offers a bafflingly uncomplicated answer to our question: 'A sea is a general gathering of waters.'[12] Isidore's definition is governed by the expectations of his readers who wanted to understand the world in which they were living. And, to make matters simple, he includes the ocean but excludes rivers and other inland waterways that are not gathered in the sea. So far, so good. Later on, however, Isidore complicates matters by introducing the abyss, and by the time he assures his readers that the ocean derives its name partly from the purple colour of the sky which it reflects, he is enlisting myth to embellish his definition of the sea.[13]

Another, seemingly more evasive answer is that the sea is not land. This reply serves to illustrate the sea's often perplexing existence in cultural memory. Its nature defies comprehension just as its substance slips through one's fingers. The sea's nature is – paradoxically – best captured in some of the most celebrated passages in occidental writing where the sea appears to be solid: a furious Xerxes has the sea whipped in punishment for its complicity with the Greeks; Christ walks over the sea to rescue his disciples; Hamlet realises the futility of taking up arms against a sea of troubles.

Until the unequivocal formulation of the notion of territorial waters in legal and political thought, literary and wider artistic images of the sea owed much to the sea's essential dissimilarity in *kind* to land: whereas land is immobile and stable, the sea is in constant movement. Land is permanent; it can be walked and built on (and rode upon). The sea, on the other hand, can merely be traversed by man or, for purposes of fishing, visited. No lasting habitation in it is possible. For Pliny the Elder (23/24–79), the constant struggle between land and sea expresses *Naturae dimicatio*, the fundamental conflict in nature.[14] It is the sea's elemental unsuitability as a direct habitat for human beings that led Plutarch (*c.* 46–120) to describe the Egyptians' perception of the sea as 'an element that is in no way related to us'.[15] He goes on to describe their view of the sea as 'alien to man's nature,

---

12 'Mare est aquarum generalis collectio', *Isidori Hispalensis episcopi etymologiarum sive originum*, ed. W. M. Lindsay (Oxford, 1911), Book 13, Chapter 14. For the translation, see *The Etymologies of Isidore of Seville*, ed. and trans. Stephen A. Barney, W. J. Lewis, J. A. Beach and Oliver Berghof (Cambridge, 2006), p. 277. Unless otherwise noted, all translations will be taken from this edition.

13 *Isidori Hispalensis episcopi*, Book 13, Chapter 14.

14 Mary Beagon, *Roman Nature: The Thought of Pliny the Elder* (Oxford, 1992), p. 159.

15 Plutarch, *Quaestiones convivales*, Book 8, question 8, quoted from *Moralia in Fifteen Volumes,*

deeply hostile and even despised'.[16] Being 'alien to man's nature', the sea is considered ungovernable in the classical and early Judaeo-Christian tradition, and, consequently, remained ungoverned (but, in the case of the Roman Mediterranean, not unpoliced) by man. It is present as a principal ingredient in a culture's macrospatial imagination, which, in turn, forms that inventive reservoir from which myths spring.

It is all too easy to entangle oneself in definitions of 'myth', tempting though it may be in this context. My use of this concept essentially combines the Greek meaning of *muthos* as 'speech', 'tale', 'narrative' with Lévi-Strauss's regard for a myth's structural properties as central to its purpose. A myth, therefore, is a fully translatable aetiological narrative. In this causal sense, myth embodies the narrative capacity for resolving contradictory notions or, in a Christian universe, explaining the actions of Providence. It is the sea's difference to land, regulated by tidal variation and constant inconstancy, that makes it so suitable as a myth of the inexplicable.

The overwhelming awe experienced when contemplating the sea's vastness and its protean nature finds articulation in Gregory of Nazianzus's (325–89) admiring words, perhaps as a rebuff to the philosophers and 'Greek' thinkers with whom early Christians had such a fraught relationship:

> And with respect to the Sea even if I did not marvel at its greatness, yet I should have marvelled at its gentleness, in that although loose it stands within its boundaries; and if not at its gentleness, yet surely at its greatness; but since I marvel at both, I will praise the Power that is in both. What collected it? What bounded it? How is it raised and lulled to rest, as though respecting its neighbour earth? How, moreover, does it receive all the rivers, and yet remain the same, through the very superabundance of its immensity, if that term be permissible? How is the boundary of it, though it be an element of such magnitude, only sand? Have your natural philosophers with their knowledge of useless details anything to tell us, those men I mean who are really endeavouring to measure the sea with a wineglass, and such mighty works by their own conceptions?[17]

Centuries later, Bernard of Clairvaux (1090–1153) would invoke the sea's vastness in a letter to Cardinal Guido di Castello to communicate what he perceived to be the alarming geographic spread of Abelard's teachings: 'His books cross the oceans, they leap over the Alps ... they spread through the provinces and the kingdoms, they are preached as famous works'.[18] Awe, fear

---

vol. 9, ed. and trans. Edwin L. Minar, Jr, W. C. Helmbold and F. H. Sandbach, LCB 425 (London and Cambridge, MA, 1961).

[16] Plutarch, *Quaestiones conviviales*, Book 8, question 8.

[17] Gregory of Nazianzus, *Orationes*, Oration 28, section 27 in *The Ante-Nicene Fathers: Translations of the Writings of the Fathers Down to AD 325*, ed. Alexander Roberts and James Donaldson, 10 vols (Edinburgh, 1868; reprint 1980), series 2, vol. 7). The most recent edition of Gregory's *orationes* is *Gregor von Nazianz: Orationes et theologicae, Theologische Reden*, ed. and trans. into German by Hermann Josef Sieben (Freiburg, 1996), p. 152.

[18] Quoted from C. Stephen Jaeger, *The Envy of Angels: Cathedral Schools and Social Ideals in Medieval Europe, 950–1200* (Philadelphia, 1994), p. 240.

and admiration for the sea are merely permutations of human responses to the sea's greatness and grandeur, simultaneously conveying its categorical alterity and the resulting incapability of human societies to control it, as well as the futility of all such efforts, enshrined in Xerxes' quixotic whipping of the sea.

For a long time the sea was therefore synonymous with myth. It features in foundation myths such as the Babylonian *Gilgamesh*, the Hebrew Genesis, or in the form of the primordial clash between Chronos and Ophion (later Okeanos) in the Greek myth of the beginning. The Babylonian dragon Tiamat forms the primeval body of water out of which earth is raised in the *Gilgamesh*, and, in its basic matter – water – the sea antedates God's creation of the six days in the Bible. In the same vein, Ophion, at the dawn of Greek history, is hurled into the sea with which he later becomes one. Other myths of creation, such as Ilmatar's ocean-birth of Wainamoinen in the *Kalevala* also begin with a deity being born by the sea. One may be tempted to read the apparent symbolism of these creation myths against the (admittedly anachronistic) modern scientific insight that prehistoric life had indeed begun in the sea, but it is altogether more likely that such myths of creation allowed the sea-born deity to clothe itself in some of the sea's mythopoeic attributes: its unpredictability, immeasurability, animistic force and elemental otherness. Such myths of transformation also embraced deaths by sea: as Boccaccio (*c.* 1313–75) reminds his readers in the *Genealogy of the Pagan Gods*, some writers say that Demophonte (Chaucer's and Gower's Demopho[u]n) threw herself into the sea and, through the gods' pity, was transformed into an almond tree.[19]

That the privilege of ocean-birth is not only restricted to gods is shown by the traditions that both Meroveus (eponymous founder of the Frankish royal dynasty) and Tristan, for instance, are said to have been born by sea-monsters.[20] Some have even claimed birth by sea retrospectively as a symbol of courtliness and dedication to *Frauendienst*, or courtly service in the name of love. As a true *Venusritter*, a knight of the Lady Venus, the poet Ulrich von Liechtenstein (*c.* 1200–75) emerges in the fourteenth-century *Manesse Codex* from the sea in imitation of his goddess's mythical birth near Cyprus (Figure 1). Ulrich is depicted in full tournament regalia, donning an effigy of Venus as decoration on his helmet, complete with the arrow of love and flames of passion. This miniature may very well serve as a memento of Ulrich's very literal act of romance self-fashioning, when the poet emerged from the sea near Venice, in front of courtiers, dressed as Venus (the choice of location may have served to live out a pun). As J. A. W. Bennett has shown,

---

19 See C. G. Child, 'Chaucer's *Legend of Good Women* and Boccaccio's *De Genealogia Deorum*', *MLN* 11:8 (1896), 238–45 (240).
20 Meroveus's mythical ocean-birth is implied by Fredegar (*The Fourth Book of the Chronicle of Fredegar*, ed. and trans. J. M. Wallace-Hadrill (London, 1960), Chapter 3) and Tristan says that 'ma mere fu une baleine, / En mer hantat cume sereine' (*La Folie Tristan d'Oxford*, ed. E. Hoepffner (Paris, 1963; third edn), lines 273–4).

Figure 1. Ulrich von Liechtenstein emerges from the sea (Heidelberg, Universitätsbibliothek, Co. Pal. germ. 848 (Codex Manesse), fol. 237r).

this association of Venus with the sea in a chivalric setting was not lost on Chaucer who presents a very maritime statue of Venus in the *Knight's Tale*:

> The statue of Venus, glorious for to se,
> Was naked, fletynge in the large see,
> And fro the navele doun al covered was
> With wawes grene, and brighte as any glas.[21]

With the sea nearby, however, danger is never far away: underneath Ulrich is the sea, peopled by monstrous creatures embroiled in strife to remind the reader of the nature of the sea.[22]

But the sea as a source of myth is not exhausted by foundation myths; it serves to stir the exploits of both protoplastic and heroic protagonists, justifying their claims to land.[23] At various points in time literary texts and other modes of expression have explored a range of physical manifestations of the sea's otherness, be it by means of the fantastically eccentric adventures of Brendan, or Matthew Paris's ominous descriptions of Britain as a hazardous and climatically exposed region, or in the form of Jonah's presumed place of refuge from God's inquisitive eye in the alliterative *Patience*.

The dialectical opposition of tangible substance and elusive myth is only an extension of the elemental antithesis between the two terms 'land' and 'sea', which, as 'earth' and 'water', is probably enshrined in most cultures. Being considered 'elements' – basic components of most animistic belief-systems – earth and water are considered opposites, and, as such, we like to think of them as incompatible with each other. Although it could be argued that the difference between human existence on dry land and at sea is a question of varying degrees of disparity and not so much quality of being, it would appear that maritime societies understand the world differently from farming communities. This cultural difference, for instance, is reflected in the frequency of maritime motifs in the lore of littoral peoples.[24] Chapter 2 will show how the Irish maritime tradition of the *peregrinatio pro amore Dei* dumbfounded landlubbing King Alfred, and we will struggle to identify a piece of biblical writing – writing generated by an agricultural society – that will allocate just as prominent a role to the sea as either the *Odyssey* or the various redactions of Brendan's voyage do.

In much the same way, this underlying dichotomy of land and sea can

---

21 *The Knight's Tale* in Larry D. Benson, gen. ed., *The Riverside Chaucer* (Boston, 1987), I, lines 1,955–8. See also J. A. W. Bennett, *Chaucer's Book of Fame: An Exposition of 'The House of Fame'* (Oxford, 1968), p. 15.

22 Martine Meuwese, 'Uit *de zee*', *Madoc* 13:4 (1999), 256–7.

23 It is important to distinguish the protoplastic or archetypal significance of Brutus or Meroveus, on whose mythical exploits entire civilisations, cultures or dynasties claim to have been erected, from mythical superheroes of Hercules' calibre.

24 Barry Cunliffe, *Facing the Ocean: The Atlantic and Its Peoples, 8,000 BC–AD 1500* (Oxford, 2001), *passim*, proves how similar the cultures of the different peoples dwelling along the shores of the Atlantic were. This observation is also made, albeit in passing, by Sonnfried Streicher, *Fabelwesen des Meeres* (Rostock, 1982), p. 7.

be discerned not only as lying between two cultures, but also as influencing distinctions within any given society. The otherness of those living off or 'on' the sea from those whose contacts with the sea are, at best, littoral, permeates even linguistic differences. Cicero (106–43 BC), perhaps one of the first observers of mariners' distinctive jargon, can already discern an idiosyncratic linguistic modality in seafarers:

> *inhibere* … is entirely nautical. That much to be sure I knew, but thought that when oarsmen were given the order *inhibere* they rested on their oars. That this is not so, I learned yesterday when a boat put in at my house. They don't rest on their oars, they row, but in a different way. … Now *inhibitio* of oarsmen involves motion and quite powerful motion too, rowing the boat astern.[25]

This antithesis of land and sea permeates our civilisation, ranging from the basic, elemental dichotomy to more sophisticated literary contexts. Barry Cunliffe, for example, sees in the belief, widespread in the Middle Ages and still prevalent in recent times, that a Christian priest aboard a ship 'will anger the gods of the ocean and bring bad luck' another permutation of the land/sea conflict where 'land' stands for 'Christian' and 'sea' for 'pagan'.[26] And it is remarkable how many pilgrim-badges have been recovered from the beds of watercourses in which they seem to have been thrown.

It is therefore a central objective of this book, integral to the concept of myth, to study the changing role of the sea as a mythopoeic agent. One such myth is the westward thrust of influence and culture, respectively referred to as *translatio imperii* and *translatio studii*. Ultimately indebted to the fourfold division of time in Paulus Orosius's (*c.* 380–420) *History against the Pagans*, this top-to-bottom reading of the world (for most pre-modern maps were oriented toward the east) was confirmed by generations of theologians and historiographers, including the influential Hugh of St Victor (1096–1141), who erected 'a theology of geo-history' on Orosius's model.[27] This theology of geo-history, I shall argue, bears implications for myths of the sea, a strain of which is preserved in historiographic descriptions which place the British Isles on the very frontier of salvation, the western Ocean. This liminal positioning of Britain and, therefore, of England, would contribute to narratives of Englishness that are inseparable from the sea. As the story of salvation moved from east to west, maps and histories became scripts for the growing

---

[25] Cicero, *Letters to Atticus*, ed. and trans. D. R. Shackleton Bailey, LCB 97 (London and Cambridge, MA, 1999), vol. 4, letter 351, p. 133. Juliusz Jundziłł, *Rzymianie a morze* (Bydgoszcz, 1991), lists a number of patristic and classical writers, amongst them John Chrysostom and Plutarch, portraying seafarers as 'different' from other people (p. 78, note 25).
[26] Cunliffe, *Facing the Ocean*, p. 9. Cunliffe conceives of land and sea 'as separate systems subject to their own very different supernatural powers' (p. 9).
[27] A phrase borrowed from Alessandro Scafi, *Mapping Paradise: A History of Heaven on Earth* (London, 2006), p. 126. Chapter 3 will discuss Britain's geographical position in relation to this westward movement.

territoriality of Christianised land – the territory of Christian kingdoms – and the sea's mythical potency was pushed to the western extremes of the world, where it continued its existence as the *oceanus dissociabilis*, separating the realm of the human from that of the divine.

The Anglo-Saxon Chronicle records two events for the year 891. The first hurries through an important military campaign on the Continent in just two sentences, whereas the second, politically less significant, receives somewhat more attention:

> 7 þrie Scottas comon to Ælfrede cyninge on anum bate butan ælcum gereþrum of Hibernia, þonon hi hi bestælon, forþon þe hi woldon for Godes lufan on elþiodignesse beon, hi ne rohton hwær. Se bat wæs gewohrt of þriddan healfre hyde, þe hi on foron, 7 hi namon mid him þæt hi hæfdun to seofon nihtum mete, 7 þa comon hie ymb .vii. niht to londe on Cornwalum 7 foron þa sona Ælfrede cyninge.

> [And three Irishmen came to King Alfred in a rudderless boat from Ireland, whence they had stolen away because they wished for the love of God to be on pilgrimage, they cared not where. The boat in which they set out was made of two and a half hides, and they had taken with them food for seven nights. And after one week they came to land in Cornwall, and they immediately made for King Alfred.][28]

Either 891 must have been a considerably uneventful year in the realm of the West Saxons or the *peregrinatio pro amore Dei* (sometimes also called *peregrinatio pro Christi amore*) of these three Irishmen must indeed have been remarkable news. The surprise arrival of three pilgrims, delivered by God from the perils of the sea, must have left King Alfred baffled.[29]

The cold, treacherous and tempestuous sea of northern Europe, which had twice prevented Julius Caesar's imperial war-machine from exporting Roman culture beyond the Continent, inspired an unprecedented enthusiasm for a kind of maritime and essentially monastic asceticism. The sudden arrival of the three Irishmen in ninth-century England, and the stir it created, are tokens of a clash between the pilgrims' perception of the sea and that of the Anglo-Saxons. The English were surprised by the initiative that the Irish pilgrims showed toward the sea. In a recent review article, Paolo Squatriti revives the dormant idea that, between the fifth and ninth centuries, the Irish Sea was a

---

[28] *The Anglo-Saxon Chronicle: A Collaborative Edition*, vol. 3, *MS A*, ed. Janet M. Bately (Cambridge, 1986), p. 54. I have standardised variant spellings of 'Æ' and 'æ'.

[29] It is worth contemplating to what extent Alfred comprehended the pilgrims' desire to be on a *peregrinatio pro amore Dei*, or whether he felt at all flattered by God's apparent decision to allow the Irishmen to reach his kingdom like Magi, especially as the chronicle points out that the three Irishmen were famous teachers.

'Celtic Mediterranean of the North'.[30] Squatriti suggests a number of parallels between the Irish Sea and the Mediterranean and observes that the Irish Sea 'is a manageable body of water through which communication was easy enough for "Celtic" economic and cultural unity to arise along its shores'.[31] Perhaps Squatriti is too optimistic in his assessment of the level of economic and cultural activity in the Irish Sea, but his theory shifts the focus away from fragmentation and toward a network-centric model:

> Beyond the transport of luxuries over long distances in the Irish Sea, many small-scale, short-range exchanges took place along its shores, across its waters, in its harbours, and quite far inland from its coast. Redistribution on such a scale was possible only thanks to the sea waters. The sea wove together a tapestry of interdependence, forming a true economic and cultural region.[32]

To delineate the concept of the 'Irish Sea World' further, Squatriti likens it to an Irish *mare nostrum*, characterised by cultural 'connectivity', a term borrowed from Peregrine Horden and Nicholas Purcell's masterful study *The Corrupting Sea: A Study of Mediterranean History*. Horden and Purcell employ the concept of connectivity to characterise the Mediterranean as a place of cultural and economic interchange.[33] The Mediterranean is not so much defined by the common inheritance of the various cultures inhabiting its shores as by the sea as a facilitator of multilateral exchange.

A natural reaction to such a paradigm-shifting proposition is a healthy dose of scepticism. Although the communities living on the shores of the Irish Sea may have shared a number of attributes with those living in the Mediterranean basin, there remain significant differences. One such difference, perhaps somewhat underestimated by Squatriti, is the rough nature of the Irish Sea. Gerald of Wales (1146–1223), for instance, calls the Irish Sea 'almost always tempestuous', which he attributes to 'opposing currents' (incidentally, a factor which makes cognitive navigation a good deal simpler as I hope to show below).[34] But if one considers that the various Celtic civilisations were scattered along the shores of the Irish Sea, less than a leap of faith separates this situation from the Aegean thalassocracy established by

---

[30] Paolo Squatriti, 'How the Irish Sea (May Have) Saved Irish Civilisation', *Comparative Studies in Society and History* 43:3 (2001), 615–30 (615). The phrase itself is a quotation from Peter Brown's *The Rise of Western Christendom* (Cambridge, MA, 1999).

[31] Squatriti, 'How the Irish Sea (May Have) Saved Irish Civilisation', 615.

[32] Squatriti, 'How the Irish Sea (May Have) Saved Irish Civilisation', 616.

[33] Peregrine Horden and Nicholas Purcell, *The Corrupting Sea: A Study of Mediterranean History* (Oxford, 2000), pp. 123–72. More recently, Purcell explored Mediterranean connectivity further in 'The Boundless Sea of Unlikeness? On Defining the Mediterranean', *Mediterranean Historical Review* 18:2 (2003), 9–29.

[34] *Giraldi Cambrensis Topographia Hibernica et Expugnatio Hibernica Opera*, ed. James F. Dimock, 8 vols, Rolls Series 21 (London, 1867), Distinction 2, Chapter 1. Timothy O'Neill lists a number of accounts of the difficult sailing conditions in *Merchants and Mariners in Medieval Ireland* (Dublin, 1987), pp. 116–18. I am grateful to Ad Putter for this reference.

the Greeks. All the necessary ingredients are present: navigability, economic exchange, cultural affinities. The only missing component is a naval force, but that does not strike me as a defining factor of a thalassocracy in the absence of a credible threat. Viking activity may have been precisely such a threat, but, as Benjamin Hudson has shown recently, the Vikings were instrumental in unifying the Irish Sea world as an economic zone and they succeeded in integrating this area with the trade network in the North Sea.[35]

A current trend among ethnographers studying the region of Oceania may prove helpful here as a suggestive analogy. It is a move away from under-estimating the degree of cultural exchange neighbouring island communi-ties appear to have had with each other. The isolationist view was largely based on the old, essentially ethnocentric (and even imperialist) notion that the islanders' navigational knowledge was insufficient for adequate maritime control of the waterways, a condition for a higher degree of communication, or connectivity. Anthropologists have examined navigational techniques in Polynesian as well as pre-modern European sailing communities. With regard to the latter, as early as 1985, the anthropologist Charles O. Frake argued for a high degree of precise and sophisticated intuitive navigational skills among pre-modern mariners.[36] As for the former, historians and (in partic-ular) historians of cartography admit that the spread of Polynesian culture in the Pacific (the so-called phenomenon of Pacific migration), spanning up to 4,000 miles, was achieved with remarkably accurate maps of island groups and the sea-lanes connecting them produced by Polynesian commu-nities. A well-known indigenous nineteenth-century map of the Marshall Islands employs a grid of sticks to visualise sea-routes and affixed shells to represent islands. The Marshall Islands' two main chains are over 100 miles apart and extend north–south for over 500 miles, yet these maps are, as Peter Whitfield observes, startlingly exact.[37] We must therefore permit the thought that cognitive seafaring abilities, even across such distances as those of the South Pacific, were more highly developed than has hitherto been surmised. Highly sophisticated celestial navigation, 'island looking' (a form of cabotage), an intimate knowledge of phenomena associated with a particular place in the ocean, mental maps and sea-lanes or surface currents, were techniques mastered by the Pacific voyagers. Perhaps something similar might be supposed for the essentially pre-cartographic cultures of the Irish seagoing monks? Although currents are comparatively weak in the Irish Sea,

---

[35] Benjamin Hudson, 'The Changing Economy of the Irish Sea Province', in *Britain and Ireland 900–1300: Insular Responses to Medieval European Change*, ed. Brendan Smith (Cambridge, 1999), pp. 39–66, passim. Recent research based on DNA and skeletal morphology tends to indicate that one third of Iceland's founding population came from Ireland, most likely as pris-oners and slaves imported from Dublin (D. M. L. Cooper, D. Guðbjartsson, B. Hallgrímsson, B.Ó Donnabháin, K. Stefánsson, and G. Bragi Walters, 'Composition of the Founding Population of Iceland: Biological Distance and Morphological Variation in Early Historic Atlantic Europe', *American Journal of Physical Anthropology* 124:3 (2003), 257–74).

[36] 'Cognitive Maps of Time and Tide Among Medieval Seafarers', *Man*, n.s. 20 (1985), 254–70.

[37] *The Charting of the Oceans*: *Ten Centuries of Maritime Maps* (London, 1996), p. 9.

they are nevertheless dependent on season and exact place.[38] In fact, the Irish Sea has the widest range of currents in the world, requiring mariners to draw on an intimate knowledge of shorelines as well as the sky.[39]

In an article on the Western Caroline Islands, 'Connected by the Sea: Towards a Regional History of the Western Caroline Islands', Paul D'Arcy identifies the beginning of a shift among ethnographers and anthropologists working in the South Pacific. D'Arcy reinforces the call for scholars to view the sea as a means of communication rather than as an isolating factor.[40] Perhaps without a direct awareness of similar developments in pre-modern European history, the cause of Pacific 'connectivity' had been taken up a few years earlier by Epeli Hau'ofa in his article 'Our Sea of Islands'. Hau'ofa speaks of the pre-colonial Pacific in terms very similar to those employed by Squatriti when characterising the 'Irish Sea World:' 'our sea of islands was a large world in which peoples and cultures moved and mingled, unhindered by boundaries of the kind erected much later by imperial powers'.[41]

One reason why the sea was viewed as an entity separating these Pacific island communities (Hau'ofa hints at this) was that researchers tended both to focus on the individual island cultures themselves and to view them through the prism of European colonialism. Connectivity therefore appeared to be dependent on navigational expertise, which, in turn, seemed dependent on the technological knowledge imported by the Europeans. To emancipate our perception of these islands, as well as of the Irish Sea before the arrival of Anglo-Norman colonialism, we have to sacrifice some degree of Western exceptionalism and grant that sophisticated navigational tools can be developed with means independent of occidental technology and science. As a result, we will realise that travel in a coracle across the Irish Sea is not as remarkable as it may have appeared to contemporaries dwelling within the boundaries of this Irish connectivity.

Further evidence for the high level of navigational sophistication attained by Pacific islanders is the *sawei* system, a complex network of sea-routes for the shipping of monetary tribute as well as other cultural and economic activities. The *sawei* exchange, pre-colonial in origin, is still in existence, spans some 900 nautical miles and consisted in the past of lengthy visits from entire fleets of canoes regularly carrying precious cargo.[42] Often some of the artefacts transported in these canoes (not unlike the Irish curagh) made

---

[38] R. G. V. Boelens and R. R. Dickson, *The Status of the Current Knowledge of the Anthropogenic Influences in the Irish Sea*, ICES Co-operative Research Report 155 (Copenhagen, 1986), passim.

[39] M. Baines, N. Connolly, O. Kiely, D. Lidgard, and M. McKibben, *Grey Seals: Status and Monitoring in the Irish and Celtic Seas* (Dublin, 2000), p. 2.

[40] 'Connected by the Sea: Towards a Regional History of the Western Caroline Islands', *The Journal of Pacific History* 36:2 (2001), 163–82 (164).

[41] 'Our Sea of Islands', *The Contemporary Pacific* 6:1 (1994), 153–4. Hau'ofa's approach has been taken by other academics, too: see, for example, Karen Nero, 'The End of Insularity', in *The Cambridge History of the Pacific Islanders*, ed. Donald Denoon (Cambridge, 1997), p. 441.

[42] D'Arcy, 'Connected by the Sea', pp. 165–71.

considerable demands on these boats. *Fei*, a form of stone money, could measure up to 3 feet (1 metre) across or more so that even the largest canoes were able to transport only one such item at any time.[43] Journeys were often long. A journey of 254 nautical miles required five days with good weather, and researchers have argued that some islands joined what amounted from their perspective to a loss-making venture (the *sawei* system) only to gain access to the superior navigational skills of those communities who were already active members of the *sawei*. Other scholars who have studied the *sawei* system have all commented on the advanced navigational skills of these islanders.[44]

This understanding, transferred (with all due caution) to the Irish Sea as a geographic area, which facilitated journeys perhaps more frequent and more extensive than anything our sense of maritime horizons before maps and compasses might lead us to expect, is highly significant for understanding the pilgrimage of the three Irishmen in the *Anglo-Saxon Chronicle*. One of the main cultural goods exported along the Irish sea-network was Insular Christianity. From the seventh century, all over the Continent and the British Isles, Irish 'settler-monks' built numerous religious houses and monasteries, often with royal or aristocratic support, which served to disseminate Irish ideas of monasticism, scripts and books. Some would even argue that this connectivity extended as far as the central European German/Slavic frontier.[45] The *peregrinatio pro amore Dei* is an integral part of this Irish Christian experience. It was so common, indeed, that even some Anglo-Saxons thought that the crossing of the sea to Ireland was an essential activity in the life of a pilgrim, or, indeed of a scholar, which led T. M. Charles-Edwards to state that 'it is clear that for Bede a man was not a *peregrinus* until he had left Britain for Ireland or the Continent'.[46]

With time, the connectivity of the Irish Sea experienced disruptions in the direction of cultural and economic exchange. Benjamin Hudson has argued that the Vikings' arrival integrated Ireland with the economic network of the North Sea; a marked northward shift.[47] At the same time, it appears to have weakened the cultural bonds among the various inhabitants of the

---

[43] D'Arcy, 'Connected by the Sea', pp. 170.

[44] William H. Alkire, 'Technical Knowledge and the Evolution of Political Systems in the Central and Western Caroline Islands of Micronesia', *Canadian Journal of Anthropology* 1 (1980), 229–37, and Reilly Ridgell, Manny Ikea, and Isaoshi Uruo, 'The Persistence of Central Carolinian Navigation', *ISLA: A Journal of Micronesian Studies* 2 (1994), 181–206.

[45] One etymological explanation for the name 'Brandenburg' is that it is derived from Brendan (Carl Selmer, 'The Origin of Brandenburg (Prussia), the St Brendan Legend and the Scoti of the Tenth Century', *Traditio* 7 (1949–51), 416–32).

[46] 'The Social Background to Irish *Peregrinatio*', *Celtica* 11 (1976), 43–59 (45). Quoted from Colin A. Ireland, 'Some Analogues of the OE *Seafarer* from Hiberno-Latin Sources', *Neuphilologische Mitteilungen* 92:1 (1991), 1–14 (3). One such Englishman may have been the seventh-century monk Bertuinus (see Sebastian Sobecki, 'Bertuinus von Malonne', *Biographisch-Bibliographisches Kirchenlexikon*, vol. 26 (Hamm, 2006), columns 141–3).

[47] Benjamin Hudson, 'The Changing Economy of the Irish Sea Province', *passim*.

British Isles. The emphasis that the arrival of the three Irishmen at Alfred's court receives suggests that, certainly by the ninth century, the once-shared Insular concept of the *peregrinatio pro amore Dei* appeared to be no longer current in England.[48] A Continental people like the Normans, whose maritime past had been preserved mainly in their military traditions and their longboats, must have listened with even greater disbelief to such extraordinary voyage accounts. The Normans, having long since abandoned the active maritime pursuits of their ancestors, had far less in common with the Irish understanding of *peregrinatio* than the Insular Anglo-Saxons, and gradually brought this eco-cultural system to a slow demise, as we shall see.[49]

During the time of Irish cultural hegemony in the British Isles, principally in the seventh and earlier eighth centuries, literature was an integral element of maritime connectivity. It was both a cultural good to be exchanged and a facilitator of such exchanges. The tradition of the Irish sea-voyage tales (*immrama*), to which the eighth-century Latin *Navigatio Sancti Brendani Abbatis* may belong, is a late literary witness to this Insular network of ideas and tales, but so is the *peregrinatio pro amore Dei* tradition which forced pilgrims out onto the open sea. The arrival of Anglo-Norman colonial culture redirected literary perceptions of the sea away from the Insular maritime commonwealth of images and themes, centering upon the Irish Sea, towards an increasingly sophisticated audience on either side of the English Channel. As a consequence of this development, the move eastward is very clear in Benedeit's Anglo-Norman *Voyage de Saint Brendan* where much of the sea's mythical force as a metaphor for Providence – hitherto preserved in the Insular sea-voyage – is romanticised and made illegible.

The second objective of this book is to explore how the loss of this Insular connectivity gradually transforms literary representations of the sea, allowing the unity of 'land' and 'sea' – viewed in terms of the monastic spirituality that predominates in so much Insular writing of the first millennium, and which is enshrined in the Irish *heremum in oceano*, the sea as a desert – to dissipate. Anglo-Norman colonial culture established a new hegemony of land. Although Susan Reynolds has demonstrated that the contractual relationships between nobles can no longer be called 'feudal' without considerable quali-

[48] The implications for the study of, for instance, *The Seafarer* are momentous. Dorothy Whitelock's reading of *The Seafarer* as an instance of the *peregrinatio pro amore Dei* ('The Interpretation of *The Seafarer*', in *Early Cultures of Northwest Europe*, ed. Cyril Fox and Bruce Dickins, H. M. Chadwick Memorial Studies (Cambridge, 1950), pp. 261–72) has been accepted as authoritative. But, as the extract from the *Anglo-Saxon Chronicle* shows, this reading of the poem clashes with the special emphasis on the arrival of the three Irishmen in the *Anglo-Saxon Chronicle*. I offer an alternative reading in 'The Interpretation of *The Seafarer*: A Re-examination of the Pilgrimage Theory', *Neophilologus* 91:4 (2007), forthcoming.

[49] To some extent, Anglo-Norman writers were also eager to adapt Insular motifs for their purposes. The Normans regularly attempted to 'insert' themselves into an English past in order to legitimise the cultural validity of their presence. For a detailed discussion, see Susan Ridyard, '*Condigna Veneratio*: Post-Conquest Attitudes to the Saints of the Anglo-Saxons', *Anglo-Norman Studies* 9, ed. R. Allen Brown (Woodbridge, 1987), pp. 180–206, and David Townsend, 'Anglo-Latin Hagiography and the Norman Transition', *Exemplaria* 3 (1991), 385–433.

fication,[50] these nevertheless involved the giving of land to Norman families and tended to ignore the sea as a component in such contracts. And there has been a plethora of books and studies on feudal and post-feudal contexts since the dawn of medieval studies that, taken together, amount to a narrative of land as a proxy for power, wealth and influence. In a society where furlongs of land constituted the barons' coveted currency, the sea, which could not raise armies or yield tax revenues, could not compete in political negotiations. This social marginalisation of the sea, in turn, created the terms that were needed for the literary role the sea would subsequently play as an emblem of unpredictability, Fortune and the fallen world. In the centuries following the Conquest and, in particular, towards the close of the Hundred Years War, writers would begin to associate Englishness with insularity in a general as well as Insularity in a particular sense, itself defined against the presence of the sea.

Omissions and Slippages: A Biography of the Sea

The lines from the Middle English *Guy of Warwick*, quoted at the beginning of this Introduction, do not suggest that we may have much to gain by exploring the presentation of the sea in English writing after the Conquest. In much the same way, Chaucer does not appear to have an interest in Aeneas' sea-travels:

> But of his aventures in the se
> Nis nat to purpos for to speke of here,
> For it acordeth nat to my matere.[51]

Indeed, there is a chapter-sized lacuna in Jonathan Raban's *Oxford Book of the Sea*. After covering fragments from *Beowulf* and *The Seafarer*, Raban teleports the reader to Spenser's *Faerie Queene*.[52] The *Oxford Book of the Sea* is an anthology, the product of negotiations between Raban's choices on the one hand and suggestions and 'favourites' gathered from a range of people on the other. It is not an academic work aimed at an expert audience, yet it still illustrates the way the sea is absent from our awareness of pre-modern literature and its horizons in every sense.

---

[50] Since the publication of Susan Reynolds's *Fiefs and Vassals: The Medieval Evidence Reinterpreted* (New York and Oxford, 1994) the term 'feudalism' has lost much of its currency. Reynolds argues that 'vassalage … is a term that no longer matches either the evidence we have available or the conceptual tools we need to use in analysing it' (p. 47). Whereas model feudalism may never have existed, some form of hierarchical bond between lords and their barons that involved the granting of land subject to conditions appears to have frequently been in place, at least on a contractual level. It is in this loose sense that I use the words 'feudal' and 'feudalism' throughout.

[51] *The Legend of Good Women*, lines 953–5, in Benson, *The Riverside Chaucer*.

[52] Raban, *Oxford Book of the Sea*, pp. 35–9.

Admittedly, the *Oxford Book of the Sea* is perhaps an eccentric example with which to begin, but the harvest of more obviously scholarly work is relatively disappointing. With the exception of one book chapter and less than a handful of articles (the 'youngest' contribution is almost fifty years old) there has been no comprehensive exploration of the sea in pre-modern English literature for very many years. Even the existing treatments hardly amount to more than preliminary surveys. By the time Raban compiled his selection, the sea had receded from the critical discourse to the margins of literary perception where it remains largely invisible.

Frederic W. Moorman laid a foundation with *The Interpretation of Nature in English Poetry from Beowulf to Shakespeare* in 1905.[53] Moorman's study, which has been particularly influential among *Beowulf*-scholars, offers a first descriptive glance at the sea in pre-modern literature. Bold as this attempt was, its contribution was to gather material rather than to interpret it. Eighteen years later, John Holland Rose created the specific subject of the sea in English literature with 'Chivalry and the Sea', although it is difficult to view this contribution, again, as very much more than an exploratory attempt to survey the field.[54] Rose focuses on naval battles and knightly conduct at sea. His sources, including Herodotus, Thucydides, Chaucer and Froissart, express the literary continuity of the ancient fear of the sea and, on the grounds of his unsurprising claim that 'in ancient times there is no trace of chivalry among the maritime peoples' (p. 181), he concludes that the sea 'was the abode of lawlessness, perfidy and violence, except where some powerful ruler like Minos of Crete enforced order by a powerful fleet'.[55] Rose reaches the conclusion that the laws of chivalry did not begin to apply to naval warfare until the sixteenth century, a conclusion that duly reveals the faintness of the Middle Ages in his work.[56]

Shortly afterwards, in 1926, Anne Treneer published the first chronological study of the sea in English literature.[57] Treneer's book dedicates an entire chapter to Middle English writing, somewhat pessimistically named 'Glimpses of the Sea in Middle English', spanning fifty-six pages, during which she briefly introduces a selection of (by now) well-known Middle

---

[53] F. W. Moorman, *The Interpretation of Nature in English Poetry from Beowulf to Shakespeare* (Strasbourg, 1905; repr. 1992), pp. 45–134.

[54] John Holland Rose, 'Chivalry and the Sea', in *The Indecisiveness of Modern War and Other Essays* (Port Washington, NY, 1968; originally published 1927; first read as a lecture on 25 April 1923), Chapter 11, pp. 180–95. I have taken the liberty of omitting Volume 4, *Prose and Poetry: Sir Thomas North to Michael Drayton*, of *The Cambridge History of English and American Literature*, ed. A. W. Ward, A. R. Waller, W. P. Trent, J. Erskine, S. P. Sherman and C. Van Doren (Cambridge, 1907–21). Chapter 4, 'The Literature of the Sea, Old and Middle English sea literature', offers a brief survey of relevant texts. However, it adds very little to our overview of critical treatments of the sea.

[55] Rose, 'Chivalry and the Sea', p. 181.

[56] Rose, 'Chivalry and the Sea', pp. 180 ff.

[57] Anne Treneer, *The Sea in English Literature – From Beowulf to Donne* (Liverpool, 1926). To this can be added Lena B. Morton's *The Influence of the Sea upon English Poetry* (New York, 1976), which mostly repeats Treneer's insights.

English texts including Laȝamon's *Brut, King Horn, Havelok the Dane, Sir Tristrem, Bevis of Hamtoun, Guy of Warwick, Richard Coeur de Lion*, Gower's *Confessio Amantis*, Chaucer's *The Man of Law's Tale, Cleanness, Patience*, John Trevisa's translation of the *Polychronicon*, Malory's *Morte Darthur, The Libelle of Englyshe Polycye*, the *Pilgrims' Sea-Voyage* as well as the plays *Noah and the Flood* and *The Building of the Ark*. Being the first such work, Treneer's book maintains the breadth of a survey and none of the texts is analysed save in passing. As a result, her conclusions did not persuade others to pursue the subject:

> Many of the sea-pictures in Middle English are conventional in phrasing. There is no attempt to realise in imaginative words various aspects of the sea, nor is there the preoccupation with its wild moods which we notice in Old English poetry.[58]

Treneer traces the relative brevity of the majority of Middle English sea descriptions to a lack of interest in the sea in the thirteenth, fourteenth and fifteenth centuries. To be fair, she never pretends to venture beyond noting the presence of the sea in the texts she selects. Her interest is not so much directed towards the literary presentation of the sea as to the frequency and quantity of references to the sea.

In the same year, Robert Ashton Kissack, Jr. published his essay 'The Sea in Anglo-Saxon and Middle English Poetry'.[59] Even though his treatment of the sea lacks the formidable scope of Treneer's survey, he juxtaposes a selection of pre-Conquest texts with Middle English passages (texts, I must add, that are largely covered by Treneer's range). He draws similar conclusions. Again, the same unfavourable comparison with pre-Conquest literature is made: 'to the Anglo-Saxons the sea was cold salt water; yet it was also the *seȝl-rad*. To Laȝamon it is cold water and very little else.'[60] Kissack also provides a sweeping (and surely questionable) explanation for the supposed lapse in the attention post-Conquest writers paid the sea:

> There has been an immense change since Anglo-Saxon times, a change, in fact, from a wintry to a spring climate, and the people who live in such a climate and who are affected only by calm, peaceful scenes naturally enough find a wild unrestrained thing like the sea somewhat uninteresting.[61]

As far as comprehensive or diachronic studies of the sea in medieval English literature are concerned, this completes the tally of significant work. Hence the first phase in the twentieth century's evaluation of the sea in pre-modern

---

[58] Treneer, *The Sea in English Literature*, p. 101.
[59] *Washington University Studies: Humanities Series* 13 (1926), 371–89.
[60] Kissack, 'The Sea in Anglo-Saxon and Middle English Poetry', p. 380.
[61] Kissack, 'The Sea in Anglo-Saxon and Middle English Poetry', p. 382.

English literature ends with a consensus: the scant attention afforded to the sea by post-Conquest writers, most of whom found the sea 'somewhat uninteresting', does not call the modern reader to look any closer. This largely one-dimensional 'archaeology of the sea' in critical literature has revealed little about the sea as a culturally charged and changing literary topos in pre-modern England.

Despite the failure of these broader approaches to invigorate the subject, there have been a number of focused studies that have allowed some space for inquiries into various maritime topoi, such as descriptions of storms, allegorical ships and rudderless boats. J. Reinhard has prepared the ground for much of this work. His 1941 article investigates in depth the topos of the rudderless boat and its legal connotations.[62] The same topos forms the core of a chapter in V. A. Kolve's *Chaucer and the Imagery of Narrative* where the development of the topos is linked (perhaps somewhat implausibly) to the allegory of the Church (*ecclesia*) as a ship.[63] Much more recently, in *The English Romance in Time: Transforming Motifs from Geoffrey of Monmouth to the Death of Shakespeare*, Helen Cooper has dedicated an entire chapter to the lasting tradition of rudderless boats in English romance (this will be discussed at greater length below).[64] Identifying three variants of the topos (setting adrift, voluntary exile or pilgrimage by sea, and transport by a self-propelled magical ship), Cooper documents how prominent sea-voyages and boats were in the English romance tradition. An article by Nicholas Jacobs, 'Alliterative Storms: A Topos in Middle English', published in 1972, has opened up the discussion of the vital storm descriptions in *Patience*, amongst other texts, besides highlighting the importance of this theme in medieval English literature.[65] Further afield, Peter Dronke's contribution to *Growth of Literature: The Sea and the God of the Sea* traces the development of the fear of the sea in early Insular literature with particular attention to Johannes Scotus Eriugena.[66] This completes a first survey of significant published work on the sea in English literature.[67]

Outside the narrow context of medieval English literature, there have been

[62] J. Reinhard, 'Setting Adrift in Medieval Law and Literature', *PMLA* 56 (1941), 33–68.
[63] V. A. Kolve, '*The Man of Law's Tale*: The Rudderless Ship and the Sea', in *Chaucer and the Imagery of Narrative* (London, 1984), Chapter 7, pp. 297–358.
[64] Helen Cooper, 'Providence and the Sea', in *The English Romance in Time: Transforming Motifs from Geoffrey of Monmouth to the Death of Shakespeare* (Oxford, 2004), Chapter 2, pp. 106–36. See also Carolyn Hares-Stryker, 'Adrift on the Seven Seas: the Medieval Topos of Exile at Sea', in *Florilegium* 12 (1993), 79–98.
[65] Nicholas Jacobs, 'Alliterative Storms: A Topos in Middle English', *Speculum* 47:4 (1972), 695–719.
[66] 'Part 1', in *Growth of Literature: The Sea and the God of the Sea*, Peter Dronke and Ursula Dronke, H. M. Chadwick Memorial Lectures 8 (Cambridge, 1997), pp. 1–26.
[67] To this must be added three unpublished theses: James Peter Conlan, 'Marvellous Passages: English Nautical Piety in the Middle Ages and the Renaissance' (unpublished PhD thesis, University of California Riverside, 1999), Insung Lee, 'The Tradition of Christian Sea-Symbolism in Medieval English Poetry and Milton' (unpublished PhD thesis, University of Oklahoma, 1996), and Robin M. Ward, 'An Elucidation of Certain Maritime Passages in English Alliterative Poetry of the Fourteenth Century' (unpublished MA thesis, University of Keele, 1991). All research on

a number of focused studies of the sea, as well as a range of historical and archaeological explorations of the ocean. The most noteworthy of those is perhaps Titus Heydenreich's study of literary attitudes towards seafaring, *Tadel und Lob der Seefahrt: Das Nachleben eines antiken Themas in der romanischen Literatur*, which remains the only attempt to analyse this subject in its appropriate temporal and spatial breadth despite its rather perfunctory choice of material.[68] Heydenreich's most important contribution to the subject lies in documenting how influential and long-lasting the Golden Age motif of the fear of the sea was.

Maritime historians and archaeologists continue to pay attention to the significance of the sea for medieval societies, to which the rich field of medieval ship archaeology testifies.[69] But the most significant recent treatments of the sea as a shaping cultural force in and beyond the medieval period have been offered by historians with an interest in archaeology, economics and cultural change. First and foremost among these contributions to our understanding of the sea is Horden and Purcell's already mentioned concept of 'connectivity', which serves as one of the conceptual markers in this book.[70]

The object of inquiry here is accordingly the 'sea' in two senses: geographically, as the ocean and the seas surrounding the British Isles; symbolically, as the range of metaphorical and allegorical uses of the sea in the literature of pre-modern England. My conceptual terms of reference are, as indicated above, the mythopoeic vigour of the sea, enshrined in the classical concept of the *oceanus dissociabilis*, and the literary afterlife of the cultural connectivity that had marked the British Isles before the Norman Conquest.

Similarly, the range of texts covered requires an explanation. A chapter on classical, biblical and patristic traditions will precede my discussion, given the continued use of this material by English writers. An altogether more intriguing set of problems is posed by the treatment of English and Insular writings composed before the Norman Conquest. I have decided to include Insular works where textual or topical continuity can be ascertained in post-Conquest England. This includes the Latin *Navigatio sancti Brendani*, the historiographical descriptions of Britain by Gildas (*c.* 504–70), Nennius

---

the sea in medieval English literature is of course indebted to Bertil Sandahl's invaluable work *Middle English Sea Terms*, 3 vols (Uppsala, 1951–82).

[68] Titus Heydenreich, *Tadel und Lob der Seefahrt: Das Nachleben eines antiken Themas in der romanischen Literatur* (Heidelberg, 1970). Worth mentioning also are Samuel Eliot Morison's 'The Sea in Literature', *Atlantic Monthly* 196 (1955), 67–77 and Albrecht Classen's 'Storms, Sea Crossings, the Challenges of Nature, and the Transformation of the Protagonist in Medieval and Renaissance Literature', *Neohelicon* 30:2 (2003), 163–82.

[69] Beside the work of Richard Unger, this area has been excellently served in recent years by Ian Friel's *The Good Ship: Ships, Shipbuilding and Technology in England, 1200–1520* (London, 1995) and Gillian Hutchinson's *Medieval Ships and Shipping* (London and Washington, DC, 1994).

[70] Horden and Purcell, *The Corrupting Sea*. Two more studies must be mentioned here: Cunliffe, *Facing the Ocean* and Michael McCormick, *Origins of the European Economy* (Cambridge, 2001).

(eighth century) and Bede (672/73–735) as well as writings of a legal nature. As far as vernacular material is concerned, I have considered the Conquest as forming a caesura, albeit not an absolute one, and I will therefore briefly discuss the sea in some pre-Conquest writings in English to contrast treatments of the sea composed after the arrival of Anglo-Norman culture.

The transition from the Latin *Navigatio sancti Brendani* to Benedeit's *Le Voyage de Saint Brandan*, composed before 1118, stands at the beginning of post-Conquest fiction written in England.[71] And whilst the poem draws on earlier material, cross-fertilising existing traditions with recently imported tastes, it presents a natural break with Anglo-Saxon culture and ushers in the very first generation of Anglo-Norman literature. Finding appropriate texts with which to conclude this book is somewhat more difficult, but those relating to the first successful voyages of Atlantic discovery obviously come to mind. These ventures into macrospace, hitherto the land of myth and uncertainty, expanded the frontiers of knowledge and imagination in an irreversible way.[72] The latest text in this book, Shakespeare's *Tempest*, postdates Columbus's first voyage by more than one hundred years and, because it no longer shares the traditional boundaries found in the earliest texts studied here, offers an illuminating commentary on the development of maritime topoi after the traditional onset of early modernity. From the perspective of this enterprise, these starting and finishing points span a period that embraces both the upheaval of the Norman Conquest with all its political or cultural consequences and the discovery of the New World. After the Conquest, Anglo-Norman replaced English as the vernacular language of most writing for the wealthy, as for the literate; after Columbus's voyage the new globe replaced the old view of the Earth and the Atlantic Ocean received new shores.

For the purpose of selecting texts, I have consciously taken a liberal view of the term 'literature' and viewed it as synonymous with 'writing' in the broadest sense. To ensure an ample width of genres and modes of writing, and to reduce the risk of relying too heavily on texts that may be deemed 'obscure', or whose currency in their own day cannot be assessed, the texts chosen here cover mainly but not only hagiography, romance, historiography, biblical paraphrase and political poetry. A number of these texts were widely read, such as Benedeit's *Le Voyage de Saint Brandan*, or gained entry into the households of influential people, such as the *Libelle of Englyshe Polycye*, or have an ambitious, universal scope, such as Matthew Paris's thirteenth-century chronicles.[73] The remaining texts either deal with widely

---

71 R. L. G. Ritchie's dating of the poem is largely accepted ('The Date of the *Voyage of St Brendan*', *Medium Aevum* 19 (1950), 64–6).

72 For an elucidation of 'macrospace' and 'microspace', see Dick Harrison, *Medieval Space – The Extent of Microspatial Knowledge in Western Europe During the Middle Ages*, Lund Studies in International History 34 (Lund, 1996), passim.

73 Benedeit's poem continued to be copied as late as the fourteenth century. A Picard version has also been produced, and, more importantly, it has even been translated back into Latin (assuming that Benedeit's poem is a translation of the immensely widespread Latin *Navigatio Sancti Brendani Abbatis*). G. A. Lester argues convincingly that Sir John Paston owned a copy of the

disseminated stories, notably the tales of Tristan, or treat well-known biblical maritime themes, such as the tale of Jonah and the whale.

By seeking temporal and generic breadth, this book covers texts composed in all three major written languages in the period concerned: Anglo-Norman, Latin and English. Can a specific view of the sea be associated with a particular language? One would expect ecclesiastical and early legal documents to be composed in Latin, for example. Religious writing in Latin was produced by monks and clergy, who, it is plausible to surmise, would interpret the sea by negotiating with more than a millennium of writing in Christian (to say nothing of classical) Latin, although it does not follow that their views can be isolated from other perceptions of the sea. Similarly, English literature composed in the twelfth and thirteenth centuries for less weighty or formal purposes tended to be predominately composed in Anglo-Norman, whereas Middle English was increasingly used after the thirteenth century. If one expects literary representations of the sea to evolve with time, then it follows that Latin texts might treat the sea differently from later, Anglo-Norman compositions and that Middle English writing would be different again. Nevertheless, I have chosen to treat the associations of the three languages with specific approaches to the sea not as 'automatic' but rather as contingent upon the circumstances of a given work's production or dissemination.

Although this book discusses the development of literary representations of the sea, the chapters do not form a strictly chronological sequence to avoid running the risk of creating an illusion of comprehensiveness. The sheer volume of texts that refer to the sea during the 1,000 years that separate Gildas from Shakespeare is overwhelming. Rather than grouping texts into chronological 'clusters' – an approach that would only frustrate this endeavour by creating arbitrary categories that cut across genre distinctions – the chapters will focus on modes of writing, most of which have at their core two to three seminal texts. By 'mode of writing' I refer to a broad and dynamic category of writing that can span a number of contiguous genres, with sub-sets that may change over time. It is in this sense that I understand the term 'romance' against which so much of pre-modern literature and, as Chris Cannon argues, even the very notion of 'English literature' is defined.[74]

The writings chosen are not necessarily themselves representative of the understanding of the sea in a given period of time, but they are employed

---

Libelle of Englyshe Polycye in 'The Books of a Fifteenth-Century English Gentleman: Sir John Paston', *Neuphilologische Mitteilungen* 88 (1987), 200–17 (205). See also Andrew Breeze, 'Sir John Paston, Lydgate and the *Libelle of Englyshe Polycye*', *Notes and Queries*, n.s. 48:3 (2001), 230–1.

74 Cannon sees the origin of the process that will lead to 'the canon' and 'English literature' as lying in the rise of romance (*The Grounds of English Literature* (Oxford, 2004), passim). I will therefore use 'romance' as a mode of writing that can span both 'romance' as a narrow genre as well as the lai, which is often written along the lines of romance expectations: 'the romance genre – any genre, indeed – is best thought of as a lineage or a family of texts rather than as a series of incarnations or clones of a single Platonic idea', Cooper, *The English Romance in Time*, p. 8.

here as illustrations of a particular perception that concentrates on one but often spans different genres, placing these in a diachronic context. One of the most rewarding insights hopefully yielded by this approach is that – from the perspective of exploring a narrative topos in relation to modes of writing – maritime topoi tend to emerge as remarkably mobile across genres, pointing toward the existence of cultural associations of the sea beyond a given literary configuration. And it is the development of this cultural life of the sea, as mediated by literature, that I wish to chart.

1

Traditions

[The Egyptians] also consider it a religious duty to avoid salt, so that neither cooked food nor bread seasoned with salt from the sea is served. Various reasons are given for this, but only one is true: their hatred for the sea as an element unrelated and alien, or rather completely hostile to man by nature.

Plutarch (c. 46–120), Quaestiones conviviales, 8, 8

He will cast all our sins into the bottom of the sea.

Micah 7.19

Classical Readings of the Sea

Mult fu hardiz, mult fu curteis
Cil ki fist nef premierement
E en mer se mist aval vent,
Terre querant qu'il ne veeit
E rivage qu'il ne saveit.

[How bold and skilled was the man who first made a ship and put to sea before the wind, seeking a land he could not see and a shore he could not know.][1]

Wace's (*c.* 1115–*c.* 1183) tribute to the audacity of the first seafarer is heir to a long literary tradition of uneasiness and ambiguity concerning the sea. The blend of admiration and incredulity betrays the narrator as an observer of the sea, an islander but a land-dweller. And although I believe that the parallel has not been noticed before, it should come as no surprise that another land-dweller, Seneca (*c.* 4 BC–AD 65), provided the source for the above passage from the *Roman de Brut*:[2]

---

[1] The text and translation are taken from Judith Weiss, ed., *Wace*: Roman de Brut – *A History of the British* (Exeter, 1999), lines 11,234–8, p. 282 (p. 283 for the translation). See also *Le Roman de Brut de Wace*, ed. Ivor Arnold, 2 vols, Société des Anciens Textes Français (Paris, 1938, 1940), vol. 2, p. 587.

[2] Given the popularity of the *qui primus* construction in classical poetry, Wace's 'Cil ki fist nef premierement' is certainly no coincidence. Titus Heydenreich, *Tadel und Lob der Seefahrt: Das Nachleben eines antiken Themas in der romanischen Literatur* (Heidelberg, 1970), argues for Horace as a potential source (p. 83), but the Senecan passage offers a closer parallel. E. Baum-

25

Audax nimium qui freta primus
rate tam fragili perfida rupit
terrasque suas post terga videns
animam levibus credidit auris,
dubioque secans aequora cursu
potuit tenui fidere ligno.

[Too bold was he who first broke
the treacherous waves with so frail a raft
and, looking back at his land behind him,
committed his soul to fickle winds;
cleaving the ocean with uncertain course,
he could set his trust in a thin piece of wood.][3]

As Peter Dronke rightly remarks in his comment on Seneca's Argonaut chorus, the *Argo* 'made the unknown sea "become a part of our fear" (*partemque metus fieri nostri*)'.[4] This fear of the sea, sometimes referred to as *phobos nautilias*, has its roots in the wisdom of the Golden Age, encapsulated in the divinely willed separation of the world of gods from the world of mortals by means of what Horace (65–8 BC) terms *oceanus dissociabilis*, the 'dividing sea':

nequiquam deus abscidit
prudens Oceano dissociabili
terras, si tamen impiae
non tangenda rates transiliunt vada.

[In vain in his wise foresight did God cut off
the lands of the Earth by means of the dividing sea

gartner and I. Short, eds, *La Geste du Roi Arthur* (Paris, 1993), p. 336, note 44, have suggested that Wace's passage refers to the *Argo* and that the poet derived this information from the beginning of Benoît de Sainte-Maure's *Roman de Troie*. Benoît's poem, however, does not seem to feature a *qui primus* construction with regard to the *Argo*. Otto Zwierlein ('Spuren der Tragödien Senecas bei Bernardus Silvestris, Petrus Pictor und Marbod von Rennes', *Mittellateinisches Jahrbuch* 27 for 1987 (1989), 171–96 (171–2)) adduces evidence that Seneca's tragedies were known in northern France by the late twelfth century: 'Somit waren also Senecas Dramen um 1180 in Nordfrankreich bekannt' (p. 172). He also shows that even earlier echoes of Seneca's tragedies are traceable in the works of French writers: in a later version of this article Zwierlein pushes this date as far back as 1096, 'Spuren der Tragödien Senecas bei Bernardus Silvestris, Petrus Pictor, Marbod von Rennes und Hildebert von Le Mans. Mit einem Nachtrag: Seneca als Wegbereiter der *tragoediae elegiacae* des 12. Jahrhunderts', in *Otto Zwierlein, Lucubrationes Philologae*, ed. R. Jakobi, R. Junge and C. Schmitz (Berlin, 2004), vol. 1, pp. 337–84 (p. 374). The other sources of the *Argo*'s exploits, Ovid's *Metamorphoses* 7 as well as *Heroides* 6 and 12, are unlikely to have supplied Wace with the above lines as they do not contain a similar construction or passage.

3   *Medea*, lines 301–5, in *Seneca in Ten Volumes*, vol. 8, *Tragedies*, ed. F. J. Miller, LCB 62 (Cambridge, MA, and London, 1917), pp. 254–5. I have chosen Peter Dronke's elegant translation from *The Growth of Literature*, pp. 1–26 (p. 8). Although the tone of Seneca's passage appears to contrast with the excerpt from Wace's *Roman de Brut*, it is important to note that Wace is working in the *qui primus* tradition (see Baumgartner and Short, *La Geste du Roi Arthur*, p. 336, note 44).

4   Peter Dronke, 'Part 1', in *Growth of Literature: The Sea and the God of the Sea*, Peter and Ursula Dronke, H. M. Chadwick Memorial Lectures 8 (Cambridge, 1997), pp. 1–26, p. 8.

if impious ships yet leap
across waters which they should not touch.][5]

Titus Heydenreich has shown that the history of portraying seafaring as a Promethean offence against divine will has its sources in Hellenic antiquity.[6] The Greeks believed the sea to be the ancient dwelling-place of the titan Ophion from whom all life was supposed to have sprung. After a clash with Chronos, Ophion was hurled into the sea and banished there forever. Roman mythology replaced Ophion with Oceanus (via the Greek *okeanos*) who became the *arbiter orbis* and ruler of the underworld, conveniently located in his abode at the bottom of the sea.[7] Many Roman writers, conscious of their Aegean heritage, adopted this foundation myth and continually referred to the sea as a sacred realm from which mere mortals should refrain: 'linquite, terrae, / spem pelagi sacrosque iterum seponite fluctus' [Leave all hope of seafaring, ye dwellers upon land, and once more shun the holy waves].[8] Those foolhardy ships that followed the *Argo* (*qui primus*), and despite all minatory verses dared to transgress the maritime frontier between the mortal and the immortal realms, were branded by Horace in the ode quoted above as 'impiae'. Even Pliny the Elder, mindful of the force of the winds, calls the adding of more and bigger sails to ships 'provocari mortem'.[9] Although Pliny uses this phrase in the context of unnecessary risk-taking, to him the sea was part of *divina Natura* and his use of *audacia* to characterise such actions aligns him closely with the idea of seafaring as a transgression.[10] One scholar who has explored the classical perception of the 'holy sea' goes even further in his evaluation of this belief:

daß möglicherweise das Meer eine dem Menschen prinzipiell gesetzte und daher unüberwindbare definitive 'Grenze' sei, die zu überspringen 'Hybris' und eine Verletzung und Besudelung der heiligen Reinheit des Meeres bedeute.

[that the sea could perhaps be a fundamental and insurmountable divide for mankind, which to overcome would mean hubris as well as a violation and defiling of the sea's holy purity.][11]

---

5 Horace, *Odes*, 1. 3, lines 21–4. Both the text and the translation are taken from *Horace 'Odes I'-Carpe Diem*, ed. and trans. David West (Oxford, 1995). Horace's use of the singular 'deus' does not need to indicate a neo-Platonic monotheistic god. Heydenreich, *Tadel und Lob der Seefahrt*, deals at length with the *oceanus dissociabilis*, pp. 28 ff.
6 *Tadel und Lob der Seefahrt*, Chapter 1, 'Antike', passim. Heydenreich dedicates an entire section to the *qui primus* tradition, pp. 44 ff.
7 Hugo Rahner, *Symbole der Kirche* (Salzburg, 1964), pp. 281–2.
8 Valerius Flaccus (first century AD), *Argonautica*, lines 631–2, quoted together with the translation from *Valerius Flaccus*, ed. and trans. J. H. Mozley, LCB 286 (London and Cambridge, MA, 1934).
9 Mary Beagon, *Roman Nature: The Thought of Pliny the Elder* (Oxford, 1992), p. 179.
10 Beagon, *Roman Nature*, pp. 178–9. On *audacia*, see p. 180.
11 Dietrich Wachsmuth, '*Pompimos o daimon* – Untersuchungen zu den antiken Sakralhandlungen bei Seereisen' (unpublished PhD thesis, FU Berlin, 1967), p. 226. Quoted from Heydenreich, *Tadel und Lob der Seefahrt*, p. 14.

It was the *Argo*'s transgression, perhaps more so than other human inventions, that disturbed the fragile perfection of the Golden Age. The invocation of the first ship, and of Jason as its proud captain, is the hallmark of the classical *qui primus* tradition nurtured by Seneca and Horace, among others.[12] Writers like Benoît de Sainte-Maure (1154–73) and Wace continued this literary tradition in their own historiographic works, and through Ovid and the *Ovide moralisé* this current would reach later poets such as Chaucer, whose short poem *The Former Age* echoes the Golden Age peace on the sea: 'No ship yit karf the wawes grene and blewe'.[13]

Unfortunately, it has become common practice to view the Romans (and by extension the ancient Greeks) as more or less incapable of expressing other, not to mention positive, sentiments about the sea. Hence the argument that the Romans' interest in the sea was invariably practical.[14] To some extent, this is justified. To Pliny the sea was at 'at best, *incerta* [uncertain], at worst, *saevissima* [wild]'.[15] E. de Saint-Denis, for instance, maintained that Graeco-Roman writers showed no inclination to explore any further meanings for the sea in their writing, being content to copy Homer whose poetry is so intensely concerned with maritime movement in the Mediterranean.[16] Nevertheless, many independent voices can also be heard: 'How great is the beauty of the sea!' exclaimed Cicero (who feared sea-travel in all seasons of the year).[17] This sentiment is endorsed by Virgil (70–19 BC) and Martial (AD 40–120) among others.[18] Some aspects of the pre-Christian, positive perception of the sea may have survived in late pre-modernity. One such tradition is the exceptional *sposalizio del mare* or 'wedding-ceremony' performed at the accession of the Venetian Doge.[19] And even Pliny's views on seafaring were not monolithic: 'Pliny allows his enthusiasm [for contemporary navigation]

[12] Heydenreich, pp. 15 ff. He quotes, beside other instances, Horace's Ode 1. 3, lines 9–12: 'illi robur et aes triples / circa pectus erat, qui fragilem truci / commisit pelago ratem / primus, nec timuit praecipitem Africum' [Oak and triple bronze / were round the breast of the man who first committed / a fragile ship to the truculent sea. / He was not afraid of the swooping sou'wester], West, *Horace's 'Odes 1'*, p. 15.

[13] Larry D. Benson, gen. ed., *The Riverside Chaucer* (Boston, 1987), p. 651, line 21.

[14] G. Wissowa (continued W. Kroll, et al.), *Paulys Realencyclopädie der classischen Altertumswissenschaft*, 84 vols (Stuttgart and Weimar, 1894–1980), series 1, vol. 16, column 1817, entry 'Naturgefühl', argues that the Romans were insensitive to a non-utilitarian exploitation of the sea. See also Michel Reddé, *Mare Nostrum: les infrastructures, le dispositif et l'histoire de la marine militaire sous l'empire romain* (Rome and Paris, 1986).

[15] Beagon, *Roman Nature*, p. 177 (for Pliny's view of the sea, see Chapter 5, 'Land and Sea', in particular pp. 177–80).

[16] E. de Saint-Denis, *La rôle de la mer dans la poesie latine* (Paris, 1935), pp. 471–86.

[17] Cicero, *De Natura Deorum*, Book 2, section 100 (cf. *Letters to Atticus*, letter 246). *De Natura Deorum* and *Academica*, ed. and trans. H. Hackham, LCB 268 (London and Cambridge, MA, 1933).

[18] Virgil, *Georgics*, Book 3, lines 236–41, and Martial, *Epigrammaton*, Book 10, section 51, lines 9–10. Juliusz Jundziłł, *Rzymianie a morze* (Bydgoszcz, 1991), provides a more comprehensive list of classical writers who expressed pleasure at the sight of the sea, p. 135, note 1.

[19] At the culmination of a sumptuous procession, the new Doge is ferried onto the sea, where, as part of a solemn ritual, he utters the formula: 'Desponsamus te mare in signum veri perpetuique dominii' (Thomas Wemyss Fulton, *The Sovereignty of the Sea: An Historical Account of the Claims of England to the Dominion of the British Seas* (Edinburgh and London, 1911), p. 4).

to overrule his feeling that land was the only element unambiguously benign towards man.'[20] Nevertheless, it was the dominant stream of mistrust of the sea that fell on fertile ground in the thought of the Church Fathers.

And it is only a small step from the classical *fear of the sea* to the patristic condemnation of seafaring as an act of pride. Ironically, since Christianity began as the faith of peoples perched on the Mediterranean littoral, Horace's *oceanus dissociabilis*, the 'dividing ocean' which parts gods from mortals, became an equally insurmountable border separating humanity from Paradise.[21] The Earthly Paradise or *terra repromissionis* was routinely, though not always, placed in the east (usually located at the top of Mappae Mundi) separated from the *oikumene*, the known and inhabited world of Africa, Asia and Europe, by the great ocean that encircles all creation. Consequently, Augustine (354–430) expresses the thought of circumnavigating the ocean as 'absurd': 'Nimisque absurdum est, ut dicatur aliquos homines ex hac in illam partem, Oceani immensitate traiecta, nauigare ac peruenire potuisse.' [And it would be too absurd to say that some men might have sailed from one side of the Earth to the other, arriving there having crossed the immense tract of the ocean.][22] To Augustine, and many generations of Christians, it seemed impossible to cross the (non-Mediterranean) waters of the ocean in search of land or inhabitants.[23] This ancient portrayal of seafaring as a transgression contributed to a distinctively Christian myth of the sea's impassability and inappropriateness for man, aptly termed *nautische Erbsünde* by Heydenreich.[24] This 'dividing sea', with frontiers stretching into the realm of macrospatial imagination, continued to exert its influence as a perennial source of fear as well as an object of speculation to those pre-modern writers who wrote about the formerly barbarian seas of northern Europe.[25]

A further reason for mistrust of the sea lies in the relative inadequacy of seafaring technology available to navigators from antiquity to the early Middle Ages and some time beyond. On the one hand, shipbuilding, including the comparably plain Norman and Viking keel-type vessels (longboats), was

[20] Beagon, *Roman Nature*, p. 185.
[21] Titus Heydenreich, *Tadel und Lob der Seefahrt*, pp. 67–8.
[22] *De Civitate Dei*, Book 16, Chapter 9, ed. J. E. C. Welldon, 2 vols (London, 1924), vol. 2, p. 201. The translation is taken from *The City of God Against the Pagans*, trans. R. W. Dyson (Cambridge, 1998), p. 711.
[23] Of course, this belief was directly challenged by the fourteenth-century *Travels of Sir John Mandeville* (cf. p. 82).
[24] Heydenreich, *Tadel und Lob der Seefahrt*, p. 30. It is, of course, the same tradition as that which underlies Dante's *Paradiso*, Canto 33, lines 94–6: 'Un punto solo m'è maggior letargo / che venticinque secoli a la 'mpresa / che fè Nettuno ammirar l'ombra d'Argo' [A single moment makes for me greater oblivion tha[n] five and twenty centuries have wrought upon the enterprise that made Neptune wonder at the shadow of the *Argo*]. The text and translation are taken from *Dante: The Divine Comedy*, ed. and trans. Charles S. Singleton, 3 vols (in 6) (London, 1971–75), vol. 3, *Paradiso*, p. 377.
[25] The *oceanus dissociabilis* in the tradition of British historiography forms part of the discussion of Chapter 3. The mythical genesis of the Atlantic is sketched by Paul Butel, *The Atlantic*, trans. Iain Hamilton Grant (New York and London, 1999), Chapter 1, 'Atlantic Legends and Atlantic Reality before the Iberian Discoveries', pp. 5 ff.

among the most advanced fields of pre-modern technology.[26] The great technological developments, like the moving of the rudder from the starboard
side (the quarter rudder) to the stern, began in the second half of the twelfth
century, but even before this time the construction of sea-going vessels was
highly complex and expensive.[27] In marked contrast stands the scarce knowledge of the sea itself in many of its non-Mediterranean observers. Much was
conjectured and little was known for certain. The western sea had no end, or
its limit lay out of reach, and only a resolute ship could breach the unknown.
This combination of the barely possible, the undiscovered and a confident
technology with scope for expansion generated an early mirror-image of
what is now called 'science-fiction': dazzling tales of the seafaring exploits
of saintly heroes and heroic saints such as Alexander or Brendan that were
even more daring than those of their Mediterranean counterparts, Odysseus
and Sinbad.

To the southern outsider, the seas of northern Europe seemed particularly
inhospitable, and there are many Mediterranean expressions of mistrust triggered by the sight of them. Among these, the 'sea of perpetual gloom', coined
by the Arab geographer Al Idrisi (*c.* 1100–65/66), is perhaps one of the most
memorable.[28] Albinovanus Pedo participated in the abortive expedition of
Drusus Germanicus' fleet to the northern ocean in AD 16. A storm thwarted
the voyage's success, and Albinovanus deduced that the gods must have been
opposed to this attempted transgression of the *sacras aquas*:

> di revocant rerumque vetant congnoscere finem
> mortales oculos: aliena quid aequora remis
> et sacras violamus aquas divumque quietas
> turbamus sedes?
>
> [The gods are calling us back, and forbid mortal eyes to know
> the end of things. Why are we violating alien seas and sacred
> waters with our oars and troubling the calm abodes of the
> gods?][29]

In his otherwise perceptive article on the complexities of coastal navigation
in the northern seas, Charles O. Frake juxtaposes the contrasting and, at
times, stereotypical perceptions of the northern sea and the Mediterranean:

> These seas, the North Sea, the English Channel, the Irish Sea, the coast
> of Brittany and the Bay of Biscay, present conditions that are in marked

---

[26] Gillian Hutchinson, *Medieval Ships and Shipping* (London, 1994), p. 4.
[27] Hutchinson, *Medieval Ships*, pp. 11 ff., charts the changes in shipbuilding technology throughout the Middle Ages.
[28] Butel, *The Atlantic*, p. 8.
[29] Seneca, *Suasoriae* 1.15, lines 20–3. Quoted from *The* Suasoriae *of Seneca the Elder*, ed. and trans. William A. Edward (Cambridge, 1928), p. 6, section 15 (line-numbering restarts on each page as the verse account of Drusus Germanicus' voyage is embedded in a prose text). The trans-lation appears on p. 45.

contrast to those of the relatively benign, generally sunny and virtually tideless Mediterranean.[30]

Neither Seneca nor Horace had the ferocious waters of northern Europe in mind when writing about the perils of seafaring. Their sea was the Mediterranean, the Roman *mare nostrum*, and was at a world's remove from the impenetrable sea of the barbarian north.[31] Yet there is, of course, no single 'attitude' towards the sea in classical thought. Whereas the Roman and, later, Christian mistrust of the sea was largely reserved for the seas of northern Europe, legal and political theories began to conceive of the sea as an entity in their respective discourses.

Legal theory and practice now widely acknowledge that the sea must be treated differently from dry land, although they share some properties.[32] This was considered self-evident during the founding phase of European maritime law, and it was only during the later Middle Ages and the early modern period that this difference between the two elements was called into doubt for political reasons. To appreciate fully the significance of this term, it is necessary to map the history of this concept.

Historians like to describe Greek hegemony over the Aegean as a thalassocracy.[33] Being dispersed throughout the Mediterranean basin from at least the sixth century BC, the Greek communities used cabotage not only to maintain trade relations, like the Phoenicians, but also to foster kinship and political ties between mainland Greece and other Hellenic communities.[34] Already the *Iliad* and the *Odyssey* document the centrality of sea-voyages, islands and navigation in Greek culture.[35] The Greeks partly inherited and partly established new trade routes along Mediterranean shores, connecting Hellenic outposts in Egypt, Asia Minor, Iberia, Sicily, as well as what is now France with the Greek heartland. Not only did trade flow along these routes but merchants also exported Greek culture – indeed, a Greek eco-system of trees and plants (for example, the olive and vine in Magna Graecia)

---

30 Charles O. Frake, 'Cognitive Maps of Time and Tide Among Medieval Seafarers', *Man*, n.s. 20 (1985), 254–70 (257). Frake appears to be thinking of the sailing season on the Mediterranean. Crossing the sea during the winter can be very hazardous, indeed.

31 The name 'Mediterranean' is, ironically, a coinage of the Christian encyclopaedist Isidore.

32 See p. 40, n. 1.

33 Already the Greek historians of the fifth century BC discerned sea-powers as separate, powerful entities, coining the term 'thalassocracy' (Peregrine Horden and Nicholas Purcell, *The Corrupting Sea – A Study of Mediterranean History* (Oxford, 2000), p. 26).

34 Horden and Purcell's remarkable *The Corrupting Sea* offers an excellent cultural overview of history *in* the Mediterranean basin. For an earlier approach to the subject, consult Fernand Braudel's *The Mediterranean and the Mediterranean World in the Age of Philip II* (*La Méditerrannée et le monde méditerrannéen à l'époque de Philippe II*, first edn 1949, second rev. edn 1966), 2 vols (New York, 1972–3; repr. Berkeley, 1995). Albin Lesky's *Thalatta – Der Weg der Griechen zum Meer* (Vienna, 1947) remains a good treatment of the Greeks' deep cultural involvement with the Mediterranean Sea.

35 The sacrifice of Iphigenia to obtain favourable winds and Odysseus' ill-fated ten-year voyage home are only two of the many well-known maritime aspects of Homeric and post-Homeric legends.

– returning home with 'barbarian' artefacts and produce. A thalassocracy in the truest sense, Greek civilisation was characterised by the centrality of the sea or, rather, by their centrality in the sea. Amongst other aspects of this civilisation's maritime enterprise, the Greeks' pioneering spirit in the field of navigation and shipbuilding survives in the legend that Jason's *Argo* was the first ship to have parted the waves.

The Romans expanded the maritime infrastructure of the Aegean thalassocracy to span the entire Mediterranean. The Roman Empire eventually united all shores of the Mediterranean (and stretched even to the Atlantic and the North Sea by the time of Augustus) and sea travel became indispensable for the purposes of provincial administration, the maintaining of supply routes to military forts and, of course, the securing of trade. Naturally, this elaborate network also included rivers as vital inland waterways for a number of reasons. Smaller rivers can be more easily policed than the sea and the possibility of erecting bridges represents the land's ability to 'conquer' rivers.[36]

One historian observes that the most powerful cities in the late Empire – Rome, Alexandria, Antioch, Byzantium, Carthage – were all either situated by the sea or close to it.[37] It should be added that the significance of these cities encompassed a range of spheres, political, economic and spiritual, as four of them were eventually Christian patriarchates. This *mare nostrum*, as the Romans called it, was not administered directly by Roman authorities, nor were there any successful lasting attempts to enforce maritime control over the Mediterranean.[38] The great repository of Roman law, the *Corpus Iuris Civilis*, preserves and codifies this *laissez-faire* attitude to the sea. Compiled during the reign of Justinian (528–34), the *Corpus Iuris Civilis* represents the codification of the body of Roman law. It consists of three main components: the *Codex*, the *Digestae (Pandectae)*, and the *Institutiones*. The *Codex* contains the various Imperial constitutions (the oldest dates back to the time of Hadrian), the *Digestae* or Digest consists of fifty books containing fragments written by Roman lawyers, and, finally, the *Institutiones* compile various items of legal information.[39] Book 2 of the *Institutiones* very clearly lays out the status of the sea:

> Et quidem naturali iure communia sunt omnium haec: aer et aqua profluens et mare et per hoc litora maris. nemo igitur ad litus maris accedere prohi-

---

36 As such, in terms of both jurisdiction and cultural perception, rivers lie outside the scope of this study. Nevertheless, it must be mentioned that some of the larger rivers could instil fear in inexperienced travellers that were not entirely dissimilar from the perils encountered at sea.

37 Jundziłł, *Rzymiane a morze*, p. 81.

38 Reddé, *Mare Nostrum*, passim. On the genesis of this term, see V. Burr, *Nostrum Mare: Ursprung und Geschichte der Namen des Mittelmeeres und seiner Teilmeere im Altertum* (Stuttgart, 1932).

39 A fourth element, the *Novellae* (a collection of Justinian's constitutions) wasadded later. The name *Corpus Iuris Civilis* itself is a sixteenth-century creation. All citations refer to the following standard modern editions: *The Digest of Justinian*, ed. T. Mommsen and P. Krueger, trans. Alan Watson, 4 vols (Philadelphia, 1985) and *Justinian's Institutes*, ed. Peter Birks and Grant MacLeod (London, 1987).

betur, dum tamen villis et monumentis et aedificiis abstineat, quia non sunt iuris gentium, sicut et mare.

[The things which are naturally everybody's are: air, flowing water, the sea and the sea-shore. So nobody can be stopped from going on to the sea-shore. But he must keep away from houses, monuments and buildings. Unlike the sea, rights to those things are not determined by the law of all peoples.][40]

This understanding of the sea as a *mare liberum* assumes that the sea cannot be easily contained, that its moving surface and contents are constantly shifting and that nobody can legally call it 'ours'. As a concept, it endured the next two thousand years.[41] According to this notion, everyone enjoys an equal right to the sea, or, in the words of the twelfth-century Bologna Glossators, 'mare est commune'.[42] Ultimately, the sea's ungovernability underlies this legal construct, a concept which forms a familiar topos in descriptions of the Golden Age. An element so powerful, it would seem, must lie outside the control of human beings and belong to the realm of the gods. If the sea lies beyond human control, as Horace and Valerius Flaccus appear to imply, it also falls beyond the remit of any single human being, and is therefore public. It would appear ridiculous to claim water and, by extension, the sea for oneself:

> 'quid prohibetis aquis? usus communis aquarum est.
> nec solem proprium natura nec aera fecit
> nec tenues undas
>
> [Why do you deny me water? The use of the waters is a common right. Nature has not made the sun private, nor the air, nor the gentle waves.][43]

The tenor of this passage corresponds to the perception of the sea as an indivisible public good in the *Corpus Iuris Civilis*: 'Et quidem naturali iure omnium communia sunt illa: aer, aqua profluens, et mare, et per hoc litora maris' [And indeed by natural law the following belong in common to all men: air, flowing water and the sea, and therewith the shores of the sea].[44]

---

40 *Institutiones* 2.2.1.1. The translation is taken from Birks and MacLeod, *Justinian's Institutes*, p. 55. Cf. *Digestae* (henceforth *Dig.*) 1.8.2.1. This point is also noted by Percy Thomas Fenn, Jr, in 'Justinian and the Freedom of the Sea', *The American Journal of International Law* 19:4 (1925), 716–27 (727).

41 It should be pointed out that the term *mare liberum* itself is anachronistic. It is the title of Hugo Grotius's influential treatise of 1609.

42 Percy Thomas Fenn, Jr, 'Origins of the Theory of Territorial Waters', *American Journal of International Law* 20:3 (1926), 465–82 (465).

43 Ovid, *Metamorphoses*, Book 6, lines 349–51; the text is from *Ovid – Metamorphoses*, ed. and trans. Frank Justus Miller, 2 vols, LCB 42 (Cambridge, MA, 1916; third edn 1977; repr. 1984) vol. 1, p. 313. The translation is my own.

44 *Dig.* 1.8.2.1. in Mommsen and Krueger, *The Digest of Justinian*, vol. 1, the translation faces p. 24 (the continuous pagination excludes the translation).

It is this theoretical view of the use of the sea as open to all (despite the fact that, in practice, all Mediterranean shores were eventually under Roman control) that formed the basis of Roman legal thought on the sea.[45] To the Romans, and to the barbarian kingdoms that inherited the western reaches of the Mediterranean Sea from the Roman Empire, the sea was not territory. The sea, that is, at first, the Mediterranean, was the Roman *mare liberum* and free to all, at least in theory.

From the Bible to the Fathers

Orthodox Christian teaching (in sharp distinction to 'Gnostic' and other 'heretical' voices that were eventually silenced) maintains that God's creation is innately good because the matter of creation is good in itself. Yet a careful reading of Genesis leaves open the (not necessarily mutually exclusive) possibility that creation is good because God imposed order on chaos. Hence, creation is defined as the act of disciplining and shaping matter rather than of generating matter itself. The distinction bears directly upon the question of evil and its source. If chaos predated God's work of creation in six days, evil could be shown to have its roots in primeval disorder, and hence the task of justifying the perpetuation of evil in a world created by a God conceived of as absolute good ceases to be necessary. This understanding of creation, it will be shown below, hinges on the place of the sea in the work of the six days.

The Vulgate resorts to three principal terms for the sea: *aqua* [water], *abyssus* [the deep] and *mare* [sea].[46] The first, *aqua*, normally in the plural, denotes the primeval matter that predates the creation in six days.[47] In the beginning, darkness covers the *abyssus* and God's spirit hovers over the *aquas*: 'terra autem erat inanis et vacua et tenebrae super faciem abyssi et spiritus Dei ferebatur super aquas' (Genesis 1.2) [And the Earth was void and empty and darkness was over the face of the deep; and the spirit of God moved over the waters]. And although Genesis 1.1 introduces Heaven and Earth, the former is not shaped and named *caelum* until the second day (Genesis 1.8) and the latter is not called *mare* until the third day (Genesis 1.9). In the narrative of divine creation, water is simultaneously the substance of the sea as well as the matter of Heaven: 'et fecit Deus firmamentum divisitque aquas quae erant sub firmamento ab his quae erant super firmamentum et factum est ita' (Genesis 1.7) [And God made a firmament, and divided the waters that

---

45 'Quod in mare aedificatum sit, fieret priuatum, ita quod mari occupatum sit, fieri publicum' [that just as a building erected in the sea becomes private property so too one which has been overrun by the sea becomes public], Dig. 1.8.10. The translation is from Mommsen and Krueger, *The Digest of Justinian*, facing page.

46 *Pelagus* sometimes replaces *mare* in the Vulgate (e.g. Jonah 2:6).

47 A point noted by Insung Lee, 'The Tradition of Christian Sea-Symbolism in Medieval English Poetry and Milton' (unpublished PhD thesis, University of Oklahoma, 1996), p. 9.

were under the firmament, from those that were above the firmament, and it was so]. Both *aqua[e]* and *abyssus* are therefore older than creation. *Mare*, however, is the result of binding the waters together and moulding them into form (Genesis 1.10: 'congregationesque aquarum appelavit maria' [and the gathering together of the waters, he called Seas]), constituting thus a part of creation.

This understanding of the formation of the sea as the taming of a formidable primordial element, rather than as a creation *ex nihilo*, is also found in Job 38.8: 'quis conclusit ostiis mare quando erumpebat quasi de vulva procedens' [Who shut up the sea with doors, when it broke forth as issuing out of a womb] and it will play a role in pre-Conquest poetry.[48] Similarly, we can find the same chastising containment of the waters in Psalm 103.9: 'terminum posuisti quem non transgredientur neque convertentur operire terram' [Thou hast set a bound which they shall not pass over; neither shall they return to cover the Earth] (cf. Proverbs 8.29).[49] Hence, as a direct consequence of creation, the ferocious waters are charged with suppressing the deep (*abyssus*), which is now located at the bottom the sea. This concept of the hostile *abyssus* may be indebted to the Babylonian creation myth, where, similarly to the later Jewish Genesis, a vast and dark body of water existed at the dawn of time. This body of water, pictured as the dragon Tiamat (a possible source for the Hebrew word *tehom*, which has been translated as *abyssos* in Greek and *abyssus* in Latin), is then divided into two halves, Earth and the Heavens.[50]

As a potent and primeval force, the sea continued to be both an echo of, and a repository for, everything that was deemed undesirable after creation – including sin (as in Micah 7.19). But these are not the only voices in the Bible. Although the sea is not viewed in positive terms, the sea-episodes in the Gospels and, in particular, Paul's remarkable sea-journey in Acts of the Apostles 27 (which may have influenced the Brendan-voyage) indicate at least some form of engagement with the sea. It is therefore important to bear in mind that although the view of the sea in the Bible is overwhelmingly negative, the Old Testament perception of its main component, the waters, is by no means consistently disapproving. Genesis 1.20, for instance, testifies to the life-giving power of the sea, as it is from the *aquae* that all life gushes forth. And in 3 Esdras 4.22–5, which formed part of the pre-Tridentine

---

48 Discussing the Exeter Book poem *Christ*, Fabienne Michelet speaks of the 'creative act of transformation' (*Creation, Migration and Conquest: Imaginary Geography and Sense of Space in Old English Literature* (Oxford, 2006), p. 57).

49 In keeping with medieval practice, I follow the 'Gallican' Psalter, rather than Jerome's later translation, *Psalterium iuxta Hebraeos*, which gradually fell out of use after Alcuin (AD 735–804) re-introduced Jerome's earlier version (the 'Gallican' Psalter).

50 Various such similarities between Jewish and Babylonian cosmogony have been noted in the nineteenth century by, first and foremost, Friedrich Delitzsch, *Das Babylonische Weltschöpfungsepos* (Leipzig, 1896), passim, Peter Jensen, *Kosmologie der Babylonier: Studien und Materialien* (Strassburg, 1890), pp. 263–364, and Heinrich Zimmern, in Hermann Gunkel, *Schöpfung und Chaos in Urzeit und Endzeit* (Göttingen, 1896), pp. 401–28.

Vulgate, Zorobabel even says that men sail over the sea to impress women.[51] One could add to this the fact that some of Christ's disciples (Peter, Andrew, James and John) were fishermen and hence reliant on the sea for their livelihoods. Besides, the Gospels style the disciples themselves as 'fishers of men' (Matthew 4.19 and Mark 1.17).

In the highly selective corpus of proto-Orthodox and Orthodox writing that we call 'patristic', representing only a fraction of Christian literature before AD 500, the sea, separating humanity from Paradise, assumed very rapidly an equally influential metaphorical role as the sea of the world (an image that would be spread through allegorical writings such as Guillaume de Deguileville's fourteenth-century *Pèlerinage de la vie humaine*). The sea was thought to be governed by the Devil who administered humankind's sins, which, according to Micah 7.19, will be hurled by God into the sea: 'proiciet in profundum maris omnia peccata nostra' [He will cast all our sins into the bottom of the sea]. Origen (185–c. 254) is generally credited with having devised the influential image of the sea as the world, *in mari vitae*, which therefore reaches back almost to the beginnings of Christian preaching.[52] Naturally, the sea of the world could only be braved by a ship that was built of the unsinkable wood taken from Christ's cross. This ship was the Church itself: *ecclesia*.[53] Hugo Rahner's seminal analysis of Christian sea symbolism in *Symbole der Kirche* provides a detailed overview of the development of the Sea-of-the-World-allegory in patristic sources.[54] He differentiates between the Bitter Sea (*mare amarum*), an essentially Mediterranean reading of the sea as a metaphor for the inconstancy of life derived from classical tradition, and the Evil Sea, a conception of the sea as the seat of demonic and hostile forces. Rahner argues that the latter has been far more influential in Christian tradition and he puts forward and defends classical antecedents for this theory. However, this second understanding of the sea as the seat of evil (the location of the abyss or *tehom*, often denoted by *sheol* in Hebrew) is ultimately biblical and pre-Pentateuchal.[55] This allegorical and essentially pessimistic reading of the sea influenced later theologians who expanded it so that Christ was thought to be the ship's helmsman and the saints and heavenly curia assumed the roles of crew and sailors, respectively. G. R. Owst identifies the first post-classical use of this allegory in one of Anselm's

---

51 On this passage, see Alcuin Blamires, *The Case for Women in Medieval Literature* (Oxford, 1997), p. 53.

52 *Origenes Werke*, vol. 3, *Homiliae in Ieremiam, Fragmenta in Lamentationes*, ed. Erich Klosterman, second edn rev. by Pierre Nautin, GCS 6 (Berlin, 1983), p. 391, line 27.

53 The use of this allegory in medieval English literature is discussed by V. A. Kolve, 'The Man of Law's Tale: The Rudderless Ship and the Sea', in *Chaucer and the Imagery of Narrative* (London, 1984), Chapter 7, pp. 297–358, in particular pp. 307–19. As the underlying inspiration one might suppose Noah's Ark, itself an established image for the Church.

54 Rahner, *Symbole der Kirche*, pp. 272–303.

55 On a more fundamental level, Rahner's differentiation between the Bitter and the Evil Sea has a largely arbitrary component since many of the biblical examples which he adduces for the Bitter Sea (e.g. Isaiah 57.20, Lamentations 2.13, Psalms 68.3) depict a violent, hostile and, ultimately, evil force.

(*c.* 1033/34–1109) sermons, and points out that the Church-as-ship allegory became commonplace in pre-modern preaching.[56] By the twelfth century, a detailed, allegorical reading was already established as the following extract from a sermon by Achard, the Abbot of St Victor and later Bishop of Avranches (*c.* 1100–72), reveals:

> To cross that sea we must have a ship, mast, sail, etc. The ship signifies the Faith; the sentences of Holy Scripture are its planks, and the authorities of the Holy Doctors its rudder. The ship is narrow in prow and stern and broad in the middle; so is the Faith.[57]

There would even emerge original variations of this theme that seem to express the sea as the time elapsed between two shores. This anonymous, sixth-century copyist of the Gospel throws his analogy off-balance by allowing his mistrust of the sea to turn what should be the 'final' or 'destination port' into 'nearest port':

> Sicut navigantibus proximus est portus,
> Sic et scriptori novissimus versus.
> Tres digiti scribunt et totum corpus laborat.
> Hora pro me scribtore, sic deum habeas protectorem.

> [What the nearest port is to sailors the last verse is to the scribe. Three fingers write and the whole body works. Pray for me – the scribe – and may you have the Lord as your protector.][58]

It is against the background of this tradition of the brave Christian soul guided by faith as it sails over the sea of the wicked world – as well as the larger allegories of Christian life as a pilgrimage or journey – that the Brendan-voyage and many other westward voyages must be understood. Brendan sails over the trials of the worldly sea, complete with all its pitfalls, temptations and divine interventions, to reach the physical and spiritual realm of Paradise.[59] And in the thirteenth-century French *Estoire del Saint Graal*, Christ explains that 'par la meir [dois tu entendre] le monde'.[60]

From the fourth century onwards, when the main (that is to say orthodox)

56 Owst regards this allegory as being very frequent in medieval English sermons, *Literature and Pulpit in Medieval England – A Neglected Chapter in the History of English Letters and of the English People* (Cambridge, 1933; repr. Oxford, 1961), p. 69. This allegory flourished throughout the Middle Ages and extended beyond sermons into other expressions of literature.

57 Owst, *Literature and Pulpit in Mediaeval England*, p. 68.

58 MS Würzburg, Universitätsbibliothek, M.p.th. f. 68, fol. 170v. Such explicits were not uncommon: 'quia sicut navigantibus dulcis est portus, ita scriptori novissimus versus' [but just as the port seems sweet to the sailor, so does the last line to the writer], Bibliothèque Nationale, lat. 12,296, fol. 162r.

59 Chapter 2 discusses Brendan's voyage. Traditionally, the Church-as-ship allegory culminates in the reaching of the harbour of salvation.

60 *Estoire del Saint Graal* in H. Oskar Sommer, ed., *The Vulgate Version of the Arthurian Romances* (Washington, 1909), vol. 1, p. 139. On this passage, see Michelle Szkilnik, 'Seas, Islands and Continent in *L'Estoire del Saint Graal*', in *Romance Languages Annual* 1 (1989), 322–7 (324).

tradition of Christian writing gained its strengths and vanquished its opponents, the *abyssus* began to subsume more and more of the semantic field once claimed by the sea. Jerome (*c.* 347–420) and Hilary of Poitiers (*c.* 300–67) viewed the *abyssus* as the primeval floods enveloping everything,[61] and Augustine's *profunditas impenetrabilis* articulated for countless generations of Christians Origen's understanding of the sea as the seat of the Devil and, in its metaphorical form, the depths of sin.[62] Early Christianity, to be sure, was too dependent upon ports and sea-lanes for any simple or emphatic consensus to be possible. Tertullian (*c.* 155–230), for example, contemplating much the same reaches of the Mediterranean as Augustine, followed the ancient Greeks and preferred a Hades deep under the Earth's surface as the Devil's dwelling.[63] Nevertheless, the view of the sea as the abode of all evil runs deep in early Christian writings and can still be found in such seminal works as Isidore's *Etymologies* and Gregory the Great's (*c.* 540–604) *Moralia*. Isidore echoes Augustine's phrase *profunditas aquarum impenetrabilis* [impenetrable depth of waters] in his *Etymologies* and Gregory judges the sea to be the *aeternae mortis profunda* [the depths of everlasting death].[64] Hilary of Poitiers can assert that 'Profundum maris sedem intelligimus inferni' [We construe the bottom of the sea to be the seat of Hell].[65] Gradually, the abyss became a synonym for the sea, a tradition that persisted in the pre-modern period.[66]

By the mid-fourteenth century, therefore, commentators can freely oscillate between *abyssus* ('abime', 'abyme' in Middle English) and the primeval *aquae*.[67] Hence, the *Midland Prose Psalter* (*c.* 1350) refers to the waters gathered together (*aquae* in the Vulgate) as *abyssi*: 'þe abimes [L abyssi] ben

---

[61] Jerome, *Tractatus In Psalmos* 103, in *S. Hieronymi Presbyteri Opera*, ed. M. Adraien, 2 vols, CCSL 72 (Turnhout, 1959), vol. 1, p. 163: 'Abyssus circumdat universam terram quam dicunt Oceanum'; Hilary, *Tractatus super psalmos*, ed. A. Zingerle, CSEL 22 (Vienna, 1891), p. 61.

[62] *Ennarationes In Psalmos*, ed. E. Dekkers and J. Fraipont, CCSL 38 (Turnhout, 1956), p. 470. Although, if one wants to believe the non-Thomistic continuation of *De regimine principum*, Augustine appears to have been familiar with sea and ships, since he compares prostitution to a ship's bilge (see Henry Ansgar Kelly, 'Bishop, Prioress and Bawd in the Stews of Southwerk', *Speculum* 75: 2 (2000), 342–88 (343, note 3)).

[63] *De anima* 55, CSEL 20, p. 387, lines 22–7.

[64] *Isidori Hispalensis episcopi*, Book 13, Chapter 20 and *Homily* 11, in *Homiliae in evangelia*, ed. R. Étaix, CCSL 141 (Turnhout, 1999), p. 76, respectively.

[65] Hilary of Poitiers, *Tractatus super psalmos* 68, 28, CSEL 22, p. 337, line 6.

[66] Largely through Wyclif's influence, the Middle English *depthe* became a current term for 'the deep sea' by the last quarter of the fourteenth century (*MED*). The *MED* lists two main meanings of *depthe*: '(a) Deep water, the sea; the primeval waters that preceded creation; also *fig.*; (b) the bottom of the sea.' However, certain biblical passages such as Exodus 15.8 offer a similarly undifferentiated understanding of *abyssus* and *maris*: 'et in spiritu furoris tui congregatione sunt aquae stetit unda fluens congregatione sunt abyssi in medio mari' [And with the blast of thy anger the waters were gathered together: the flowing water stood, the depths were gathered together in the midst of the sea]. Here, it is impossible to separate the *abyssi* from the sea itself.

[67] 'Abyss' has entered English first via Old French *abisme/abime* in the first quarter of the fourteenth century (*OED/MED*) in the forms 'abyme' and 'abime'. It is noteworthy that *Cleanness*, *Patience*, and *St Erkenwald* all deploy this rare word, which provides a further argument for the shared authorship of the these poems. Slightly later, in 1398, John Trevisa introduced the Latinism *abyssus* (cf. p. 39 below), providing the initially rarer but ultimately dominant form of the word.

gadered to-gidres a-middes þe see'.[68] This (by now) orthodox conflation of *abyssus* and *aquae* is reiterated by John Trevisa (1342–1402) in his translation of Bartholomaeus Anglicus's (*fl.* 1250) *De Proprietatibus Rerum*. It is also noteworthy that Bartholomaeus considers the deep to be the primordial matter of creation that is, as yet, without form. As rendered by Trevisa

> *Abissus* is depnesse of water vnsey, and þerof cometh and springeþ welles and ryuers. ... Þe primordial and firste matere [þ]at was in the bygynnynge of þe worlde noȝt distingued by certeyne forme is yclepid *abissus*.[69]

The biblical sea, therefore, preserves an echo of uncreated primeval chaos, the first a priori and all-encompassing *abyssus* that, because it predates time, is immeasurable by the dimensions of the creation of the six days. And because it had not been created by God during the six days, its matter and essence, as well as its form (as a result of theological conflation) was deemed by some to lie outside divine jurisdiction.

The mythical placing of the sea in the Judaeo-Christian continuum is perhaps best illustrated in this last example. Two of the most compelling scriptural references to the sea can be found in the Books of Ezekiel and Job. In Ezekiel 28, the fall of Tyre – a great seagoing power – serves as an example of hubris. Ezekiel is summoned by God to seek out the King of Tyre and to proclaim God's judgement to the apostate ruler. Predictably, the divine verdict is harsh (Ezekiel 28.2):

> fili hominis dic principi Tyri haec dicit Dominus Deus eo quod elevatum est cor tuum et dixisti Deus ego sum in cathedra Dei sedi in corde maris cum sis homo et non Deus et dedisti cor tuum quasi cor Dei.

> [Son of man, say to the prince of Tyre: Thus saith the Lord God: Because thy heart is lifted up, and thou hast said: I am God, and I sit in the chair of God in the heart of the sea: whereas thou art man, and not God: and hast set thy heart as if it were the heart of God.]

The heart of the sea as the seat of pride ultimately goes back to the long description of Leviathan in Job 41. This primordial sea-giant exceeds in power and age any other creature and has his abode in the depths of the ocean. After a long, simile-enriched portrayal of its terrifying physical features, the final lines of Job 41 (41.22–5) lay the foundation for Ezekiel 28.2:

> fervescere faciet quasi ollam profundum mare ponet quasi cum unguenta bulliunt. Post eum lucebit semita aestimabit abyssum quasi senescentem.

---

[68] *Midland Prose Psalter* in *The Earliest Complete English Psalter*, ed. K. D. Bülbring, EETS 97 (London, 1891; repr. Woodbridge, 1987), p. 189.

[69] *On the Properties of Things, John Trevisa's Translation of Bartholomaeus Anglicus De Proprietatibus Rerum, a Critical Text*, gen. ed. M. C. Seymour, 3 vols (Oxford, 1975–1988), vol. 1, Chapter 13, paragraph 20, p. 664.

Non est super terram potestas quae conparetur ei qui factus est ut nullum timeret. Omne sublime videt ipse est rex super universos filios superbiae

[He shall make the deep sea to boil like a pot, and shall make it as when ointments boil. A path shall shine after him, he shall esteem the deep as growing old. There is no power upon earth that can be compared with him who was made to fear no one. He beholdeth every high thing, he is king over all the children of pride.]

It becomes apparent why the Church Fathers and the more bookish-minded clerics of the European Middle Ages associated misfortune, pride and, finally, the enemy of the faith with the sea. From patristic times onwards, Leviathan was thought to be Satan himself, and thus one can imagine without great difficulty why John saw the first beast of the Apocalypse ascending from the sea.

Yet, conceivably the most telling passage for this negative portrayal of the sea in the Bible is John's potent vision of the new Jerusalem in Apocalypse 21.1: 'et vidi caelum novum et terram novam primum enim caelum et prima terra abiit et mare iam non est' [And I saw a new heaven and a new earth. For the first heaven and the first earth was gone, and the sea is now no more]. In God's realm there is no place for the sea. Next to the macrospatial perfection of one faith, no other myth can be tolerated. This emphatic exclusion of the sea, the last great residue of pagan animism, from the city of eternal bliss is a conclusive argument for the fervent biblical condemnation of the ocean.[70] But Apocalypse 21.1 also expresses the heritage and the ideological triumph of a land-dwelling civilisation that harbours a deep mistrust of the sea. There is not much seafaring in the Bible, and the little sea-travel that transpires is either immoral (Jonah) or utilitarian (fishing).[71] The people of Israel were farmers and land-dwellers and tended not to be maritime merchants,[72] but many, like Peter, were certainly fishermen, and depended on the sea for their livelihood and, at least pragmatically, must have paid close attention to the sea. And this renders the final exile of the sea in Apocalypse 21.1 so absolute. 'And the sea is now no more' contains plain spite and contempt for the sea, perhaps as a result of mistrust and, ultimately, fear. In the heavenly Jeru-

---

[70] One of the Church Fathers who noted this elementary opposition of the sea and God was Ephraim of Syria. In the second of his *Seven Hymns on the Faith*, the wise pearl admonishes the listener that he should not be so foolish as to seek God in the deep: 'Search not out the Lord of the sea. ... Who would linger and be searching on into the depths of Godhead?' *Select Works of Saint Ephrem*, trans. J. B. Morris (Oxford and London, 1847), p. 87.

[71] Their kings, however, could be another matter. In *The Phoenicians and the Sea: Politics, Colonies and Trade* (Cambridge, 2001), Maria Eugenia Aubet observes that Solomon entered into an economic partnership with Hiram of Tyre: 'The second stage in Hiram's expansionist policy coincides with the organization of a joint naval enterprise with Israel aimed at opening up a new market: the Orient', p. 44 (see also pp. 43–6). The sources, very rich, are Isaiah 23, Ezekiel 26–8, and 1 Kings, passim.

[72] A point also noted by Bernard McGinn, 'Ocean and Desert as Symbols of Mystical Absorption in the Christian Tradition', *Journal of Religion* 74:2 (1994), 155–81, who describes the Jews of antiquity as 'landlubbers from the Mediterranean littoral', p. 156.

salem fickleness and uncertainty have been transmogrified into stability and certainty; truth has vanquished doubt; land has encroached upon water. In this sense, the absence of the sea from the topography of perfection-to-come is the ultimate expression of expanding land at the sea's expense. No longer will the sea host Leviathan or the Beasts of the Apocalypse or the vindictive members of the 'pagan' pantheon; nor will it produce shipwrecks, sponsor floods and sea-borne invasions; nor will God require the sea as a vehicle to execute Providence. In Heaven, the divine truth can be experienced directly. Here, the sanctity of land has territorialised the unholy sea – land has purified the sea by turning it into land. The battle, elemental in every sense, is over. Naturally, this spiritual mastery of the sea not only spells the end of the sea but it also brings to an irrevocable conclusion all myths of the sea.

One such myth is the perception of the ocean as a desert.[73] Inherited from the Church Fathers, this tradition is indebted to the notion of the sea as the seat of the Devil. Among Irish seaborne *peregrini* in search of an ascetic experience, the sea, resting-place of all sins committed by human-kind, will gain particular currency as a substitute for the monastic desert. This change in the spiritual value of the sea as desert, *heremum in oceano*, can be observed in the two earliest Insular versions of Brendan's voyage, the pre-Conquest Latin *Navigatio Sancti Brendani Abbatis* and the post-Conquest Anglo-Norman *Voyage de saint Brandan* by Benedeit. But before I discuss these two texts, a brief glance at Old English writings will be necessary.

A Note on English Writings before the Conquest

That the Conquest did not immediately bring to a halt the dissemination of English writings is documented by the considerable number of twelfth-century manuscripts written in English. So significant in terms of codicological activity is the first century and a half following the Conquest that Seth Lerer judges it 'one of the most productive for the dissemination of Old English writing'.[74] Lerer, mindful of the distinction (or lack thereof) between literary and non-literary texts, qualifies his assessment by prefacing it with a somewhat bleak observation about the harvest of literary writings: 'from a literary standpoint, the period is marked by minor forms'.[75] 'Minor', I should add, means 'short' or 'lyrical' in this context since 'no single, long, sustained narrative survives from the time of *Beowulf* (*c.* 1000) to that of Laȝamon (*c.* 1189–1200) and the *Orrmulum* (*c.* 1200)'.[76]

To use the absence of something as evidence for the existence of some-thing else is always fraught with dangers. The particular problem with the

---

[73] On the sea as desert see McGinn, 'Ocean and Desert', passim.
[74] Seth Lerer, 'Old English and Its Afterlife', *The Cambridge History of Medieval Literature*, ed. David Wallace (Cambridge, 1999), pp. 7–34 (p. 8).
[75] Lerer, 'Old English', p. 8.
[76] Lerer, 'Old English', p. 8.

above evaluation is the validity of these three texts as markers: both *Beowulf* and the *Orrmulum* each exist in only a single manuscript, whereas Laȝamon's *Brut* has reached us in two manuscripts. To this one could add that the *Orrmulum* is actually a compilation of homilies which ought to disqualify it, at least partly, from being considered 'a single, long, sustained narrative', so that Laȝamon must hold his ground alone in this assessment of the yield of twelfth-century literature written in English. If, however, the scarcity of these existing witnesses is anything to go by, then the odds of a text not having reached us must only be marginally higher than those of finding another manuscript of a known text. My point, in other words, is that there is not enough evidence to make statistical inferences of this type. We simply do not know whether or how many such works have been produced. What one can say, though, is that this type of text was not produced in any significant number, provided, of course, that there was no targeted destruction of such texts. I understand that my view may be less satisfactory than existing theories about the role of vernacular writings during this period but it has the benefit of erring on the side of caution. Because an absence of evidence (be it positive or negative) spells a lack of foundations on which to erect stable arguments, I suggest that if we need to speak of literary form at this stage, we talk of its instability, both individually and statistically.[77]

My reasons for offering a prolix introduction to a section that promises brevity are the difficulties I have encountered in answering the simple yet pertinent question 'did thirteenth- and fourteenth-century writers read pre-Conquest works written in English?' Even where seemingly demonstrable continuities exist, such as the codicological activity in the twelfth century or alliteration (albeit inflected by an exposure to much more influential French traditions), evaluating the existing evidence is, as I have tried to show, a different matter altogether. And this is especially valid for alliteration in its contentious guise as the 'Alliterative Revival'.[78] The answer, therefore, must be a cautious and, by definition, unstable one. Taken together, the absence of positive evidence on the one hand and the presence of codicological and stylistic continuities on the other only lend support to the statement that in the twelfth century a good range of pre-Conquest works in English continued to be read and copied.[79] But there is a dearth of evidence for the subsequent centuries so that it would appear safe to say that Old English works did

---

[77] In a broader context, Christopher Cannon considers oddness the norm in early Middle English literature (*The Grounds of English Literature* (Oxford, 2004), passim).

[78] For an intelligent approach to this problem, see Ralph Hanna, 'Alliterative Poetry', in Wallace, *The Cambridge History of Medieval Literature*, pp. 488–512.

[79] This range spans Ælfric's homiletic and hagiographic writings as well as translations of the Gospel, the Rule of St Benedict, laws, dialogue literature and much more (Mary Swan and Elaine M. Treharne, Introduction to *Rewriting Old English in the Twelfth Century*, ed. Swan and Treharne, Cambridge Studies in Anglo-Saxon England 30 (Cambridge, 2000), pp. 1–10 (pp. 1–2). I am grateful to Christopher Cannon for sharing with me his thoughts on this question and for drawing my attention to Swan's and Treharne's volume.

not continue to be understood or used in any significant number during the remainder of the pre-modern period.

It is on those grounds that I have decided to marginalise pre-Conquest writings in English in my wider discussion of the sea in English literature. Still, some Old English works need attention, if only to illustrate how much the arrival of the newly polarised connectivity and, therefore, multilinguality of the post-Conquest centuries had affected maritime topoi in literature. I should add that 'multilinguality' is a problematic and, in my view, not always helpful concept in the first two centuries after the Conquest since it is commonly called upon to define the period against the state of affairs in England before the coming of the Normans. But Anglo-Saxon England was not monolingual – after all, Latin was used by the Church – nor were the twelfth and thirteenth centuries necessarily governed by some kind of unchecked diffusion among the three languages of England. English was simply not significant enough to be on a par with French or Latin.

Almost every genre of Old English writing features texts that assign considerable narrative space to the sea: elegies (*The Seafarer* and *The Wanderer*), the epic poem (*Beowulf*), biblical translations and variations (*Exodus*, *Genesis*, *Christ*), riddles (the 'storm'), homilies (the story of Jonah) and the traveller accounts/geographical treatises of Ohthere and Wulfstan. This list is, of course, not exhaustive.[80] A closer look at some of these texts, however, will betray the Insular connectivity that generated many of these narratives. Dorothy Whitelock argued as early as 1950 that *The Seafarer* (composed before 975) represents an Anglo-Saxon instance of the Irish *peregrinatio pro amore Dei*.[81] *Beowulf*, for instance, narrates events taking place in Denmark and Sweden, whereas Ohthere (*fl.* late ninth century) was a Norwegian traveller and visitor to England who recounted his experience of North Atlantic whaling at King Alfred's court.[82]

There are, of course, parallels between pre- and post-Conquest treatments

---

[80] On the sea in Old English literature, see F. W. Moorman, *The Interpretation of Nature in English Poetry from Beowulf to Shakespeare* (Strasbourg, 1905; repr. 1992); Amy Bullock, 'The Sea in Anglo-Saxon Poetry' (thesis, Boston University, 1909); Anne Treneer, *The Sea in English Literature – From Beowulf to Donne* (Liverpool, 1926); Adelem Barker, 'Sea and Steppe Imagery in Old English and Old Russian Epic' (thesis, New York University, 1976); Frederick Holton, 'Old English Sea Imagery and the Interpretation of *The Seafarer*' *Yearbook of English Studies* 12 (1982), 208–17; Roger Smith, 'Seafaring Imagery in Old English Poetry' (PhD thesis, Stanford University, CA, 1987); Sarah Lynn Higley, 'Storm and Mind in Anglo-Saxon Poetry: A Hard Lesson', *In Geardagum* 9 (1988), 23–39, Karin Olsen, 'The Dichotomy of Land and Sea in the Old English *Andreas*', *English Studies* 79 (1998), 385–94, and Jennifer Neville, *Representations of the Natural World in Old English Poetry*, Cambridge Studies in Anglo-Saxon England 27 (Cambridge, 1999), in particular Chapter 5, 'Representing God: Power in and against Nature', pp. 139–77.

[81] 'The Interpretation of *The Seafarer*', in *Early Cultures of Northwest Europe*, H. M. Chadwick Memorial Studies (Cambridge, 1950), pp. 261-72. For an alternative reading, see Sebastian I. Sobecki, 'The Interpretation of *The Seafarer*: A Re-examination of the Pilgrimage Theory', *Neophilologus* 91:4 (2007), forthcoming.

[82] Ohthere's account is included in the opening chapter of the *Old English Orosius*. On his whaling episode, see Vicki Ellen Szabo, 'Whaling in Early Medieval Britain', *Haskins Society Journal* 9 (2001), 137–57.

of the sea such as the (possible) *peregrinatio pro amore Dei* in *The Seafarer* and the patristic commonplace of the sea of the world, described as 'yða ofermæta' [measureless waters] in *Christ II* (composed before the tenth century) and alluded to by Jonah's motionless ship trapped in a storm in the tenth-century *Vercelli Homilies*.[83] To this one can also add the patristically inspired threatening presence of the sea in Creation narratives.[84] Yet what dominates a comparative reading of pre- and post-Conquest writings in English is the degree to which the earlier texts are permeable to the sea. There is hardly a narrative or lexical space that the sea cannot reach. In the ninth-century *Genesis B*, Adam is prepared to walk on the ocean floor if it allows him to make up for his transgression:

> þeah me on sæ wadan
> hete heofones god heonone nu þa,
> on flod faran ...
> ac ic to þam grunde genge, gif ic godes meahte
> willan gwyrcean.

> [even if heavenly God now ordered me to walk into the sea from here, to go into the water ... but I would go the bottom [of the sea] if I could perform God's will][85]

The translator of Exodus goes even further and forces Pharaoh to realise that God is the 'mereflodes Weard', the Guardian of the sea.[86]

Taking to sea becomes a natural activity for those heroically inclined. This applies not only to Beowulf's swimming contest, his submarine battle, or his sea-voyage in response to Hroðgar's call for aid, but it also holds true for hagiographic narratives such as *Andreas* (eighth to tenth century). When commanded by God to travel to Mermedonia, Andrew refers to his path as 'herestræta / ofer cald wæter' [military roads over the cold water].[87] Such martial associations are not uncommon and, in his discussion of the ninth-century *Genesis A*, Paul Battles takes it for granted that the sea invites

---

83 See Michelet, *Creation, Migration and Conquest*, p. 59 (for *Christ II*), and Paul E. Szarmach, '*The Vercelli Homilies*: Style and Structure', in *The Old English Homily and Its Background* ed. Paul E. Szarmach and B. F. Huppé (Albany, NY, 1978), pp. 241–67 (p. 249). Szarmach makes the same point in 'Three Versions of the Jonah Story: An Investigation of Narrative Technique in Old English Homilies', *Anglo-Saxon England* 1 (1972), 183–92.

84 Michelet, *Creation, Migration and Conquest*, pp. 56–7.

85 *Genesis B*, lines 830b–5a, in *The Saxon Genesis*, ed. A. N. Doane (Madison, WI, 1991). The translation is from Michelet, *Creation, Migration and Conquest*, p. 63.

86 *The Old English Exodus: Text, Translation and Commentary by J. R. R. Tolkien*, ed. Joan Turville-Petre (Oxford, 1981), line 503.

87 *Andreas*, lines 200b-1, in *The Vercelli Book*, ed. George Philip Krapp, Anglo-Saxon Poetic Records 2 (New York, 1932; repr. 1961). For the translation and a discussion of this passage, see Michelet, *Creation, Migration and Conquest*, pp. 193 ff. This passage also forms the focus of Lisa J. Kiser, '*Andreas* and the *lifes weg*: Convention and Innovation in Old English Metaphor', *Neuphilologische Mitteilungen* 85 (1984), 65–75.

such readings: 'migration, like sea-voyages and battle, constitutes heroic action'.[88]

If the number of pseudonyms is indicative of usage, then the sea is hardly a lexical taboo in pre-Conquest English poetry. There are countless words, phrases and synechdoches for the sea that would even embarrass the combined linguistic forces of the post-Conquest period. The following is a list of by no means all words for the sea or parts of the sea employed in *Beowulf* alone: 'brim', 'brimstream', 'brimwylm', 'faroð', 'flod', 'flodyð', 'garsecg', 'geofon', 'holm', 'hronrad', 'lagu', 'lagustræt', 'lagustream', 'mere', 'mere-grund', 'merestræt', 'sæ', 'sægrund', 'sæwudu', 'seglrad', 'streamas', 'sund', 'sundgebland', 'sundwudu', 'swanrad', 'wæter', 'wæteregesa', 'wæteryð', 'wylm', 'yðgeblond', 'yðgewin(n)' and 'yðlaf'.[89] To this can be added the many sea-related verbs, adjectives and compound nouns in the poem. Certainly, a number of these terms belong to a more poetic register, of which some, in turn, may be coinages of convenience permitted by the modular nature of Old English compounding. Nevertheless, this still leaves a tally of more than ten pseudonyms for the sea native to Old English prose.

This deafening presence of the sea in pre-Conquest writings in English has led some readers to think of the sea as land-like, paved by the many ways of expressing sea-voyages as paths. Karin Olsen even goes as far as suggesting that it is common in Old English poetry to regard the sea as land.[90] Perhaps this assessement of the degree to which pre-Conquest vernacular poetry allows for the integration of land and sea is too optimistic since it creates the – not necessarily accurate – impression that Anglo-Saxon writers always viewed the sea as something natural and integral to their lives. The danger with this view is that it denies a voice to the many diverse facets of the sea in Old English writings that were indebted to the Bible and patristic writings.[91] It is also easy to forget that Ohthere was a Norwegian visitor whose tales of whaling captured King Alfred's court because of their exoticism and novelty value, the same exoticism, one would suppose, that afforded the three Irish sea-pilgrims the place of honour for the year 891 in the *Anglo-Saxon Chronicle*, relegating Arnulf's victory over the Normans at the River Dyle near Leuven to second place (the pilgrims incidentally arrived at the same court as Ohthere).[92] Neither does the Scandinavian society sketched in *Beowulf* necessarily reflect that of the writer or the copyist of the poem.

Many of the earlier accounts of the supposedly triumphal march of the sea through Old English literature spring from the isolationist nationalism of late nineteenth- and early twentieth-century approaches to Old English culture as

---

[88] Paul Battles, '*Genesis A* and the Anglo-Saxon "Migration Myth"', *Anglo-Saxon England* 29 (2000), 43–66 (59). See Michelet, *Creation, Migration and Conquest*, p. 202.

[89] Lena B. Morton discusses some of these and other words for the sea in *The Influence of the Sea upon English Poetry* (New York, 1976), pp. 20–6.

[90] Karin Olsen, 'The Dichotomy of Land and Sea', p. 385.

[91] Jennifer Neville offers a good discussion of religious uses of the sea in 'Representing God'.

[92] See my discussion of this passage in the Introduction.

expressive of the quintessence of Englishness. In the romantic typology of this tendency 'Old English' prefigures the Imperial 'Anglo-Saxon', a state of being truly English, with minimal Continental influences. The language (like the culture that produced it) is viewed as simple, stoic, pragmatic, honest, home-bred, living in harmony with its environment and, at the same time, proto-Protestant and therefore free from any religious contamination from the Continent. It is remarkable how vital the sea becomes as something that is native to and expressive of such a nostalgic and essentially anachronistic 'Anglo-Saxon state of mind'. This is also what Churchill appears to have in mind when he employs the phrase 'Island race' in his *The Second World War* and, even more clearly, in the *History of the English Speaking Peoples*: 'the phrase is used ... to describe the inhabitants of Britain from Celtic society to the Norman Conquest'.[93] Although the main stage for launching and conducting such readings was the introductions to the many editions published by the learned societies, one of the best remembered applications of this sentiment is Ezra Pound's translation of *The Seafarer*.[94]

In a manoeuvre reminiscent of Matthew Arnold's equally maritime *Dover Beach*, Pound dismisses the spiritual (and most densely Christian) section of the poem, effacing religious references so systematically that he deliberately translates 'englum' [angels] in line 78 with 'English'.[95] Chris Jones notes that Pound's interest in Old English poetry does not stop at *The Seafarer*: besides translating Caedmon, Pound's juvenilia include much Saxonesque material, some of which expresses the desire to leave dry land and go to sea in possible imitation of *The Seafarer*.[96] Throughout his oeuvre, writing about and emulating Old English becomes a theme that cannot be divorced from the sea: Jones characterises the voice at the start of the *Cantos* as 'the Homeric-Saxon-Modernist voice of the sea',[97] and, when summing up Pound's Old English style, he repeatedly talks of Pound's 'Saxon(ised) sea-music'.[98]

Since some readers of Old English show a propensity for colouring their prose with alliteration and compound nouns in the manner of the texts they discuss (Jones's 'Saxon sea-music' is very much tongue-in-cheek), it is sometimes difficult to determine whether it is the poet or the reader who becomes enthralled by the sea in Old English literature. Bruce Mitchell's and Fred C. Robinson's 'sea fever' is precisely such an instance:

---

[93] Kathleen Wilson, *The Island Race: Englishness, Empire and Gender in the Eighteenth Century* (London and New York, 2003), p. 54,

[94] For a summary of the critical debate over Pound's translation, see Chris Jones, *Strange Likeness: The Use of Old English in Twentieth-century Poetry* (Oxford, 2006), p. 29, in particular, note 42.

[95] 'Deliberately' since Pounds admits so himself. See Michael Alexander, *The Poetic Achievement of Ezra Pound* (Edinburgh, 1998), pp. 75–6.

[96] Jones, *Strange Likeness*, pp. 22–3.

[97] Jones, *Strange Likeness*, pp. 55 and 57.

[98] Jones, *Strange Likeness*, p. 53.

One aspect of the seafaring life which has always captured the attention of people everywhere is the paradoxical state of mind called 'sea fever' – that irresistible call of the sea felt by experienced seamen who may on some occasions complain bitterly about the pains and trials of sea travel, but will sign on for another voyage when the opportunity presents itself.[99]

The problems such an approach can generate in *The Seafarer* (not to mention the remainder of the body of Old English literature, where such sentiments are indeed scarce) is that it clashes with the elegiac voice of the Seafarer himself, who then becomes trapped between readings of being an experienced sailor or an Insular pilgrim-by-sea. If he is pilgrim who crosses the sea in search of exile, as Dorothy Whitelock suggests, then why does he talk about life at sea? But if, on the other hand, he is a seasoned mariner as, Mitchell and Robinson appear to hint at, then why does he elaborate on the transitoriness of existence in celebration of his pilgrimage?[100]

But this is just one example of the continued grip of false continuities on the sea in Old English literature, a sea that, although significant and multivocal, has not outlived the Conquest. Pre-Conquest writings in English present a view of the sea that belongs to an alternative history of the subject, one that was stifled in its development by the overnight imposition of Continental tastes. As far as my argument is concerned, the afterlife of the Old English sea in later pre-modern literature is reduced to a set of improbable possibilities. Once rediscovered as quasi-continuities by the nineteenth century, these possibilities became operative in the discourse of Englishness at the time. But the writing of the history of the sea in that discourse lies beyond the scope of this book.

99 Bruce Mitchell and Fred C. Robinson, *A Guide to Old English* (Oxford, 1982; sixth edn, 2001), p. 276
100 I discuss this conundrum in 'The Interpretation of *The Seafarer*'.

2

Deserts and Forests in the Ocean

But north, still north, Saint Brandan steer'd;
And now no bells, no convents more!
The hurting Polar lights are near'd,
The sea without a human shore.

Matthew Arnold, 'Saint Brandan' (1860)

And when neither sun nor stars appeared for many days, and no small
storm lay on us, all hope of our being saved was now taken away.

Acts of the Apostles, 27.20

The End of the *Désert Liquide*: Benedeit's *Voyage de Saint Brandan*[1]

Benedeit's *Voyage de Saint Brandan* (*c.* 1118) has often been unjustly labelled a translation of the anonymous Latin *Navigatio Sancti Brendani Abbatis* (eighth century).[2] It cannot be readily assumed that Benedeit's skilful adaptation of his source material results from a direct translation of the *Navigatio*. M. D. Legge has even argued for a Latin version of the legend prepared by Benedeit for Henry I's first wife, Queen Maud or Matilda, which he himself translated into French as the *Voyage*.[3] As one of the more widely read poems of the pre-modern period, the Latin *Navigatio* boasts over 120 extant manuscripts and has been translated into nearly all European vernaculars.[4] Scholars of early Insular literature agree that the *Navigatio* either belongs

---

[1] Some of the material here has appeared as 'From the *Désert Liquide* to the Sea of Romance: Benedeit's *Le Voyage de Saint Brandan* and the Irish *Immrama*' in *Neophilologus* 87:2 (2003), 193–207.

[2] Benedeit's poem has been edited by E. G. Waters, *The Anglo-Norman Voyage of St Brendan by Benedeit* (Oxford, 1928), and by Ian Short and Brian Merrilees, *The Anglo-Norman Voyage of St Brendan* (Manchester, 1979). More recently, Glyn S. Burgess furnished an English translation in *The Voyage of Saint Brendan: Representative Versions of the Legend in English Translation*, ed. W. R. J. Barron and Glyn S. Burgess (Exeter, 2002). The standard edition of the Latin *Navigatio* remains *Navigatio Sancti Brendani Abbatis*, ed. C. Selmer (South Bend, IN, 1959). David Dumville has argued for a *terminus ante quem* for the *Navigatio* not later than the 'third quarter of the eighth century' ('Two Approaches to the Dating of *Nauigatio Sancti Brendani*', *Studi medievali*, third s. 29 (1988), 87–102, passim).

[3] M. D. Legge, 'Anglo-Norman Hagiography and the Romances', *Medievalia et Humanistica*, n.s. 6 (1975), 41–9 (41).

[4] Selmer, *Navigatio sancti Brendani abbatis*, pp. xxvi–xxvii.

to, or is cognate with, the Irish genre of the *immram*, or maritime voyage-tale, which David Dumville renders literally as 'rowing about'.[5] Legge has alleviated any remaining concerns as to the genre of Benedeit's work.[6] Her assessment of the *Voyage* has perhaps not gained the currency it deserves, but is has not lost anything of its accuracy: 'This is not a Life, although it is so described in the manuscripts, but might well be labelled a romance in its own right.'[7] The copious parallels she enumerates in her article are ample evidence for the *Voyage*'s profound influence on English romances. And if later Anglo-Norman poets eagerly turned toward Benedeit's work for ideas, then it is all the more conceivable that writers such as Wace or Thomas of Britain (twelfth century), whose own poems assigned considerable narrative space to the sea, had listened with great care to what Benedeit had to say about the deep.[8]

One key idea of the Irish (and, to a lesser extent, wider Insular) *peregrinatio pro amore Dei* is the enthusiastic search for remote places and extreme solitariness, or, in Matthew Arnold's words, 'the sea without a human shore'.[9] St Gall's hagiographer, Walahfrid Strabo (808/9–49), even calls it the natural state of an Irishman.[10] Arnold Angenendt classifies the first stages of the Irish *peregrinatio* as follows: first comes the wish to abandon the material world through which the designated pilgrim becomes a stranger to everything secular, *mundo alienus*. This desire culminates in the act of leaving one's homeland, *exul patriae*, and afterwards follows the quest for a remote island, *insula semota*.[11] Dumville identifies this spiritual longing with the search for a *heremum in oceano*.[12] Other scholars have called it a *Wasserwüste* or *désert liquide*, but the idea is essentially rooted in Matthew's call to the apostolic life (Matthew 19.29).[13] The setting out in an unseaworthy coracle, the refusal

---

5   David Dumville, '*Echtrae* and *Immram*: Some Problems of Definition', *Ériu* 27 (1976), 73–94 (75). Three Old Irish *immrama* have survived: the prose *Immram curaig Máele Dúin*, the *Immram Snédgus ocus Maic Riagla* and the *Immram curaig Ua Corra*. On the *immrama*, see Tom Clancy, 'Subversion at Sea: Structure, Style and Intent in the *Immrama*', in *The Otherworld Voyage in Early Irish Literature*, ed. Jonathan Wooding (Dublin, 2000), pp. 194–225. Helen Cooper, in *The English Romance in Time: Transforming Motifs from Geoffrey of Monmouth to the Death of Shakespeare* (Oxford, 2004), discusses the *immrama* and the Brendan-voyage as instances of setting adrift, pp. 122–4.

6   Legge, 'Anglo-Norman Hagiography', passim.

7   Legge, 'Anglo-Norman Hagiography', 41.

8   Elsewhere, I suggest that the description of the magical ship that has ferried the hermit Paul to his island (*Voyage*, lines 1,555–8) may have influenced Marie de France's lai *Guigemar* (Sebastian I. Sobecki, 'A Source for the Magical Ship in the *Partonopeu de Blois* and Marie de France's *Guigemar*', *Notes and Queries*, 48:3 (2001), 220–2).

9   Matthew Arnold, 'Saint Brandan', line 8.

10 Jerzy Strzelczyk, 'Społeczne aspekty iroszkockiej peregrinatio', in *Peregrinationes – pielgrzymki w kulturze dawnej Europy*, ed. Halina Manikowska and Hanna Zaremska, Colloquia Mediaevalia Varsoviensia 2 (Warsaw, 1995), pp. 39–50 (p. 41).

11 Arnold Angenendt, 'Die irische Peregrinatio und ihre Auswirkungen auf dem Kontinent vor dem Jahre 800', in *Die Iren und Europa im früheren Mittelalter*, ed. Heinz Löwe, 2 vols (Stuttgart, 1982), vol. 1, pp. 52–79 (pp. 52–8).

12 Dumville, '*Echtrae* and *Immram*', p. 78.

13 Colin Ireland, 'Some Analogues of the OE *Seafarer* from Hiberno-Latin Sources', *Neuphilologische Mitteilungen* 92:1 (1991), 1–14 (2). See also Bernard McGinn, 'Ocean and Desert as

to use one's oars and/or rudder and the fervent prayer to God acknowledge, according to Angenendt, *deus* as *gubernator*, which is the next and, often, the crucial phase of this ritualistic provocation of a miracle.[14] Angenendt's at times schematic view of the Irish *peregrinatio* is helpful, but it should be remembered that the various 'steps' do not have to occur in precisely this sequence.

Yet the religious desert is not only a place of solitude but also the home of temptation, the ultimate spiritual challenge to the sea-borne pilgrim. Doubt, fear, despair: all these 'vices' are encountered by the *peregrinus pro amore Dei*. Since Christ fought one of his greatest spiritual battles against Satan's enticing in the desert, it is no surprise to see that Brendan addresses his monks as *conbellatores* in the *Navigatio* (Chapter 2, line 3), a term which J. F. Webb translates as 'co-warriors in spiritual conflict'.[15] Benedeit lets Brendan address his monks as *seignurs* and *frere*, but reserves the rare *pelerin* for the narrator's remarks. *Seignur(s)* is the standard address of romance, and it need not have any military connotations. The result is a partial loss of the basic quality of the *peregrinatio* as a '*con-bellum*' fought together by a group of monks against the multitude of temptations unleashed by the sea of the world.

A further characteristic of the Irish *peregrinatio* seems to be the spontaneity behind Angenendt's *exul patriae*. In the *Immram Snédgus ocus Maic Riagla* the two heroes, Snédgus and Mac Riagla, after having visited a friendly ruler to offer their legal advice, suddenly decide to abandon their return to Iona. Without much ado, they discard their oars and embark on a *peregrinatio pro amore Dei*:

> Am*al* batar ina curoch imráidhset eturro dul assa ndeóin isand-ocián n-imechtrach a n-ailit*h*ri, amal dochotar in sesca lanamna, cencop assa ndeóin dochotar sidhe.

> [As they were in their coracle they bethought them of wending with their own consent into the outer ocean on a pilgrimage, even as the sixty couples had gone, though these went not with their own consent.][16]

When Barinthus and his *filiolus* Mernoc visit the Island of Delights in the *Navigatio*, they stroll along the shore after compline:

> Mihi autem pernoctanti insulamque totam perambulanti meus filiolus duxit me ad litus / maris contra occidentem, ubi erat nauicula, et dixit mihi: 'Pater, ascende in nauim et nauigemus contra occidentalem plagam ad

Symbols of Mystical Absorption in the Christian Tradition', *Journal of Religion* 74:2 (1994), 155–81.

[14] Angenendt, 'Die irische Peregrinatio', pp. 58–9.

[15] J. F. Webb, *The Voyage of St Brendan*, in *The Age of Bede*, ed. D. H. Farmer (Harmondsworth, 1983), p. 235.

[16] Whitley Stokes, trans., 'The Voyage of Snedgus and MacRiagla', *Revue Celtique* 9 (1888), 14–25 (18–19).

insulam que dicitur ‖ terra repromissionis sanctorum, quam Deus daturus est successoribus nostris in nouissimo tempore.' Ascendentibusque nobis et nauigantibus.

[When I stayed awake to walk round the island by night, my *filiolus* [Mernoc] led me to the western sea-shore, where there was a small boat, and he said to me: 'Father, let us board this boat and sail westwards to the island that is called the Promised Land of the Saints, which God will grant to our successors on the last day.' We embarked and sailed away.][17]

Later, when Brendan hears of Barinthus's voyage, he spontaneously resolves to go on a journey himself (Chapter 2, lines 1 ff.). All of this urgency is missing from the *Voyage* as Benedeit gives Brendan's pilgrimage a fixed aim:

> Mais de une ren li prist talent,
> Dunt Deu prïer prent plus suvent,
> Que lui mustrast cel paraïs
> U Adam fud primes asis.
> …
> Deu en prïet tenablement
> Cel lui mustret veablement;
> Ainz qu'il murget voldreit saveir
> Quel sed li bon devrunt aveir,
> Quel lu li mal aveir devrunt.
> Quel merite il recevrunt.   (lines 47–50; 59–64)

[But he had one particular desire, concerning which he began to pray to God repeatedly, asking him to show him the Paradise where Adam was lodged in the beginning. … Brendan prayed fervently to God that he would show him this place clearly; before he died, he longed to see the future abode of the good, as well as the place where the evil would dwell and the reward they would receive.][18]

Perhaps Benedeit judged the Irish *désert liquide* too alien a concept for a courtly Anglo-Norman audience when he removed the militancy and the spontaneity from Brendan's pilgrimage. In doing so, he aligns his poem much more closely with Paul's sea-voyage in Acts 27.[19] Both the biblical episode

---

17 Chapter 1, lines 30–6. All citations from the *Navigatio* are taken from Selmer, *Navigatio Sancti Brendani Abbatis*. The translation is my own. The word *filiolus* presents some problems of translation here. Webb renders it into English as 'spiritual son' and is probably very close to its actual meaning. It might well correspond to a novice who is formally placed under the auspices of a more experienced monk. This relationship cannot have been one of strict authority of the mentor over the *filiolus* as it is Barinthus who follows the impulsive suggestion of Mernoc, his *filiolus*. I have decided not to translate *filiolus*, given the difficulties of finding an accurate equivalent.
18 I shall refer to E. G. Waters's line numbering throughout. All translations from Benedeit's poem are taken from *The Voyage of Saint Brendan*, ed. Barron and Burgess.
19 There are a number of striking parallels between the Brendan-tradition and Acts 27: at various points in the episode, Paul displays prophetic qualities, admonishes the crew, fasts, and stresses

and the *Voyage* foreground the adventure at sea at the expense of spiritual aspects.

At other instances, Benedeit defuses the exuberant spirituality that characterises the *Navigatio*-tradition. In the Latin poem Brendan's seven-year odyssey is structured by the liturgical year as all major feasts are allocated to specific islands and are therefore observed each year at the same place. This sense of spiritual coherence and divine guidance is removed from Benedeit's poem, so that the *temporale* and *sanctorale* are no longer Brendan's compass, and the frequent quoting of hymns and antiphons has been banished from the *Voyage*, making it a less musical and, hence, less liturgical work. Nevertheless, Brendan's pilgrimage is not to be confused with the purpose-driven, penitential journeys of the Continental tradition. Benedeit's sea may have lost most of its quality as *heremum*, but the seeming arbitrariness of the saint's enterprise heralds the coming of romance questing.

Unlike the writers of the *immrama*, Benedeit betrays himself to be, like Wace and Seneca before him, an observer of the sea. He awakens one attribute of the ocean which lay dormant in the *Navigatio* and which constituted only a minor element of the *immrama*: the fear of the sea. The words *turment/ turmente* and *tempestes* appear far more often in the *Voyage* than their Latin equivalents in the *Navigatio*. A number of examples will illustrate this cognitive shift. Before their visit to the Isle of Ailbe, the monks show their *fear of the sea* as soon as the wind begins to blow stronger:

> Vunt s'en mult tost en mer siglant,
> De tant bon vent Deu gracïant.
> Crut lur li venz, e mult suvent
> Crement peril e grant turment.   (lines 623–6)

> [They sailed swiftly over the sea, thanking God for such a favourable wind; then the wind increased and they were in constant dread of danger and great suffering.]

Immediately Seneca's *partemque metus fieri nostri* comes to mind as Benedeit makes the ocean part of the monks' horror.[20] The sea-monsters cause not only panic among the pilgrims but also a great storm: 'Sul les undes que il muveit, / Pur grant turment plus ne stuveit' (lines 919–20) [On the surface, the waves which it churned up were like those created by a great storm].

And storms continue to harass the traumatised monks. After the harrowing fight of the two sea-monsters, Brendan's crew lands on an island and the pilgrims set up their tent (lines 969–72). Just as they reach land, another storm begins to rage on the sea (lines 973–6) and the circumspect abbot immediately realises the imminent danger: 'Li venz lur est cuntresailiz, /

---

the importance of the number fourteen. It is difficult to imagine that the writer behind Brendan's Latin voyage would not have been familiar with this biblical narrative.

20   See pp. 25 ff.

E li cunreiz lur est failiz' (lines 977–8) [a gale had got up and their provisions were running low]. From one disaster they are tossed into another until the sea imprisons them on an unknown island. It is under these adverse circumstances that God works his miracle by washing ashore a third of the vanquished monster's carcass to feed the exhausted pilgrims. In the *Navigatio*, on the other hand, the monks land on this island precisely because they make out a fragment of the dead creature's carcass on the shore, which prompts the indiscriminately hungry abbot to articulate his relief:

> Appropinquantibusque illis ad ipsius litus atque ascendentibus de naui, uiderunt posteriorem partem illius belue que erat interfecta. Ait sanctus Brendanus: 'Ecce, que uoluit uos deuorare. Ipsam deuorabitis.'
>
> [As they came by its shore and left their boat, they saw the abdomen of the killed beast lying on the beach. 'There,' exclaimed St Brendan: 'that one wanted to devour you. Instead, you will eat it.][21]

This miraculous feeding is independent of the storm in the *Navigatio*. Once the pilgrims are nourished and refreshed, the writer informs us in passing that their stay on the island is lengthened by *tres menses* because 'tempestas in mari et uentis fortissimus et inequalitas aeris' (Chapter 16, lines 44–5) [a storm at sea and a strong wind and changeable weather] prevented them from departing sooner. On a larger scale, the fear of storms is part of the increased danger of the sea conveyed by the *Voyage*. It also removes the Anglo-Norman text even further from the spirituality of the *Navigatio* where biblical passages, such as Christ's archetypal calming of the storm in Luke 8.23–5, always seem to have been at the back of the writer's mind.

The other notable shift in Benedeit's portrayal of the sea is the frequency with which it serves as a locus for *merveilles*. To some extent, this change of emphasis is facilitated by Benedeit's discreet removal of one of the central reasons for the epic length of Brendan's odyssey in the *Navigatio*:

> Ecce terram quam quesisti per multum tempus. Ideo non potuisti statim [illam] inuenire quia Deus uoluit tibi ostendere diuersa sua secreta in oceano magno.
>
> [Behold the land you have been seeking all that long time. You could not find it immediately because God wished to reveal to you the abundance of His wonders in the great ocean.][22]

This information is not contained in Benedeit's poem, and, as a result, Brendan's quest for a closer look at Paradise is at times reduced to a maritime paperchase as the *merveilles* of the sea move into the foreground at the expense of the *Navigatio*'s spirituality.

---

[21] Chapter 16, lines 24–8.
[22] Chapter 28, lines 24–7.

In this respect, the battle of the sea-dragons displays not only Benedeit's astonishing virtuosity as a visual poet, but the scene's length and amount of detail demonstrate his interest in *aventure*. When the rapidly approaching second creature challenges the initial attacker, the Latin text passes over the ensuing clash quickly:

> His finitis duobus uersibus,[23] ecce ingens belua ab occidente iuxta / illos transibat obuiam alterius bestie. Que statim irruit bellum contra illam, ita ut ignem emisisset ex ore suo. ... His dictis, misera belua que persequebatur famulos Christi interfecta est in tres partes coram illis.

> [When he finished his two sentences, a great beast approached from the west towards the first monster. At once it attacked the other one by spewing fire out of its mouth. ... As Brendan said this, the wretched monster that had pursued Christ's servants was torn into three parts as all could see.][24]

The corresponding passage in the *Voyage* (lines 931–54) spans twenty-four lines and is charged with a vivacity that easily outplays the Latin text. Benedeit fills the scene with lively similes, e.g.: shield-like fins (*lur noës, / Tels cum escuz*) [their fins, which they used as shields] and *denz* which are as sharp as swords (lines 943–4). The fire ejected by the nostrils reaches up to the sky: 'Des narines li fous lur salt, / Desque as nües qui volet halt' (line 939–40) [fire spewing from their nostrils and rising swiftly up towards the clouds] and the waves of the sea are coloured red by the monsters' blood. Benedeit's effective use of these literary devices achieves a highly dramatic and spectacular effect, shifting the emphasis from the spiritual vanquishing of the sea serpent to the graphic details of the battle itself.

A second passage that contrasts both in length and in intensity with the above sea-battle is the observation of the ocean bed on St Peter's Day. This is one of the rare moments when the sea itself is being looked at – indeed into – by the pilgrims. After witnessing yet another nerve-wrecking clash of monsters, Brendan celebrates Mass for St Peter's Day on the high sea:

> Quodam uero tempore, cum sanctus Brendanus celebrasset Sancti Petri Apostoli festiuitatem in sua naui, inuenerunt mare clarum ita ut possent uidere quicquid subtus erat. Cum autem aspexissent intus in profundum, uiderunt diuersa genera bestiarum iacentes super arenam. Videbatur quoque illis quod potuissent manu / tangere illas pre nimia claritate illius maris. Erant enim sicut greges iacentes in pascuis. Pre multitudine tali uidebantur sicut ciuitas in girum, adplicantes capita ad posteriora iacendo.

---

23 Selmer's text has *tribus uersibus* but Brendan's preceding prayer has only two sentences that parallel each other. Two manuscripts, MS Stadtbibliothek, Berne Codex 111 and MS Hofbibliothek Stuttgart Codex 152, have *duobus uersibus* instead. As it does not conflict with the preceding prayer, I prefer the latter reading.

24 Chapter 16, lines 15–18; 21–3.

[One time, when St Brendan celebrated the feast of St Peter the Apostle in his boat, [the monks] found the sea to be so clear that they could discern everything that was underneath its surface. And when they glanced into the deep, they saw different kinds of animals lying on the sand. Because the sea was so clear, it seemed to them as if they could touch them with their hands. The animals were lying head to tail and looked like flocks at pasture, and they saw so many of them that it appeared like a city in motion.][25]

The worried monks entreat Brendan to sing Mass quietly out of fear that the animals on the ocean bed might attack them (lines 9–11). In the *Voyage*, the situation is less peaceful. The monks speak of 'peissuns … granz e crüels' (line 1049) [so large and fierce are the fish], and the sheep-like flocks of the *Navigatio* ('Erant enim sicut greges iacentes in pascuis') are transformed by the monks' anguish into scene of activity: 'veum … Peissuns tante guerre' (line 1048) [such a confusion of fish].[26] Where the writer of the *Navigatio*, which is believed to be of Irish origin, paints a scene of peace on the sea-bed, Benedeit perceives commotion and danger at the heart of the ocean.

The fear of storms and the exploitation of the *merveilles* of the sea are two aspects of the *Voyage* that are foregrounded by Benedeit at the expense of the ascetic sea-desert which survives only in Brendan's wish to venture off into the unknown. This subtle but revealing shift in the perception of the sea between the *Navigatio* and the *Voyage* could be read as a careful articulation of the Normans' cultural difference, an echo of *Normannitas*. Marjorie Chibnall has argued that as the Normans increasingly absorbed their English host culture, their traditional networks of familial and contractual relationships began to suffer. As a reaction to this development, Chibnall discerns a heightened demand for the creation of a myth of Normanness. Historiography and romances took on the task of articulating this myth.[27] At the same time, Benedeit's poem is perhaps the earliest example of the Normans' insatiable hunger for Celtic tales that would continue for the next century. Moreover, the *Voyage* could be read as a metaphor for the cultural dimension of the Conquest itself which has carefully nurtured some native tales and, at the same time, manipulated their implied cultural values. The transformation of the sea from the religious desert of patristic and Irish spirituality to a landscape of adventure not only heralds the coming of romance, but also is evidence of the Normans' osmotic process of assimilation: 'Even as a domi-

---

[25] Chapter 21, lines 1–8.

[26] Short and Merriless, *The Anglo-Norman Voyage of St Brendan*, recommend this translation in their note to this line. In the *Physiologus* and Bestiary tradition, the ocean floor is said to be permanently turbulent (see Chapter 5, p. 126, n. 18).

[27] Marjorie Chibnall, *The Normans* (Oxford, 2000), in particular 'The Norman Myth', pp. 107–24, and passim. This was especially important for a people as ethnically heterogeneous as the Normans: 'the Norman people were the product, not of blood, but of history' (p. 3). For an overview of the scholarly debate in this area, see Chibnall's *The Debate of the Norman Conquest* (Manchester and New York, 1999).

nant minority, the Normans could assimilate the English people and their culture only by changing their own nature.'[28]

By unhinging the *peregrinatio pro amore Dei* from its strictly spiritual context, the early Anglo-Norman text detaches the received material from the Irish Sea world. In the wider, anthropological context of this work, Insular connectivity begins to weaken and the *Voyage* serves as a fine specimen of the arrival of cultural *dis*connectivity in the wake of the Conquest. The *Voyage* articulates an Anglo-Norman writer's alertness to the perilous northern seas and creates a transitional English sea of romance which supplied a model sea for the first generation of Anglo-Norman courtly narratives before being ultimately subsumed by the growing uneasiness towards the deep.

Tristan's Bitter Sea of Romance

When, in Benedeit's *Voyage*, the monks set out into the unknown and the wind ceases after two weeks of sailing, Brendan urges his anxious fellow pilgrims to place their trust solely in God's spiritual navigation:

> 'Metez vus en Deu maneie,
> E n'i ait nul qui s'esmaie.
> Quant averez vent, siglez sulunc;
> Cum venz n'i ert, nagez idunc.' (lines 225–8)

> [Put yourselves under God's protection and let none of you be afraid. When the wind is blowing, sail along with it; when there is no wind, then you must row!]

Without delay, the monks put Brendan's admonition into practice:

> As aviruns dunc se metent,
> La grace Deu mult regretent,
> Quer ne sevent quel part aler,
> Ne quels cordes deient haler,
> Quel part beitrer, quel part tendre,
> Ne u devrunt lur curs prendre. (lines 229–34)

> [So they took to the oars, calling upon the grace of God. For they did not know which way to head or which ropes to haul, in which direction to steer or set their course.]

Essentially, this ritualistic calling on God not only to protect but also to guide the pilgrims through their voyage, is an instance of what Angenendt classifies as *deus gubernator* in his analysis of the Irish *peregrinatio pro amore Dei*. In the Irish *immrama*, the reliance upon *deus gubernator* manifests itself,

---

28 Chibnall, *The Normans*, p. 109.

amongst other actions, in the giving up of one's oars. In the Irish voyage-tale, *Immram Snédgus ocus Maic Riagla*, the protagonists spontaneously decide to go on pilgrimage and they refuse to employ the rudder:

> Atlaighit buidhe do Dia, 7 asb*er*[*a*]t: 'Lecam ar n-imrum do Dia, 7 tabrum ar rama inar nói.' *Ocus* leac[ad] iarsin a n-imrom aænur, 7 doberad a rama ina nói.

> [They render thanks to God and say: 'Let us leave our voyage to God, and let us put our oars into our boat.' And thereafter their voyage was left alone, and their oars were put into their boat.][29]

In a similar fashion, in the *Immram curaig Ua Corra* the bishop aboard the boat of the Húi Corra suggests the voyagers cease rowing: 'An leth a mb*er*a in gaeth sinn,' ar an t-eascab. IArsin nos-tocbat na ramhada *cucu* isin cur*ach*, 7 nos-idhbratar iat fein do Dia' ['Whithersoever the wind shall take us,' says the bishop. Thereafter they shipped their oars and offered themselves to God].[30] The late twelfth-century poem *Tristan* by Thomas of Britain expresses a similar sentiment after Tristan suffers a near-mortal wound during his clash with Morholt.[31] Thomas's account of Tristan's duel with Morholt and Tristan's ensuing sea-voyage has been preserved in a number of translations and reworkings, most importantly in the thirteenth-century Old Norse translation prepared by Friar Robert for the Norwegian King Haakon Haakonsson (reigned 1217–63). When the seemingly fatally wounded Tristan, poisoned by Morholt's sword, decides to set out in a ship, he does so voluntarily and his words of unbending trust in God echo those uttered by Irish pilgrims:

> 'Enginn vill nú mínna frænda né vina til mín koma né mik sjá eðr mik hugga, ok því vil ek héðan burt fara, hvar sem guð lætr mik niðr koma með sínni háleitri miskunn eptir mínni þurft.'

> [Not one of my friends or kinsmen want to visit me or see me or console me. Therefore I wish to go away, wherever God in his infinite grace may let me land to obtain help.][32]

Assuming that the Old Norse redaction does not alter the basic content of this passage, Tristan's setting adrift is extraordinarily similar to the precedents

---

[29] 'The Voyage of Snedgus and MacRiagla', 18–19.

[30] 'The Voyage of the Húi Corra', ed. and trans. Whitley Stokes, *Revue Celtique* 14 (1893), 22–69 (40–1).

[31] The composition of the poem is generally placed in the mid-1170s (see Gesa Bonath, ed. and trans., *Thomas Tristan* (Munich, 1985), pp. 16–18)). Despite Joseph Bédier's remarkable attempt to recreate an *Ur*-text in *Le Roman de Tristan par Thomas: Poème du XIIe siècle* (Paris, 1905), it remains nearly impossible completely to reconstruct Thomas's text, and the following discussion will be based on three versions of the Tristan-romance: Friar Robert's Old Norse *Tristrams saga ok Ísöndar*, Gottfried of Straßburg's *Tristan* and Eilhart of Oberge's *Tristrant*.

[32] *Tristrams saga ok Ísöndar. Mit einer literaturhistorischen Einleitung*, ed. Eugen Kölbing (Heilbronn, 1878), p. 37. All translations from the Old Norse text are my own.

discussed above. A number of parallels emerge. To start with, Tristan does not venture off alone:

> Nú var því næst skip Tristram búit með gnógum vistum ok því, sem hann þurfti at hafa, ok fylgðu hánum þá allir til skips ok hormuðu burtferð hans; ok sigldu nú burt í haf út; báðu nú allir fyrir hánum, sem eptir váru, at guð skyldi gæta hans ok miskunna hánum.

> [Therefore Tristram's ship was now equipped with sufficient victuals and with whatever else he needed. Everyone followed him down to the ship and grieved at his leaving. They sailed out onto the sea, and those who stayed behind prayed that God should watch over him and be merciful to him.][33]

There can be no doubt that some of the people who went with him to the shore boarded his ship and departed with the sick hero.

Gottfried of Straßburg, whose unfinished version of Thomas's poem is thought to have been composed around 1210, provides further detail on Tristan's passage. However, it must be borne in mind that Gottfried is generally less reliable than the Old Norse *Tristrams saga* since his text diverges at times considerably from Thomas's in those sections of both poems that can be compared (one should add that the passages that can be compared amount to less than 5 per cent of Thomas's poem, namely the Carlisle, Cambridge and Sneyd fragments).[34] On the other hand, Gottfried often copies long sequences from Thomas nearly verbatim and with a greater degree of congruence than that achieved by Friar Robert.[35] In particular, Gottfried tends to flesh out passages in instances where Friar Robert shortens the text. In the corresponding passage in Gottfried's text, eight men board the boat with the dying hero and trusted Curvenal:

> unde als [ez] abendende wart,
> nu bereite man in zu zir vart
> eine barke unde ein schiffelin
> unde schuf in vollen rat dar in
> an lip nar unde an spise,
> [an] anderre schifwise.
> da wart der arme Tristan
> mit maniger clage getragen an
> vil tougenliche unde also,
> daz dirre schifunge do
> vil lutzel ieman wart gewar,

---

33 *Tristrams saga*, ed. Kölbing, pp. 37–8.
34 Walter Haug reassesses the relationship between Gottfried and Tristan, following the discovery of the Carlisle fragment, in favour of Gottfried's sophisticated and innovative understanding of the text: 'Gottfrieds von Straßburg Verhältnis zu Thomas von England im Licht des neu aufgefundenen *Tristan*-Fragments von Carlisle', *Mededelingen van de Afdeling Letterkunde*, n.s. 62:4 (1999), 5–19.
35 Bonath, *Thomas Tristan*, pp. 14–15.

wan die man ouch besande dar.
…
hie mit so stizsens anden se.
sus vuren si von dannen
niuwan mit ahte mannen;
die selben heten ouch ir leben
ze borgen [*und*] ze phande geben
unde ouch versicheret bi gote,
das si us ir zweier gebote
niemer vuz getreten. (lines 7,339–50 and 7,362–9)

[And when it was evening a barge and a small ship were prepared for their journey, and supplies of food, victuals, and other equipment were stored in plenty. Then the suffering Tristan was carried with much lamenting, secretly and in such a way that his embarkation remained unnoticed, except by those who went with him. … Thus they set out into the sea. They sailed off with only eight men. Those pledged their lives [to him] and swore by God that they would not stray from orders from the two [Tristan and Curvenal].][36]

'Sigldu' [they sailed] in the Old Norse text, is clarified here further by Gottfried, who adds that eight men accompanied Tristan and Curvenal. Furthermore, the passages also correspond in their account of the provisions taken on board the ship (although only one boat departs in the *Tristrams saga*): the Old Norse text has 'gnógum vistum' [sufficient victuals] and 'sem hann þurfti at hafa' [whatever else he needed], and Gottfried provides 'an lip nar unde an spise,/[*an*] anderre schifwise' [supplies of food, victuals and other equipment].

Most importantly, however, the rationale and the exact process of Tristan's decision are made not entirely clear in either text. Friar Robert states that Tristan sets out because 'not one of [his] friends wants to visit [him]' (nú mínna frænda né vina til mín koma) and Gottfried adds that the poisoned wound, given to him by Morholt, has developed such a 'grulichen' [abominable] stench that his own body became repelling to him ('sin e*i*gen lip umarete') (lines 7,276–8). In Gottfried, as in the Old Norse text, Tristan leaves because he perceives his condition as a burden to his friends:

ouch was sin meistez ungemach,
das er das alle zit wol sach,
das er den begunde swaren,
die sine vriunde [*e*] waren (lines 7,279–82)

[His greatest sorrow was that he was well aware that he had become a burden to those who were his friends.]

---

[36] All quotations from Gottfried's *Tristan* are taken from Spiewok's edition: *Das* Tristan-*Epos Gottfrieds von Strassburg mit der Fortsetzung des Ulrich von Türkheim*, ed. Wolfgang Spiewok, Deutsche Texte des Mittelalters 75 (Berlin, 1989). The translations are my own.

As a consequence, Tristan places his trust in God's will and, having lost his own will to live ('so were [im] also mere / der lip gewaget oder tot', lines 7,304–5), he wishes for his fate to be as God would want it to be ('swie got wolte', line 7,309), thus rendering God, and Providence, his helmsman (*deus gubernator*). It is a noteworthy detail that Curvenal, who himself surrenders to God ('er wolte mit ime wesen, / mit ime ersterben oder genesen' [he wanted to stay with him, / to die or be saved with him], lines 7,337–8), becomes Tristan's *de facto* helmsman.[37]

Tristan's lack of enthusiasm for life ('im das leben swarete' [his life became a burden to him], line 7,276), and the subsequent handing himself over to God's mercy, renders him a sea-pilgrim in the tradition of setting adrift, and corresponds to the first stage of the *peregrinatio pro amore Dei*, which Angenendt calls *mundo alienus*. This originally religious wish leads to the yearning for exile, for becoming an *exul patriae*, and, ideally, the target of the journey becomes a remote island where spiritual salvation may be granted, the *insula semota*. Even this final aspect is reflected in the destination of Tristan's journey as the hero decides to sail to Ireland ('er ze Yrlanden wolte' [he wanted [to sail] to Ireland], line 7,328) because he was aware of Iseut's reputation as a healer (lines 7,295–7). Although Friar Robert removes the clear destination, Tristan leaves in the hope that he may find help and he arrives in Ireland:[38]

> Nú rak þá svá lengi í hafi fyrir vindi ok straumi, at þeir vissu ei, hvar þeir fóru; en um síðir kómu þeir at Írlandi.

> [And so the strong currents and winds tossed them on the sea for such a long time that they did not know where they were sailing. But finally they came to Ireland.][39]

The destination is also missing from *Sir Tristrem*, preserved in the fourteenth-century Auchinleck Manuscript:

> 'Em,' he seyd, 'Y spille.
> Of lond kepe Y namare.
> A schip thou bring me tille,

---

37 This may be a pun on Curvenal's/Governal's name ('Governal' in Beroul) which is synonymous with the Old French word for rudder/steer, *governail* from the Latin *gubernaculum* (at this time this was most likely a stern- or quarter-rudder). See Bertil Sandahl, *Middle English Sea Terms*, 3 vols (Uppsala, 1951–82), vol. 1, pp. 119–21.

38 Such an act of self-inflicted exile, as in the case of the Irish *immrama*, does not need to have an overtly religious motivation at the journey's outset: Snédgus and MacRiagla leave their course for Iona and hand themselves to the mercy of the waves, and Mael Duin leaves initially on a journey of revenge (see H. P. A. Oskamp, ed., *The Voyage of Mael Duin* (Groningen, 1970); Whitley Stokes, trans., 'The Voyage of Mael Duin', *Revue Celtique* 9 (1888), 447–95; 10 (1889), 50–95, and 'The Voyage of Snedgus and MacRiagla'). In a recent essay, Tom Clancy argues that the journey itself has a religious motivation ('Subversion at Sea: Structure, Style and Intent in the *Immrama*').

39 *Tristrams saga*, p. 38.

Mine harp to play me thare,
Stouer ynough to wille
To kepe me, son you yare.'
Thei Marke liked ille,
Tristrem to schip thai bare
And brought.
Who wold with him fare?
Governayle no lete him nought.[40]

With Governail/Curvenal accompanying him, Tristrem knowingly sails into the unknown. Bédier has given Tristan's voyage for healing the title 'navigation à l'aventure'.[41] *Aventure*, it would seem, stands here for chance encounters with the unknown and the unexpected. Tristan's quest is for solitude, rest and healing. He seeks God's intervention on matters of life and death, and, more precisely, perhaps, he wants to be healed.

The fact that neither Friar Robert nor Gottfried suggests that Tristan leaves behind any oars, brings these two accounts closer to Benedeit's *Voyage* than to some of the *immrama*, including the Latin *Navigatio*. This observation gains importance when compared with Eilhart of Oberge's late twelfth-century *Tristrant*, which not only happens to be the earliest complete telling of the Tristan-legend, but also features the first account of Tristan's voyage of healing:

he bat daz man in nême
und trûge in in ein schiffelîn:
dâ wolde he eine inne sîn
und ûf dem irsterbin.
he wolde eir vorderbin
ûf dem wazzer eine,
den he die lûte gemeine
vorterbete mit gestanke:
des wârin sîne gedanke.
…
grôz jâmir dâr geschach,
dô sie in trûgen an den sê.
dô bat der hêre nicht mê
mit im an daz schif tragin,
wen sîne harfin, hôrte ich sagin,
und sîn swert des he begerte.

---

[40] *Sir Tristrem*, ed. Alan Lupack, TEAMS (Kalamazoo, MI, 1994), lines 1,145–55.

[41] Bédier, *Le Roman de Tristan par Thomas*, vol. 2, p. 328. Bédier cites the prose *Tristan* in his appendix to the second volume of his work, and it is there that he uses this heading. Titus Heydenreich, *Tadel und Lob der Seefahrt: Das Nachleben eines antiken Themas in der romanischen Literatur* (Heidelberg, 1970), p. 81, draws on Bédier's phrase as the subheading for one section of his book.

[[Tristan] asked to be taken and carried into a small boat in which he wanted to die alone. He preferred to perish on the sea rather than disgust the people with the stench of his wound. Such were his thoughts. … There was much lamenting as they bore him to the sea. As I have heard, the knight asked no more of them than his harp and his sword which he greatly desired.][42]

The striking difference between the previously discussed accounts and Eilhart's text is that the latter has Tristan leaving on his own. This is his explicit wish: 'dâ wolde he eine inne sîn'. In addition, the text implies that Tristan does not desire anything else but his *harfin* and his *swert*. In marked contrast to the *Tristrams saga*, Eilhart's Tristan refuses to take aboard victuals, sailors or even basic equipment such as oars. Here, the wounded hero places his life entirely at God's mercy (*deus gubernator*). There is, of course, a difference between abandoning oars and not mentioning them, but Eilhart takes four lines to emphase that Tristan wished 'nicht mê / mit im an daz schif tragin,/wen sîne harfin … und sîn swert'. And although this emphasis, it would appear, stresses Tristan's refusal to take with him a number of essential items, it is impossible to know with any certainty which items Eilhart may have had in mind when resorting to the phrase 'nicht mê' in line 1134. Thomas, or, to be precise, the *Tristrams saga*, makes the hero's setting adrift less an act of seeking divine arbitration on matters of life and death than an expression of Tristan's trust in God to find a way out of his prolonged misery.

Yet there is sufficient common ground between the three versions to assume shared ancestry: in all three accounts Tristan's embarkation is accompanied by lamenting and, like Gottfried, Eilhart mentions the unbearable stench of the hero's wound. In fact, Eilhart emphasizes the stench ('gestanke'), and states that Tristan would rather die than 'disgust the people with the stench of his wound'. This accentuation of Tristan's illness and the stench of his wound as the decisive reason for his setting adrift, is an echo of the quasi-religious character of Tristan's 'pèlerinage à l'aventure,' which is indebted to the Insular tradition of the *peregrinatio pro amore dei* and contributes to the secularisation of the sea.[43] Like Benedeit's removal of much of the Brendan-

---

42 *Eilhart von Oberge*, ed. Franz Lichtenstein, Quellen und Forschungen zur Sprach- und Culturgeschichte der germanischen Völker 19 (Strasbourg, 1877), pp. 70–1, lines 1,096–1,104 and 1,132–7. The translation is my own. On the complexities of reconstructing Eilhart's text as well as on the date, see Hadumod Bußmann's introduction to his synoptic edition of the oldest fragments of the poem (*Eilhart von Oberg: Tristrant*, Altdeutsche Textbibliothek 70 (Tübingen, 1969), pp. vii–lxiv).

43 J. R. Reinhard, in his discussion of the custom of setting people adrift in (often unseaworthy) boats ('Setting Adrift in Medieval Law and Literature', *PMLA* 56 (1941), 33–68), identifies a second category that would be appropriate for Tristan's motivation: 'II. Persons unwanted in the community', 39–47. A detailed discussion of rudderless boats in English Romance can be found in Cooper's *The English Romance in Time*, Chapter 2, 'Providence and the Sea: "No Tackle, Sail, nor Mast"', pp. 106–36.

voyage's spirituality for the sake of adventure, the earliest redactors of the Tristan-legend adapted an Insular tradition to meet the expectations of a courtly audience. As a consequence, spiritual wandering on the sea becomes a journey into *aventure*.

Eilhart's version is regarded, together with Beroul's work, as belonging to the so-called 'non-courtly' tradition of the legend, and it is unlikely that Eilhart would have read Benedeit's *Voyage*. However, the German poet may have had access to one of the Continental copies of the *Navigatio* with which his setting adrift episode shares the parallel of abandoning the oars. In fact, Eilhart's version can be seamlessly inserted into the old rudderless boat tradition of the *immrama*:

> 'Fratres, nolite formidare. Deus enim adiutor noster est et nautor et gubernator atque gubernat. Mittite intus omnes remiges et gubernaculum. Tantum dimittite uela extensa et faciat Deus sicut uult de seruis suis et de sua naui.'

> [Brethren, have no fear, for God is our helper, our helmsman and our captain. And He will guide us. Put down all your oars and the rudder. And leave the sails and let God do as He wishes with His servants and His ship.][44]

It is suggestive that both the *Voyage* and Robert's Old Norse translation of Thomas's *Tristan* do not feature the abandoning of the oars, reducing the risk incurred by the monks and Tristan's 'crew' greatly. Unfortunately, no early fragments of Thomas's Anglo-Norman poem survive that could validate this part of the *Tristrams saga*, but it seems striking that both the *Voyage* and the *Tristrams saga* should make the same changes to an Irish tradition which has continued uninterruptedly on the Continent as Eilhart's rendering documents. The idea of voluntary exile on the sea, *exul patriae* in Angenendt's words, formed an integral element of Insular pilgrimages and Tristan's 'pèlerinage à l'aventure' constitutes one of the last acts of pilgrimage *by* sea as opposed to the later pilgrimage *across* the sea.[45] Tristan's voyage for healing occupies the narrative space common to both the (westward) quest of romance and the Insular pilgrimage tradition. Bédier's heading 'pèlerinage à l'aventure' shows the semantic contiguity and overlap of both forms of travel. At the same time, Tristan's hybrid voyage encompasses the two meanings Jacques Le Goff proposes for the sea in pre-modern literature: that of the desert and that of the forest.[46]

---

[44] Selmer, ed., *Navigatio Sancti Brendani Abbatis*, Chapter 6, lines 4–9.

[45] Pilgrims' accounts of the sea concentrate on their personal experience of the voyage rather than on the sea itself. Particularly noteworthy texts are Saewulf's voyages (*Peregrinationes tres*, ed. R. B. C. Huygens (Turnhout, 1994); for the translation, see Thomas Wright, ed., *Early Travels in Palestine* (London, 1848; repr. New York, 2003)) and the celebrated Pilgrims' Sea-Song to Compostella (*IMEV* 2148), printed in *The Stacions of Rome* and *The Pilgrims' Sea-Voyage*, ed. F. J. Furnivall, EETS, o.s. 25 (London, 1867; repr. Cambridge, 2003).

[46] Jacques Le Goff, 'Le Désert-forêt dans l'Occident médiéval', in *L'Imaginaire médiéval* (Paris,

There is no need to document the shaping role the Tristan-legend played in the development of romance motifs and patterns, and Tristan's crossing into the unknown may be one of the first instances of a chivalric hero taking on the sea. There are, particularly in the tradition of Arthurian romances, a number of instances where knights board ships to unknown or otherwordly destinations. Albrecht Classen sees such crossings as bringing about 'profound effects, if not the radical transformation of the protagonist within the courtly world'.[47] This transformation is needed to allow the hero to grow: a knight whose abilities are out of this world requires challenges that are similarly out of this world. To a writer, the sea offers the narrative advantage of transforming the means by which the questing protagonist travels into a part of the quest proper. And there are, of course, many such voyages that force the questing knight to return as a transformed entity: for instance, the protagonists of Marie de France's *Guigemar* and of the anonymous *Partonopeu de Blois* (both late twelfth century) are ferried into an Otherworld by self-propelled magical vessels.[48] That the sea or the crossing of it becomes the ultimate testing ground for the knight is also shown by Marie de France's *Eliduc* where, in a freak incident, Eliduc kills a sailor critical of the protagonist's moral misconduct: when faced with the legitimate accusation of adultery, Eliduc responds with a fit of sea-rage, showing an altogether uncourtly side.[49] There is no shortage of crossings, magical ships and mysterious islands in the early thirteenth-century French prose romance *Estoire del Saint Graal*, which forms part of the *Vulgate Cycle*, but the poem's most remarkable voyage surely must be that of the Grail's first owner, Josephé, who sails on his shirt to Britain and even manages to find space for the Grail and his companions.[50]

But the transformative power of the sea in the Tristan-legend is not restricted to quests by sea: storms, already important aspects of Benedeit's sea as well as of the maritime *peregrinatio pro amore Dei*, become a narrative focus in Thomas's poem. Early in Tristan's life, a storm on the coast of Norway saves him from the sinister designs of the merchants who have abducted him. The fear of the merchants, who seem to be experienced mariners, is gripping:

> Hrygðust allir ok hræddust, grétu ok illa létu, svá at hinir, er harðastir váru í þeirra liði, gørðust hugsjúkir, ok hugðu allir, at þeir mundi týnast, þvíat rekstr þeirra var hinn harðasti, ok alla viku rak þá sá stormr ok leiddi, svá

1985), pp. 59–85. On the forest in the romance tradition see Corinne Saunders, *The Forest of Medieval Romance* (Cambridge, 1993).

[47] Albrecht Classen, 'Storms, Sea Crossings, the Challenges of Nature and the Transformation of the Protagonist in Medieval and Renaissance Literature', *Neohelicon* 30:2 (2003), 163–82 (165).

[48] On the similarities between the magical ships in the two poems, see Sebastian I. Sobecki, 'A Source for the Magical Ship in the *Partonopeu de Blois* and Marie de France's *Guigemar*', *Notes and Queries*, 48:3 (2001), 220–2.

[49] *The Lais of Marie de France*, trans. Glyn S. Burgess and Keith Busby (London, 1986), pp. 121–2.

[50] Michelle Szkilnik, 'Seas, Islands and Continent in *L'Estoire del Saint Graal*', *Romance Languages Annual* 1 (1989), 322–7, p. 322. Szkilnik's entire article is dedicated to the sea and islands in the *Estoire del Saint Graal*.

(at) þeir sá hvergi lond, ok fengu þeir byr jafnhræddir ok hryggir, ok vissu hvergi til landa né hafna.

[Everyone was screaming and feared for his life. They wept and whined in such a way that even those who were the toughest among them made great distress, and all feared that they were lost because they were in the greatest hardship. A whole week they were driven and tossed by the storm so that they saw land nowhere. When they caught a favourable wind they found themselves in equal terror and misery for they did not know where to look for shore or harbour.][51]

The tempest itself is not so compelling in this passage as the psychological impact it has on the merchants. Even the hardiest of the crew, 'er harðastir váru', succumb to the sheer violence of the foul weather. Immediately afterwards, the moral implications of this storm begin to surface as the merchants interpret it as a punishment for their sins and implore their captain to abandon Tristan on the next shore.[52] Providence has pronounced God's judgement. Or, at least, the merchants think so.

At the end of the romance, the mortally wounded hero calls his trusted *amis*, Kaherdin, to his sick-bed. His words echo those spoken earlier to King Mark before Tristan went on his pilgrimage of healing:

'Entendez, beal amis:
Jo sui en estrange païs,
Jo në ai ami ne parent,
Bel compaing, fors vus sulement. (lines 2,392–5)

[Listen to me, fair friend of mine:
Here I am in a foreign land,
Without friend or man of my kin,
Except you alone, fair companion.][53]

All this sounds very familiar, only this time the hero is actually dying: 'Perc jo, bels dulz compainz, la vie' (line 2401) [I am on the point of death, fair companion]. Tristan then implores Kaherdin to seek out Ysolt, in the course of which he, seemingly casually, includes the portentous reminder that their disastrous, unfulfilled love has been sealed 'en la mer':

Del beivre qu'ensemble beümes
En la mer, quant suppris en fumes.
El beivre fud la nostre mort,
Nus n'en avrum ja mais confort. (lines 2,490–3)

---

[51] *Tristrams saga*, p. 19.

[52] *Tristrams saga*, p. 19.

[53] *Thomas of Britain: Tristan*, ed. and trans. Stewart Gregory (New York, 1991), p. 122. All translations are taken from Gregory's edition.

[The potion we drank together
At sea, which took us unawares.
Our death lay in that potion,
And never shall we have relief from death]

As the Carlisle fragment reveals, Ysolt herself has prophetically woven the
sea's bitterness into their newfound love as the pun on *l'amer / la mer / amer*
leaves Tristan in the dark about whether she means their love, the sea or, in
fact, the sea's bitterness:

> 'Merveille est k'om la mer ne het
> Qui si amer mal en mer set,
> E qui l'anguisse est si amere!
> Si je une foiz fors en ere,
> Ja n['i] enteroie, ce quit.'
> Tristran ad noté [ch]escun dit,
> Mes el l'ad issi forsvëé
> Par 'l'amer' que ele ad tant changé
> Que ne set si cele dolur
> Ad de la mer ou de l'amur,
> Ou s'el dit 'amer' de 'la mer'
> Ou pur 'l'amur' dïet 'amer'. (lines 40–52)

> ['It is a wonder that man does not hate the sea when he knows
> that such bitter evil is at sea, and that its sorrow is so bitter!
> If I cannot escape it, I think I will never enter it again.' Tris-
> tran has heard every phrase, but here she has confused him by
> *l'amer* which she has imbued with such ambiguity that he does
> not know whether this pain she has is caused by the sea or by
> love, or if she is referring to 'the sea' as 'bitter or is saying that
> 'love' is 'bitter'.][54]

Since the discovery of the Carlisle fragment in 1995, this passage has attracted
considerable attention which has led to a number of articles and book chapters. Of these, perhaps most noteworthy are Gérard Brault's and Marie-José
Heijkant's essays, published in 1998 and 1999, respectively.[55] Although both
Brault and Heijkant note the ambivalent role of the sea in this episode, the
religious and moral roots of the sea's ambivalence have not been explored.
Like Juliet's persistent emphasis on the distance between the two lovers in
Act 2, Scene 2 of *Romeo and Juliet*, Ysolt's surprise that her compatriots
do not hate the sea ('Merveille est k'om la mer ne het / Qui si amer mal en

---

[54] 'Un nouveau fragment du *Tristan* de Thomas', ed. Michael Benskin, Tony Hunt and Ian Short, *Romania* 113 (1995), 289–319.
[55] Gérard Joseph Brault, 'L'Amer, l'amer, la mer: La scène des aveux dans le Tristan de Thomas à la lumière du fragment de Carlisle', in *Miscellanea Medievalia: Mélanges Philippe Ménard*, ed. Claude Faucon, Alain Labbé and Danielle Quéruel, 2 vols (Paris, 1998), pp. 215–226, and Marie-José Heijkant, '*Merveille est k'om la mer ne het*: de ambivalente rol van de zee in de liefdesgeschiedenis van Tristan en Isolde', *Madoc*: 13:4 (1999), 205–12.

mer set, / E qui l'anguisse est si amere, and that its sorrow is so bitter!') [It is a wonder that man does not hate the sea / When he knows that such bitter evil is at sea!] is an instance of a lady exercising her *daunger*, or distance from the optimistic words of her suitor (which may often be not much more than a veiled admission of being in love with the suitor). However, unlike Juliet, who stands at the end of the ceremonial tradition of exacting love's vows from her courtly suitor, Ysolt's words are shrouded in an oracular mist, a veil of ambiguity: love blends with the sea blends with bitterness blends with love. This vague yet premonitory cluster of meanings shows an awareness of the sea's role in deciding their fate both now and in the future. One vital component of this fate is the sea's potency as the causal nucleus of their love and as its final judge, thus marking both the beginning and the end of their passion.

The underlying etymology of the sea's capacity for inspiring bitterness leads, like so many etymologies, to Isidore and, ultimately, reflects those established classical sentiments that led this optimistic hoarder of knowledge to assert that *mare* is derived from *amarum*: 'Proprie autem mare appellatum eo quod aquae eius amarae sint' [But strictly speaking something is called sea (*mare*) because its waters are bitter (*amarus*)].[56] In his influential book, *Symbole der Kirche*, Hugo Rahner devotes a section to the bitter sea (*mare amarum*), and, charting its development, demonstrates that this understanding of the sea is a literary expression of the Mediterranean and quintessentially classical belief in the sea's inconstancy and fickleness.[57] Hence, Ysolt's wordplay on the sea's bitterness expresses love's volatility, and, once more, the heroine passes through another stage of a ritualised, courtly verbalisation of love. There are even wider semantic connotations that result from patristic and scholastic attempts to decipher Semitic names by means of Latin stems, and, surely, the understanding of *Maria, stella maris* as, at least pseudo-etymologically, 'star of the bitter sea', may have imbued Ysolt's words with a presaging quality. The association of Mary with bitterness and the bitter sea is old, and is thought to have been derived from the Hebrew *mar* [bitter] and *yam* [sea]. Perhaps Jerome's *pikra thalassa* [bitter sea] in combination with Isidore's *mare amarum* etymology provided the inspiration for writers to link Mary's name to bitterness, but, in any case, by the thirteenth century it was current: 'This word "Marie" so is brightnesse and bitokne the steorre of the se, / And soruwe also and biturnesse, ase the bok tellez me'.[58] The circle may be drawn even wider: like God's divine love for humanity (Mary), human

---

[56] *Isidori Hispalensis episcopi*, Book 13, Chapter 14.

[57] See p. 36.

[58] *Early South English Legendary Life of Mary Magdalen*, lines 10–11 in *Middle English Legends of Women Saints* ed. Sherry L. Reames (Kalamazoo, MI, 2003). Reames suggests that this explanation for Mary's name was ultimately derived from Jerome's *Liber de nominibus hebraicis* (explanatory note to lines 11–16). Similarly, Conrad of Saxony explains that the name 'Mary' denotes the bitter sea in the third chapter of his *Speculum Beatae Mariae Virginis* (*Conradi de Saxonia Speculum seu Salutatio Beatae Mariae Virginis ac Sermones mariani*, ed. P. de Alcántara Martínez, Bibliotheca Franciscana Ascetica Medii Aevi 11 (Grottaferrata, 1975)). *Maris stella*, on

love has also sprung from the sea in the shape of Aphrodite/Cythaerea/Venus. When Ysolt taps into the large reservoir demarcated by love, the sea and bitterness, she summons a string of mythopoeic, moral and spiritual ambiguities that all articulate the finely balanced semantic core of the romance, which revolves around the sea. The physical articulation of the sea, such as storms, can both rule love and be ruled by love as the tradition of praying to Mary, the star of the bitter sea, in times of danger at sea, testifies. The following passage from John Gower's *Vox Clamantis* illustrates this customary plea: 'In my prayers, I called out for Christ, Whom the wind and the sea revere, to give me a calm voyage over the sea: Go Thou before me, O Star of the Sea, wherever I may be borne by the waves. Take charge of me; I shall be safe with thee as my guide.'[59]

In the lines quoted above (lines 2,392–7), Tristan summons the sea to witness what appears to be his dying speech. His words are permeated by 'mort', and as line 2,495 ('A nostre mort l'avum beü') [that we drank with it our death] mirrors line 2,492 ('El beivre fud la nostre mort') [our death lay in that potion] his thoughts appear trapped in regret, bestowing on his utterances a final quality. Despite its bitterness, this farewell to the world represents to some degree what Angenendt calls *mundus alienus*, the first stage of Tristan's final journey. What follows then is a lover's testament giving vent to years of suppressed emotions until Tristan reaches an insurmountable thought that forces him to place his trust in God as he had done in his journey of healing, or as Brendan had done on the high seas: 'Se Deu n'en pense, jo murrai' (line 2,543) [I shall die of it, unless God intervenes]. His gaze is firmly directed overseas (*exul patriae*), to Ysolt's shore, and it is as if the weary hero placed himself in a rudderless boat making only the most necessary provisions:

> Vus en merrez ma bele nef
> E porterez i duble tref:
> L'un en ert blanc e l'altre neir.
> Se vus Ysolt poez aver,
> Qu'el venge ma plaie garir,
> Del blanc siglez al revenir;
> E se vus Ysolt n'amenez,
> Del neir siglë idunc siglez. (lines 2,558–65)

> [Take my fine ship
> And carry with you two sails,
> One white and the other black.
> If you do manage to have Yseut
> Come and heal my wound,

the other hand, may have its origin in a scribal error (*Middle English Marian Lyrics*, ed. Karen Saupe (Kalamazoo, MI, 1997), footnote 1 to poem 9).

59   John Gower, *Vox Clamantis*, in *The Major Latin Works*, ed. and trans. Eric W. Stockton (Seattle, 1962), p. 85. Other instances of a tribute to the *stella maris* in medieval England can be found in *Middle English Marian Lyrics*, numbers 9, 12 and 58.

Then make the return journey under the white sail.
But if you do not bring Yseut with you,
Then travel under the black sail.]

Once more Tristan calls on the sea to act as a vehicle for Providence as he opts for sharp contrasts, white/black and life/death, rather than carefully weighed words. Binary opposites articulate his desire for ultimate certainty. Finally, the hero places his hopes in a last pilgrimage of healing. As he cannot go himself, he cannot control the voyage: 'Ne vus sai, amis, plus que dire' (line 2,566) [my friend, I think there is nothing else to say]; God is, once more, Tristan's *gubernator*.

Contrary to Tristan's worst fears, Kaherdin's remarkable persuasion of Ysolt succeeds and the queen agrees to go Brittany. In what may prefigure Dorigen's psychological addiction to the 'grisly rokkes blake' along the sea-coast in Chaucer's 'Franklin's Tale',[60] Tristan's dependence on the sea is best expressed in his wish to have his bed set up by the shore so that he can discern Providence, like an invading fleet, from afar:

E sovent se refait porter,
Sun lit faire juste la mer
Pur atendre e veer la nef,
Coment siglë e a quel tref (lines 2,826–9)

[And often he would have himself carried there instead,
Have his bed made up by the sea
So that he could await and see the ship,
How it sailed and under what sail.]

When the time of Ysolt's return grows nearer, her ship is suddenly seized by a terrible storm ('Del sud lur salt dunques un vent', line 2,861) [suddenly a wind blew up from the south] that contrasts starkly with the preceding joy at sighting land ('Balt sunt e siglent leement', line 2,860) [they were overjoyed by this and sailed on merrily].[61]

Many critics, including Bédier, have argued that the following description of the storm is derived from Wace's *Roman de Brut*, but, as Gesa Bonath convincingly shows in her edition of Thomas's *Tristan*, Wace provided only the scheme which Thomas varied.[62] This storm is much closer to the one which

---

60 *The Franklin's Tale*, in *The Riverside Chaucer*, gen. ed. Larry D. Benson (Boston, 1987), V, line 859.

61 This two-line shift from the joy of making out land to a sudden storm coming from the land ('Del sud' as Ysolt is travelling from England to Brittany) could have laid the foundation for a similar turn of events in Dante's celebrated Voyage of Ulysses in Canto 26 of the *Inferno*: 'Noi ci allegrammo, e tosto tornò in pianto;/ ché de la nova terra un turbo nacque, / e percosse del legno il primo canto' (lines 135–7) [We rejoiced, but soon our joy was turned to grief, for from the new land a whirlwind rose and struck the forepart of the ship]. *Inferno*, vol. 1 of *Dante: The Divine Comedy*, ed. and trans. Charles S. Singleton, 3 vols (London, 1971–5), p. 279.

62 *Thomas Tristan*, ed. Bonath, pp. 391–6.

surprised the merchants earlier in Tristan's career than to Wace's tempests, which in itself is a further argument for the reliability of the *Tristrams saga*.[63] For instance, *er harðastir váru* prefigures lines 2,880–1: 'Qu'eskipre n'i ot tant preisez / Qu'il peüst estre sur ses pez' [that there was no sailor on board, however experienced, / who could stand up on his feet]. In the same manner the despair of the merchants finds its counterpart in this storm: 'Tuit i plurent e tuit se pleinent, / Pur la poür grant dolur maingnent' (lines 2,882–3) [All wept and lamented / and in their fear gave vent to great grief].

Perhaps Thomas's most noteworthy innovation in this tragic storm is the blackening of the sea: 'Levent wages, la mer nercist' (line 2,869) [the waves swelled, the sea turned black]. The sea itself is foreshadowing the almost inevitable colour of the sails. Providence's verdict is prefigured by the sea before it is delivered. Tristan's speech to Kaherdin is not one that leaves much space for hope to shimmer through, and this passage continues the theme of the protagonist's imminent demise. It would seem that the blackening of the sea is too good an idea to be Thomas's own: one reader even suggested to emend it to 'li ciels nercist' [the skies turned black] to bring it into line with Wace's frequently blackening skies.[64]

Ysolt's dramatic response to the storm is one of the psychological climaxes of the poem. Like Dante's Ulysses some 150 years later, the queen feels the sea closing above her head like a tomb and her prophetic words allow us to grasp the extent to which the two lovers' fatal relationship is interwoven with the sea:

> Se jo dei em mer periller,
> Dunc vus estuet issi neier.
> Neier ne poez pas a terre;
> Venir m'estuet en la mer quere.
> La vostre mort vei devant mei,
> E ben sai que tost murrir dei. (lines 2,912–17)

> [If I am to come to grief on the sea,
> Then you must needs drown in the same way.
> But you cannot drown on dry land,
> You shall have to come and find me at sea.
> I see your death before my eyes,
> And I know that I must die soon.]

Her fear of a death without confession, that is, a death that could very well lead to damnation, is eclipsed by her love for Tristan as she finds consolation in the anonymity of a bleak sea-grave:

---

[63] The negative portrayal of merchants can be interpreted as a token of aristocratic and courtly readership. If this is correct, then a further argument for the trustworthiness of the *Tristrams saga* emerges as Thomas's work is similarly courtly and, hence, aristocratic in bias.

[64] Walter Mettmann, 'Zu einigen nautischen Termini im Tristan-Roman von Thomas', in *Verba et Vocabula: Festschrift für E. Gamillscheg*, ed. Helmut Stimm and Julius Wilhelm (Munich, 1968), pp. 319–21.

Mais jo i sui, si i murrai!
Senz vus, Tristran, i neerai!
Si m'est, beals dulz, süef confort
Que vus ne savrez ja ma mort;
Avant d'ici n'ert mais oïe:
Ne sai, amis, qui la vus die. (lines 2,936–41)

[But I am there, and shall die there!
I shall drown there, Tristan, without you!
And yet, dear, dear love, it is sweet comfort to me
That you will never know about my death.
Outside this place it will never be heard of:
I cannot think, my love, who could possibly tell you.]

But a brief spell of hope awaits Ysolt before her words come true. The storm passes and a fine wind carries her ship towards Brittany, when, all of a sudden, the sea proves unpredictable once more, painfully stretching her voyage to an odyssey. Violently alive until now, the sea seems almost dead: 'Mult süef e pleine est la mer: / Ne ça ne la lur nef ne vait' (lines 2,983–4) [the sea was very calm and flat: / their ship went neither here nor there]. As if playing on the recurring theme of contrasts, it is only at the moment of Tristan's death that the sea miraculously comes to life again:

Puis le chuchent sur un samit,
Covrent le d'un paile roié.
Li venz est en la mer levé,
E fert sei en mi liu del tref;
A terre fait venir la nef. (lines 3,045–9)

[Then they laid him down on a samite
And covered him with a striped pall.
The wind had risen at sea,
And struck the sail in the middle,
Bringing thereby the ship to land.]

In Thomas's poem Ysolt's fear of the storm is paced accordingly to the narrative rhythm which, in turn, is dictated by the sea. Like the sea itself, her fear of the tempest is a narrative tool to thicken the plot. The sea gives Tristan a last opportunity to send for a voyage of healing and the storm sets alight Ysolt's latent passion for her lover. The sea raises and crushes Tristan's hopes, and the storm awakens Ysolt's love only to turn it into grief. Perhaps Tristan's last *pèlerinage à l'aventure* fails so tragically because he could not go himself. Ysolt's words seem to imply that, at least hypothetically, he could be out at sea, looking for her: 'En mer, amis, que querreiez? / Ne sai que vus i feïssez!' (lines 2,934–5) [but what, dear love, would you be seeking out at sea?/ I cannot think what you could be doing there!].

71

3

Almost Beyond the World

Who knows, after all, how far this great sea extends, onto which sailors do not dare to sail, and, up till now, have not attempted to do so, and which surrounds Britain with furious waves and which reaches even further places that are not even accessible in legends.

Ambrose (*c.* 340–97), *Hexaemeron* 3, 3, 15
(after Basil of Caesarea)

At the farthest reaches of the world often occur new marvels and wonders, as though Nature plays with greater freedom secretly at the edges of the world than she does openly and nearer us in the middle of it.   Ranulph Higden (1299–1363/64), *Polychronicon*[1]

Britain at the 'Laste Clif of Occean'

For Gildas, things could only get worse. Disintegration and the slow but steady decline of Romano-British civilisation into chaos form the main themes of his *On the Ruin of Britain*, which was composed in the first half of the sixth century. In many ways, he cannot be blamed. After the Romans had abandoned Britannia, their cultural inheritance began to deteriorate and, with time, established British civilisation was confronted by pagan newcomers. As if this were not punishment enough, it was in times such as these that the inhabitants of the British Isles were paying the price for their frontline position in Christian geography. Drawing on Roman sources, Gildas asserts that Britain lies at the very end of the world, surrounded by an uncrossable ring of sea:

> Brittannia insula in extremo ferme orbis limite circium occidentemque versus divina, ut dicitur, statera totius ponderatrice librata ab Africo boriali propensius tensa axi ..., quae arcuatis oceani sinibus ambiuntur, tenes, cuius diffusiore et, ut ita dicam, intransmeabili undique circulo.

> [The island of Britain lies virtually at the end of the world, towards the west and north-west. Poised in the divine scales that (we are told) weigh

---

[1] Translated in *Polychronicon Ranulphi Higden monachii Cestrensis*, ed. Churchill Babington and Joseph Rawson Lumby, 9 vols (London, 1865–86), vol. 1, p. 361.

the whole earth, it stretches from the south-west towards the northern pole. … It is fortified on all sides by a vast and more or less uncrossable ring of sea.][2]

Gildas's placing of Britain at 'extremo ferme orbis limite' is of interest for two reasons: first, he does not mention that Britain lies at the edge of the *oikumene*, the known, inhabited world (the omission of Ireland is not unusual in such contexts), but that it is actually located at the end of the world as such; second, he amplifies the legendary ferocity of the British ocean by surrounding Britain with an uncrossable ring of sea, an image that will contribute to the notion of Englishness in the fifteenth century.[3] In an embryonic state, this geographical isolation of Britain 'virtually at the end of the world' contains, as I will argue below, the predisposition of the British Isles to harbour magic and invite natural disasters, so memorably expressed at the very start of *Sir Gawain and the Green Knight* (1, lines 14–19).

Nennius (eighth century), the next significant British historiographer after Gildas to describe Britain's position in the world, does not place the island in a relationship to the ocean or the *oikumene* as a whole. He just writes of its size, which he derives from Gildas, and then continues to speak of its cities and inhabitants.[4] Bede (672/73–735), however, uses his classical learning and opens up the sea to endlessness by adding that behind Britain lies the infinite Ocean.[5] Like Gildas, Bede places Britain at the edge of the world, but he is more specific in identifying Britain's location as lying almost under the North Pole.[6] As a result, Britain

> lucidas aestate noctes habet; ita ut medio saepe tempore noctis in quaestionem ueniat intuentibus, utrum crepusculum adhuc permaneat uespertinum, an iam aduenerit matutinum.

> [has short nights in summer, so that often at midnight it is hard for those who are watching to say whether it is evening twilight which still lingers, or whether morning dawn has come.][7]

The half-light in which Britain's short nights are clouded confers an enigmatic quality on the island's geographical liminality: towards the edge of

---

2   Gildas, *De Excidio Britonum*, ed. and trans. M. Winterbottom (London, 1978), paragraph 3, p. 89 and, for the translation, p. 16 (Gildas's work is better known as *De Excidio Britanniae*). On Gildas's indebtedness to Orosius's geography, see N. J. Higham, 'Old Light in the Dark Age Landscape: the Description of Britain in the *De Excidio Britanniae* of Gildas', *Journal of Historical Geography* 17:4 (1991), 363–72.
3   Examples of the sea as a 'murus Angli[a]e' appear in *The Libelle of Englyshe Polycye* and in John Capgrave's *Liber de Illustribus Henricis* (see the discussion of these texts in Chapter 6).
4   Nennius, *British History and the Welsh Annals*, ed. and trans. John Morris (London, 1978), paragraphs 7–10.
5   *Bede: Ecclesiastical History of the English People*, trans. and ed. B. Colgrave and R. A. B. Mynors (Oxford, 1991), Chapter 1, p. 14.
6   *Ecclesiastical History of the English People*, p. 14. Cf. Adam of Bremen's description of Britain, p. 97.
7   *Ecclesiastical History of the English People*, p. 16 (p. 17 for the translation).

the world order becomes blurred as night transgresses into day and day into night, preventing the diurnal cycle from restating itself clearly.

Consequently, most of the later accounts of Britain's position in the physical world or of Brutus' landing in Albion, such as the histories of Geoffrey Gaimar (*fl.* mid-twelfth century), Wace and Geoffrey of Monmouth (*c.* 1100–55) or the *Polychronicon* of Ranulph Higden, describe Britain as an island at the edge of the known world facing the endless ocean. This liminal position of Britain influenced a number of traditions explaining Britain's spiritual topography: Britain is Geoffrey of Monmouth's 'best of islands' (*insularum optima*),[8] holy and dear to God, but it is also the inhospitable stronghold of Christianity surrounded on all shores by a fierce, monster-infested ocean, an image that is informed by both the Judaeo-Christian *abyssus* and the classical *oceanus dissociabilis*. There is also a third, predominantly literary tradition in which the British Isles become a privileged outpost in the westward geography of Christianity. This association of the English or Angles with angels, famously expressed in Gregory the Great's pun that the English are called English (*angli*) because they have the beauty of angels (*angeli*), has been chosen by Kathy Lavezzo as the title of a recent book dedicated to this topic, *Angels on the Edge of the World*.[9]

The end of the known world is also the beginning of civilisation. When Brutus sets foot on Albion's shores he finds it already inhabited by uncivilised, unhuman and unworldly creatures:

> Erat tunc nomen insule Albion que a nemine exceptis paucis hominibus gigantibus inhabitabatur. … Erat ibi inter ceteros detestabilis quidam nomine Goemagog stature .xii. cubitorum. Qui tante [uirtutis] existens quercum semel excussam uelut uirgulam corili euellebat. … At Britones undique tandem confluentes preualuerunt in eos et omnes preter Goimagog interfecerunt.

> [At this time the island of Britain was called Albion. It was uninhabited except for a few giants. … Among the [giants] there was a particularly repulsive one, called Gogmagog, who was twelve feet tall. He was so strong that, once he had given it a shake, he could tear up an oak-tree as though it were a hazel wand. … However, the Britons finally gathered together from round and about and overcame the giants and slew them all, except Gogmagog.][10]

---

8 Geoffrey of Monmouth, *History of the Kings of Britain*, in *The* Historia Regum Britannie *of Geoffrey of Monmouth*, ed. Neil Wright, vol. 1, *Berne, Bürgerbibliothek, MS 568* (Cambridge, 1985), p. 2. The phrase becomes *beatissima insularum* and *insularum nobilissima* in Henry of Huntingdon's *Historia Anglorum* (Diana Greenway, ed. and trans., *Henry, Archdeacon of Huntingdon – Historia Anglorum, The History of the English People* (Oxford, 1996), pp. 10 and 12, respectively.

9 Kathy Lavezzo, *Angels on the Edge of the World: Geography, Literature and English Community, 1000–1534* (Ithaca, NY, 2006). For Gregory's comment, see page 11.

10 *Historia Regum Britannie*, ed. Wright, vol. 1, pp. 13–14. For the translation, see *Geoffrey of Monmouth: The History of the Kings of Britain*, trans. Lewis Thorpe (Harmondsworth, Middlesex, 1966), pp. 72–3. All translations are Thorpe's.

Initially, Gogmagog is only spared because Brutus' comrade, Corineus, fosters a lively passion for blood-sport and 'enjoyed beyond all reason matching himself against such monsters'.[11] Finally, Gogmagog meets his fate when Corineus hurls 'this deadly monster, whom he was carrying on his shoulders, far out into the sea'.[12] Such giants and freaks of nature usually mark the end of geographical knowledge; they inhabit the fringes and the grey areas of maps and histories, where imagination constructs otherness to compensate for the perplexing collision with the frontier of epistemology. A shrewd observer, Plutarch notices this habit when he refers to

> 'geographers', who 'when they come to deal with those parts of the earth which they know nothing about, crowd them into the margins of their maps with the explanation, "Beyond this lie sandy, waterless deserts full of wild beasts", or "trackless swamps", or "Scythian snows", or "ice-locked sea." '[13]

Here, Geoffrey's giants also help him justify Brutus' very physical *translatio imperii* from Troy to Britain, which, after all, is being 'humanised', and claw back territory from the monsters and giants who are 'by kind' hostile to the human race.[14] The compound name 'Gogmagog' itself invites the speculation that this island lies beyond the reach of time and regular history as it was widely believed that the two lost tribes of Israel, Gog and Magog, would not be found until Doomsday.[15]

Once a place on the fringe of the world had been civilised, the frontier of the *oikumene* moved further into the ocean. The giants that populated Albion have become the Cyclopes now living in the caves and crags of the exotic, western island to which the Frisian explorers in Adam of Bremen's eleventh-century history were sent after their expedition ended in a debacle.[16] Where myth blends with the individual imagination, learned writers cram the unknown with monsters from classical myth, pagan legend and Christian apocrypha. On his voyage Brendan encounters not only Judas clinging to a rock, but also the sea-monster Jascanius, devils, Purgatory and sea-serpents.

Like Nennius, Geoffrey uses Gildas's measurements and description but his emphasis on Britain as the finest of islands is a novel idea. Geoffrey's

---

11 *Historia Regum Britannie*, ed. Wright, vol. 1, p. 14.
12 *Historia Regum Britannie*, ed. Wright, vol. 1, p. 14.
13 Evelyn Edson, *Mapping Time and Space: How Medieval Mapmakers Viewed Their World* (London, 1997), p. 169, note 39.
14 Sylvia Federico discusses the function of *Troyness* in English fictions of the *translatio imperii* in *New Troy: Fantasies of Empire in the Late Middle Ages* (Minneapolis, 2003), passim.
15 Geoffrey may be thinking of Bede's location of Britain in the north, and of Gog and Magog's northern exile in Ezekiel 39.2: 'et circumagam te et seducam te et ascendere faciam de lateribus aquilonis' [And I will turn thee round, and I will lead thee out, and will make thee go up from the northern parts].
16 See pp. 89 ff., below.

notion of Britain's superiority is based on the very subjective evaluation of its natural resources:

> continens quicquid mortalium usui congruit indeficienti fertilitate minis-trat. Omni etenim genere metalli fecunda campos late pansos habet, ... in quibus frugum diuersitates ubertate glebe temporibus suis proueniunt. Habet nemora uniuersis ferarum generibus repleta ... et aduolan[tibus] apibus flores diuersorum colorum mella distribuunt. ... Porro lacubus atque piscosis fluuiis irr[i]gua est.

> [It provides in unfailing plenty everything that is suited to the use of human beings. It abounds in every kind of mineral. It has broad fields and hillsides ... and in which ... all kinds of crops are grown in their seasons. It also has open woodlands which are filled with every kind of game. ... and there too grow flowers of every hue which offer their honey to the flitting bees. ... What is more, it is watered by lakes and rivers full of fish.][17]

Bede's description is also positive, but nowhere near as idyllic as Geoffrey's.[18] One has almost the impression that Geoffrey is describing the Earthly Paradise in the east from which Britain is, at least geographically, only separated by the western Ocean, yet still at a great, and, if one recalls Augustine, 'absurd' remove.[19] When Brendan enters the Earthly Paradise at the end of his long journey, the Anglo-Norman poet Benedeit, greatly elaborating the corresponding passage in the Latin *Navigatio*, describes the following scene:

> Avant en vait cil juvenceals,
> Par paraïs vait ovoec eals.
> De beals bois e de rivere
> Veient terre mult plenere;
> Gardins est la praierie,
> Qui tuzdis est beal flurie.
> Li flur süef mult i flairent,
> ...
> Esteit süef tuzdis i est,
> Li fruiz de arbres e de flurs prest,
> Bois repleniz de veneisun,
> E tut li flum de bon peisun. (lines 1,735–41 and 1,751–4)

> [The young man moved forward, accompanying them through Paradise. They saw a very fertile land of beautiful woods and meadows; the meadows form a garden which is permanently in full bloom. The flowers there smell very sweet. ... there is permanently pleasant summer there with fruit on the trees and

---

[17] *Historia Regum Britannie*, ed. Wright, vol. 1, p. 2.
[18] *Ecclesiastical History of the English People*, Chapter 1.
[19] On the (mostly eastern) location of Paradise, see Alessandro Scafi, *Mapping Paradise: A History of Heaven on Earth* (London, 2006), passim.

flowers always in bloom. The woods are always full of game and there is good fish in all the rivers.][20]

The main difference between these two accounts is that the bliss of Geoffrey's Britain is not entirely spontaneous: its fields require human tilling and the game active hunting. Also, as a token of eternity, the cycle of the seasons is suspended in Brendan's island Paradise. Jacques Le Goff calls the universal myth of the island 'the great figure of human fancy',[21] and Michel Mollat du Jourdin goes even a step further in claiming that 'the concept of the island invokes distant shores, earlier than the inhabited earth (*extra orbem*), new worlds (*alterae orbes*) beyond the mists of the immense sea.'[22] Given that Eden, by virtue of being a garden, was also believed to have been walled, it requires only a small step to interpret the paradisiacal conditions in Britain, which is surrounded by a wall of water, as befitting an earthly Paradise. This is, after all, the image that Shakespeare's John of Gaunt develops in *Richard II* when he calls Britain 'this other Eden, demi-paradise / This fortress built by Nature for herself'.[23]

Le Goff's 'great figure of human fancy' refers not only to the Fortunate Islands, but it also works for the mythical islands of the thirteenth-century *Queste del sainte graal* and such ephemeral places as Malory's fifteenth-century 'vale of Avylyon'. Because of its relative geographical (and therefore spiritual) proximity to the presumed Paradise which Brendan and his monks have visited, Britain appears to be, at least in some part, benefiting from being pushed against the world's *ultimae fines*. Britain is pressed against the spatial and the temporal end of the world since, as Fabienne Michelet reminds us, 'the end of time will take place in the west, according to the theory of the *translatio imperii*.'[24] King Alfred's ninth-century Preface to the Old English translation of Gregory's *Pastoral Care* shows that, already for pre-Conquest writers, this outlook 'situates salvation in the west'.[25] Unlike the *translatio studii*, which denoted the carrying across of learning from the ancient East to the pre-modern West, since Geoffrey's introduction of the topos to England, the *translatio imperii* had often been interpreted as a political endeavour.[26] Nevertheless the westward shift of Orosius's *translatio imperii* through Assyria, Macedonia and Carthage to Rome continued to be read as a theological history of time and space, spanning all areas of human

---

[20] For the corresponding scene in the *Navigatio*, see Carl Selmer, *Navigatio sancti Brendani abbatis* (South Bend, IN, 1959), pp. 79–80.

[21] Michel Mollat du Jourdin, *Europe and the Sea* (Oxford, 1993), p. 41.

[22] Mollat du Jourdin, *Europe and the Sea*, p. 41

[23] *Richard II*, ed. Andrew Gurr, The New Cambridge Shakespeare (Cambridge, 1990), Act 2, Scene 1, lines 42–3. In the subsequent lines Gaunt draws on Gildas's image of the sea as Britain's wall (see pp. 3–4).

[24] Fabienne Michelet, *Creation, Migration and Conquest: Imaginary Geography and Sense of Space in Old English Literature* (Oxford, 2006), p. 17.

[25] Michelet, *Creation, Migration and Conquest*, pp. 158–9.

[26] Its development in later pre-modern England has been most recently traced by Federico's *New Troy*.

activity, including the motif of westward questing in romance.[27] One of the most influential proponents of this theory, Hugh of St Victor, emphasises the divine nature of the westward movement:

> Ordo autem loci et ordo temporis fere per omnia secundum rerum gestarum seriem concurrere videntur. Et ita per divinam providentiam videtur esse dispositum, ut que in principio temporum gerebantur, in oriente – quasi in principio mundi – gererentur, ac deinde ad finem profluente tempore usque ad occidentem rerum summa descenderet, ut ex hoc ipso agnoscamus appropinquare finem seculi, quia rerum cursus iam attigit finem mundi.

> [In the succession of historical events the order of space and the order of time seem to be in almost complete correspondence. Therefore, divine providence's arrangement seems to have been that what was brought about at the beginning of time would also have been brought about in the east – at the beginning, so to speak, of the world as space (*mundus*) – and then, as time proceeded towards its end, the centre of events would have shifted to the west, so that we may recognise out of this that the world (*saeculum*) nears its end in time as the course of events has already reached the extremity of the world in space (*mundus*).][28]

Britain's 'privileged' location rendered it somewhat special in a spiritual sense: it was closer to the geographical and temporal end of the world, and this meant greater proximity to the realm of the divine. For Ranulph Higden, Britain's alterity is a defining feature. Abbreviating Bartholomaeus Anglicus's *On the Property of Things* in his *Polychronicon*, Higden closes his list of authorities on this subject with Alfred and Solinus:

> Alfred. English Britain is called another world, which formerly Charlemagne called his own chamber because of the great abundance of good things there. Solinus. For the coasts of France would be called the end of the world if Britain did not deserve the name of almost another world.[29]

Even Leonardo Bruni (*c.* 1370–1444) would come to echo this sentiment when admiring Florentine merchants 'whose profession could lead them as far away as Britain, "which is an island in the ocean almost on the edge of the world."'[30] Hence, William of Malmesbury (*fl.* twelfth century) finds more faith in this God-favoured island than elsewhere:

---

[27] On the westward bias of romances, see Helen Cooper, *The English Romance in Time: Transforming Motifs from Geoffrey of Monmouth to the Death of Shakespeare* (Oxford, 2004), 'Questing Westward', pp. 72–7.

[28] Hugh of St Victor, *De archa Noe morali*, ed. Patrice Secard, CCCM 176 (Turnhout, 2001), Part 4, 9. The translation is Scafi's, *Mapping Paradise*, p. 126.

[29] Quoted from Lavezzo, *Angels on the Edge of the World*, p. 85. On Higden's geographical perception of England, see Lavezzo, *Angels on the Edge of the World*, Chapter 3, 'Locating England in the *Polychronicon*', pp. 71–92.

[30] David Wallace, '"Whan She Translated Was": A Chaucerian Critique of the Petrarchan Academy',

Quod ideo fieri credo caelitus, ut natio pene extra orbem posita, ex consideratione incorruptelae sanctorum, fidentius ad spem resurrectionis animaretur.

[I believe Heaven's purpose in this was that our nation, situate almost beyond the world, might by considering the incorruption of the saints be kindled to a more confident hope in the resurrection.][31]

William may even be thinking of Britain as one of the Fortunate Isles, thus alluding to an interpretation of Britain's position in the geography of salvation that persisted throughout the early modern period and beyond (as the above quotation from *Richard II* shows).[32] This is also what Ranulph Higden appears to have in mind in the passage quoted at the beginning of this chapter, and the same thought can be detected in Gerald of Wales:

Sicut enim orientales plagae propriis quibusdam et sibi innatis praeeminent et praecellunt ostentis, sic et occidentales circumferentiae suis naturae miraculis illustrantur. Quoties quippe, tanquam seriis et veris fatigata negotiis, paululum secedit et excedit, remotis in partibus, quasi verecundis et occultis natura ludit excessibus.

[Just as the countries of the East are remarkable and distinguished for certain prodigies (*ostentis*) peculiar and native to themselves, so the boundaries of the West also are made remarkable by their own wonders of Nature (*naturae miraculis*). For sometimes tired, as it were, of the true and the serious, [Nature] draws aside and goes away, and in these remote parts indulges herself in these shy and hidden excesses.][33]

Josephine Waters Bennett documents the persistence of this reading of Britain's liminal position in the sixteenth and seventeenth centuries. Bennett observes that Solinus's *Polyhistor* (fourth century) talks of Britain as being out of this world: 'The Sea coast of Gallia had beene the end of the worlde, but that the Ile of Brytaine for the largenesse thereof every way, deserveth the name almost of an other Worlde.'[34] In his *Description of Britaine*, prefixed to Holinshed's *Chronicles of England, Scotland and Ireland* (1586–87), John

---

in *Literary Practice and Social Change in Britain, 1380–1539*, ed. Lee Patterson (Berkeley, CA, 1990), pp. 156–215 (p. 159).

31 *Gesta Regum Anglorum*, ed. and trans. R. A. B. Mynors with R. M. Thomson and M. Winterbottom, 2 vols, (Oxford, 1998), vol. 1, p. 387 (cf. p. 386 for the Latin).

32 Josephine Waters Bennett has discussed this tradition as early as 1956 in her article 'Britain among the Fortunate Isles', *Studies in Philology* 53: 2 (1956), 114–40.

33 Gerald of Wales, *Topographia Hibernie*, 'Praefatio Secunda', p. 20. The translation is taken from *The History and Topography of Ireland*, trans. John J. O'Meara (Harmondsworth, 1982), p. 31 (quoted from Lorraine Daston and Katherine Park, *Wonders and the Order of Nature, 1150–1750* (New York, 1998), pp. 25–6).

34 Arthur Golding's 1587 translation, quoted from Bennett, 'Britain among the Fortunate Isles', p. 114. Bennett draws the conclusion that 'by this series of associations, the geographical "otherworld" of Britain becomes identifed with the mythological Otherworld, the land of spirits' (p. 121). See also Tristan Marshall, '*The Tempest* and the British Imperium in 1611', *The Historical Journal* 41:2 (1998), 375–400.

Harison notes that '[i]t is not certeine vnto which portion of the earth our Ilands, and Thule, with sundrie the like scattered in the north seas should be ascribed.'[35] The association of Britain with Thule goes back to Pythias of Massalia's lost work *On the Ocean* (fourth century BC) in which he claims, at least so the Greek geographer Strabo (27 BC–AD 14) tells us, that one can sail from Britain to Thule in only six days.[36]

It is therefore hardly surprising that William of Malmesbury should approach Britain not only from a spatial perspective: his *extra orbem*, apparently the same phrase Mollat du Jourdin uses above to denote a state *earlier* than the *oikumene*, suggests that Britain, owing to its extreme geographical isolation, is also closer to the Earthly Paradise, which, lying at the other end of the world, connected to and yet separated from Britain by the 'boundless ocean', also dates from a time *extra orbem*.[37] The conflation of time and space is characteristic of pre-modern geography and lies at the very heart of the problem of locating Paradise. As Alessandro Scafi has shown, the confusion about Eden's location stems from two equally valid translations of the Hebrew word *miqedem*: Jerome translates the word as *a principio* [from the beginning] whereas the *Vetus Latina* version, informing the speculations of Isidore and Bede, renders it as *in oriente* [eastward].[38]

Isidore's description of Eden's geographical location formed the starting point for many historiographers and cartographers coming after him. He says that 'Paradisus est locus in orientis partibus constitutus' [Paradise is located in the east], adding that it has been 'post peccatum hominis aditus interclusus est' [blocked off after the fall of humankind].[39] At the same time, a comment Isidore makes on the Fortunate Isles betrays the existence of an alternative tradition, certainly in classical antiquity, which interpreted the Fortunate Isles as Paradise. In Book 14, Chapter 6, 'De insulis' (*On islands*), Isidore corrects the classical belief that these islands were, in fact, Paradise.[40] The placing of Paradise in the west can already be found in Homer's *Odyssey*, where the Elysian Fields are said to lie in the Atlantic Ocean at the south-western limits of the habitable world.[41] Hesiod (*fl.* eighth century BC), Pindar (522–433

35 Raphael Holinshed, *The Chronicles of England, Scotland, and Ireland* (London, 1597), 1, 2 (quoted from Bennett, 'Britain among the Fortunate Isles', p. 115).
36 *The Geography of Strabo*, ed. and trans. H. L. Jones, 8 vols (London, 1917–32; repr. 1966–70), vol. 1, p. 233. The surviving fragments of and references to Pythias' work have been edited and translated by Christina Horst Roseman, *Pytheas of Massalia: On the Ocean: Text, Translation and Commentary* (Chicago, 1994) and Serena Bianchetti, *L'oceano* (Pisa, 1998).
37 There are also alternative locations of Paradise, some of which will be discussed below. See Scafi, *Mapping Paradise*, passim.
38 Scafi, *Mapping Paradise*, pp. 35 ff.
39 *Isidori Hispalensis episcopi*, Book 14, Chapter 3. Scafi dedicates his entire book *Mapping Paradise* to answering this question.
40 'Unde gentilium error et saecularium carmina poetarum propter soli fecunditatem easdem esse Paradisum putaverunt' [hence the mistake of pagans and the poems by worldy poets, who believed that these isles were Paradise because of the fertility of their soil], *Isidori Hispalensis episcopi etymologiarum sive originum*, ed. W. M. Lindsay, 2 vols (Oxford, 1911), Book 14, Chapter 6.
41 Francesco Relaño, 'Paradise in Africa: The History of a Geographical Myth from its Origins in

BC) and Horace continued this tradition.[42] This belief, Isidore writes, was based on the Fortunate Isles' excellent climate and their natural abundance of produce.[43] Isidore's description is marked by the same fecundity of the islands' vegetation as Brendan's Paradise, and he suggests that the woods there yield fruits naturally.[44]

But not everybody heeded Isidore's warning, as Brendan's voyage suggests. The Hereford Mappa Mundi, for instance, composed in the last quarter of the thirteenth century, includes in its representation of the Fortunate Isles (in the same place as the Canary Islands, another typical locale for the Fortunate Isles) a reference to Brendan: 'Fortunate Insulae sex sunt Insulae Sct Brandani' [The six Fortunate Islands are islands of St Brendan].[45] The account of Brendan's voyage circulated widely across Europe, and not every reader was as discerning as the Hereford Mappa Mundi would suggest: at the end of the twelfth century, Godfrey of Viterbo tells in his *Pantheon*, the same work that John Gower (*c.* 1330–1408) would rely on for his tale of Apollonius of Tyre, of a group of monks who sailed from Britain to Paradise and back again.[46] And in what must be a conflation of Homer's Elysian Fields and the tradition of placing Paradise below the equator, Dante's Ulysses sails for Paradise on a south-westerly course:

> ma misi me per l'alto mare aperto
> sol con un legno e con quella compagna
> picciola da la qual non fui diserto.
> L'un lito e l'altro vidi infin la Spagna,
> fin nel Morrocco, e l'isola d'i Sardi
> e l'altre che quel mare intorno bagna.

> [But I put forth on the deep open sea with one vessel only, and with that small company which had not deserted me. The one shore and the other I saw as far as Spain, as far as Morocco, and Sardinia and the other islands which that sea bathes round.][47]

Intriguingly, there seems to be no source for Dante's last voyage of Ulysses, unless one allows for the possibility that the poet drew on the Brendan-

---

Medieval Thought to its Gradual Demise in Early Modern Europe', *Terrae Incognitae* 36 (2004), 1–11 (1).

[42] Relaño, 'Paradise in Africa', 1.

[43] *Isidori Hispalensis episcopi*, Book 14, Chapter 6.

[44] 'Sua enim aptae natura pretiosarum poma silvarum parturiunt' [indeed, well-suited by their nature, they produce fruit from very precious trees], *Isidori Hispalensis episcopi*, Book 14, Chapter 6.

[45] *The Voyage of Saint Brendan: Representative Versions of the Legend in English Translation*, ed. W. R. J. Barron and Glyn S. Burgess (Exeter, 2002), p. 9.

[46] Godfrey of Viterbo, *Pantheon*, in *Illustres veteres scriptores qui rerum a Germanis per multas aetates gestarum historias vel annales posteris reliquerent*, ed. Johann Pistorius (Frankfurt am Main, 1613), vol. 2, pp. 55–6. The reference to Godfrey is made by Scafi, *Mapping Paradise*, p. 52 and in note 57.

[47] *Inferno*, vol. 1 of *Dante: The Divine Comedy*, ed. and trans. Charles S. Singleton, 3 vols (London, 1971–5), p. 276; p. 277 for the translation.

legend.[48] That this tradition continued unabated throughout the pre-modern period is documented by the sustained circulation of Brendan's voyage tale. Besides, in 1410, Pierre d'Ailly continues the association of the Fortunate Isles with the terrestial Paradise in his *Imago Mundi*.[49]

And although the exact location of Paradise remained contested, with the belief in a spherical earth the notion was born, at least in theory, that Paradise could be reached by means of circumnavigation. In firm opposition to Augustine, the fourteenth-century narrative persona of John Mandeville, at the end of his voyage account, tries to show that the globe could be circumnavigated: 'yif [he] hadde had companye and schippynge for to go more beyonde, we would 'haue seen alle the roundness of the firmament alle aboute'.[50] Scafi's otherwise exemplary discussion of the location of Paradise underestimates, I think, the role played by literary texts. One must account for the fact that three of the most widely read and copied pre-modern texts, the Brendan-legend, Dante's *Divine Comedy* and Mandeville's *Travels*, either demonstrate or suggest a western route to Paradise.

And so, during his third voyage (1498–1500), when Columbus landed on what is now Trinidad, he thought he had found the Earthly Paradise. His account is compelling evidence for the degree to which physical geography and spiritual topography were deemed inseparable:

> I do not find, nor have ever found, writings by any Roman or Greek that identify with certainty the location of the earthly paradise in this world, nor have I seen it on any world map, yet by authority a place was assigned to it arbitrarily. ... St Isidore and Bede and Strabo and the Master of the *Historia Scholastica* [Petrus Comestor] and St Ambrose and Duns Scotus and all the holy theologians agree that the earthly paradise was found in the east, etc. ... I believe that, had I gone under the equinoctial line rather than reaching the higher point, I would have met a regime of winds much more constant.[51]

He then surmises (on metaphysical grounds, however) that Eden would not be accessible to anyone: 'I believe that there is located the earthly paradise,

---

[48] This is a thought already entertained by Dorothy L. Sayers: 'The voyage of Ulysses, perhaps the most beautiful thing in the whole *Inferno*, derives from no classical source, and appears to be Dante's own invention. It may have been suggested to him by the Celtic voyages of Maelduin and Brendan', *The Comedy of Dante Alighieri the Florentine*, 3 vols (Harmondsworth, 1955), vol. 1, pp. 238–9, note to line 83.

[49] Relaño, 'Paradise in Africa', 1. It is noteworthy that Eden is represented as an island in the world ocean on the same map (Alessandro Scafi notes the 'contiguity of Paradise with the outer Ocean' in some traditions, 'Mapping Eden: Cartographies of the Earthly Paradise', in *Mappings*, ed. Denis Cosgrove (London, 1999), pp. 50–70 (p. 63)).

[50] The *Travels of Sir John Mandeville*, British Library, Cotton MS Titus C xvi, printed in *Mandeville's Travels*, ed. M. C. Seymour (Oxford, 1967), p. 133.

[51] *Christopher Columbus – Accounts and Letters of the Second, Third, and Fourth Voayges*, ed. Paolo Taviani, Consuelo Varela, Juan Gil and Maria Conti, trans. Luciano F. Farina and Marc A. Beckwith, 2 vols (Rome, 1994), vol. 1, pp. 87–8.

where no man may come without the will of the divine.'[52] Finally, he discards this newfangled scepticism and, with the weighty *auctoritas* of the 'santos é sanos teólogos', Columbus carefully proposes with almost scientific circumspection that the lands he has found could in fact be what Christianity had been dreaming of:

> These are excellent clues of the earthly paradise, because the place matches the descriptions of the holy and sacred theologians. Likewise, the signs very much support this idea, for I never read nor knew of so much fresh water penetrating so far inland and so near salt water, and another strong proof is the extreme mildness of the climate.[53]

Beside the two traditions of locating Paradise, Columbus may be thinking here of a third possibility, that is, a southern location. Alfred Hiatt has alerted me to a twelfth-/thirteenth-century tradition of locating Paradise at the equator, or even beneath the Tropic of Capricorn, which emerged as a result of integrating Arabic and Greek geographical knowledge of the regions below the equator with existing information. In the thirteenth century, for example, Roger Bacon's *Opus Maius* and the *Liber introductorius* of Michael Scot argue for an equatorial or sub-equatorial location of Paradise.[54] Columbus's comment that he would have found a milder, more temperate climate 'had [he] gone under the equinoctial line [here: 'equator']', suggests that he was familiar with this tradition, too.[55]

Because it was thought impossible to reach the *terra repromissionis* before the Last Judgment, the inclusion of Paradise by so many writers and mapmakers shows how easily the spatial and temporal dimensions could be collapsed. But given the interpretative framework of the *translatio studii et imperii*, this intertwining of geography and history need not be surprising. What must be stressed here is Britain's position at the end of time and space, situated between the very end of the world in the extreme west and the Earthly Paradise, the old and new beginning in the extreme east. William of

---

[52] *Christopher Columbus*, vol. 1, p. 88.

[53] *Christopher Columbus*, vol. 1, p. 88. Scafi quotes the same passage and other early-modern travellers claiming to have found Paradise (*Mapping Paradise*, pp. 240–1) but is dismissive of these accounts on the grounds that 'once full account has been taken of the context in which those travellers lived and wrote', then the question whether 'Renaissance explorers really intended to, or thought they could, discover the location of Paradise [must be answered] with "no"' (p. 241). But Scafi neither gives such a full account nor does he quote the earlier passage, where Columbus actually claims to have found Paradise. Besides, if it was not one of his intentions or hopes to find Paradise, one ought ask the question why he was so intimately familiar with the various authorities' opinions on its location, adding his own view of an sub-equatorial Paradise.

[54] Columbus had access to a number of passages from Roger Bacon's *Opus Maius* via Pierre d'Ailly's *Imago Mundi* (Pauline Moffitt Watts, 'Prophecy and Discovery: On the Spiritual Origins of Christopher Columbus's "Enterprise of the Indies"', *American Historical Review* (1985), 73–102). As I indicated above, d'Ailly also indentifies the Fortunate Isles with the terrestrial Paradise.

[55] The equatorial location of Paradise is discussed at length by Scafi, *Mapping Paradise*, in particular pp. 173–6.

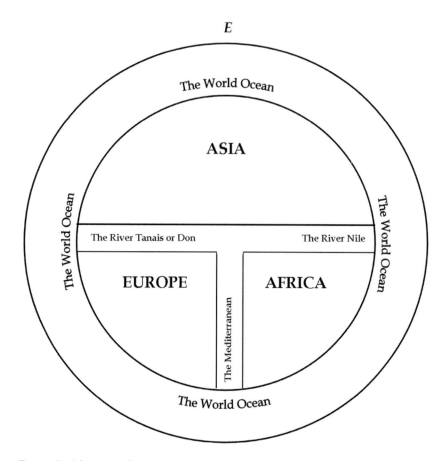

Figure 2. Diagram of a T-O map.

Malmesbury's assertion that God works miracles in Britain maintains hope in the resurrection, that is, hope that Britain will play a privileged role in the geography of the Christian story which will come to a close in the west.

Anyone looking at a T-O map or, in fact, any of the other Mappae Mundi, could not help noticing that Britain was about to fall off the table or, more precisely, into the world-encircling ocean. T-O maps show the *oikumene* (Africa, Asia and Europe forming the three 'negative' areas necessary to delineate a capital 'T'), surrounded by the world ocean (Figure 2). This ocean defines the landmasses of the three known continents and marks the end of the world. Thus, under the heading 'occean' the *MED* translates meaning 1 (a), that is, the phrase '(laste) clif of ocean', as 'the end of the world'. Certain Anglo-Norman and Old French spellings and, later, Middle English, added a second 'c' to render the term as 'occean' or 'occian'. This, together with the frequent use of 'occean' for the Atlantic, invited the association

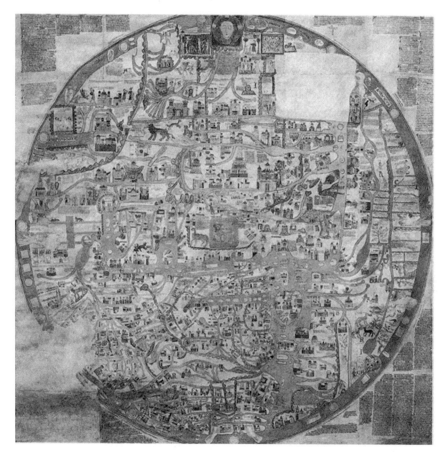

Figure 3. The Ebstorf Mappa Mundi. The four directions are represented by Christ's head (east), hands (north and south) and feet (west).

with 'west occean', especially during sunset.[56] This binding together of two distinct meanings was perhaps assisted by the etymological confusion of *occidentalis* and *occeanus*. In the context of westbound European literature, written for a very different purpose than the maps depicting the world-encircling ocean, *occean* became a name for the west, the *Abendland*, the land of the evening, but the west is also a name for the end of the day, the end of time, and ultimately, the end of the geographical world.

The largest known map of this kind (also the largest of the Mappae Mundi)

---

[56] For example, see Lydgate's *Troy Book*: 'Phebus ... gan to baþen in þe wawes wete His briȝt bemys of þe occian'. *Lydgate's Troy Book*, ed. H. Bergen, vols 1–3, EETS e.s. 97, 103, 106 (London, 1906–35; repr. as one vol., Woodbridge, 1995, 2003), Book 4, line 2,933. The image of Phebus bathing is, of course, sunset which takes place in the western ocean from Lydgate's vantage point ('occian' is not used for the Mediterranean). It is clear that 'Phebus ... baþen' can only denote sunset, hence 'occian' must stand for the west here.

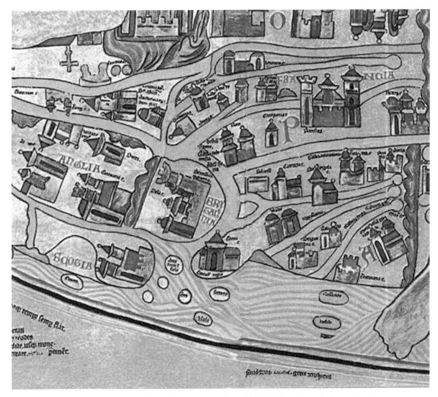

Figure 4. Detail of the Ebstorf Mappa Mundi. England and Scotland are depicted as separate islands next to Christ's left foot.

is the fourteenth-century Ebstorf map (Figure 3), sometimes ascribed to Gervase of Tilbury (*c.* 1152–1239). The orginal was destroyed in an air-raid in 1943 but facsimiles have preserved the map for posterity. Both spiritually and geographically, the Ebstorf map expresses England's position in the *trans-lationes imperii* and *studii*. Oriented towards the east, Christ's head marks the top of the map, whereas his hands designate north and south, respectively. At the very bottom of the map, his feet dip into the waters of the word-encir-cling ocean in the west. Eden, adjacent to Christ's head, marks the farthest east, *in oriente*, and the beginning of the map, *in principio*. As Christ's body enacts the history of the (Christian) world, the eye of the beholder glides from top to bottom or from beginning to end as it apprehends Christ's body from head to foot. This movement is emphasised by a fragment of an Advent antiphon placed above Christ's feet [the italicised text appears on the map]: 'O Sapientia, quae ex ore Altissimi prodisti, attingens a fine *usque ad finem, fortiter suaviter disponensque omnia*' [O Wisdom, who came from the mouth of the Most High, reaching from end *to end and ordering all things mightily and sweetly*].[57] Since only 'usque ad finem fortiter' [on its own perhaps best rendered as 'mightily towards the end'] is visible above Christ's left foot, the quotation stresses the finality of this western end of the world; at the same time, however, the use of an Advent antiphon to mark the end of the world, of time and of Christ's physical body, heralds the *adventus* or coming of Christ, synonymous with the availability of salvation, appropriately placed in the farthest west. And it is of course here, close to Christ's left foot, that we find Britain (which is synonymous with England on this map as Scotland is assigned a separate island) (Figure 4).

'Vastissimum and inuium' are the adjectives the thirteenth-century historiographer and Benedictine monk Matthew Paris uses in his inscription on the map of England in British Library Cotton MS Claudius D. VI, fol. 12v, to denote the ocean west of Britain. Orosius, Bede and the eleventh-century historian Adam of Bremen, for example, all call it *oceanus infinitus*.[58] This quality of the sea did not go unnoticed in the Bible. Deuteronomy 30.13 is perhaps the earliest equation of the sea with something equally unattainable and immeasurable as Heaven itself:

> neque trans mare positum ut causeris et dicas quis e nobis transfretare poterit mare et illud ad nos usque deferre ut possimus audire et facere quod praeceptum est?

> [Nor is it beyond the sea: that thou mayst excuse thyself, and say: Which of us can cross the sea, and bring it unto us: that we may hear, and do that which is commanded?]

Overlooking the Mediterranean from the Levant, one could have the impression of looking infinity in the eye, even though this was merely the Roman *mare nostrum*: 'Like mountains and deserts, the sea invites reflection; because it is immense it can draw the spirit towards the infinite.'[59] But one must wonder what kind of infinity the sea could represent for a thirteenth-century scholar. In a finite, fallen world infinity is a contradiction in terms. And yet there is no doubt that the 'pelagus vastissimum et inuium' invited speculation about the physical and, precisely because Paradise was supposed to lie beyond the ocean, the anagogical topography of the ocean. So how does the infinity of the *ultimae fines*, the 'last clif of occean', square with the finitude of the physical world? The rejection by Augustine, mentioned above, of any

[57] *Corpus antiphonalium officii*, ed. Dom René-Jean Hesbert, 6 vols (Rome, 1963–79), vol. 1, pp. 28–9 (16a) and vol. 2, pp. 56–7 (16).

[58] For Orosius, see *The Seven Books of History Against the Pagans*, trans. Irving Woodworth Raymond (New York, 1936), Book 1, passage 2, p. 43; for Bede, see p. 12, n. 5; and for Adam, p. 97, n. 96. In addition, the same phrase (*occeano infinito*) appears in Henry of Huntingdon's *Historia Anglorum*, p. 12.

[59] Mollat du Jourdin, *Europe and the Sea*, p. 198. Bernard McGinn explores a number of 'Christian uses of the sea as a symbol for divine infinity' (p. 158) in 'Ocean and Desert as Symbols of Mystical Absorption in the Christian Tradition', *Journal of Religion* 74:2 (1994), 155–81, pp. 158 ff.

attempt to cross the ocean testifies to its perceived vastness as infinite. Yet, the ocean was a part of this world, and Augustine himself (as well as many pre-modern writers coming after him) held that this world had clear limits and was finite.[60]

Isidore, in describing the source of all seas, the *abyssus*, refers to it as 'profunditas aquarum inpenetrabilis' [impenetrable depths of waters] to which 'omnes aquae ... per occultas venas ... revertuntur' [all waters return through hidden passages].[61] Isidore's definition of the mechanics of the ocean was copied (and sometimes modified) by many encyclopaedists, so that it would still be recognisable centuries later. This allows Gower to express a comparable idea of almost infinite, circular motion in his fourteenth-century *Confessio Amantis*:

> But thilke See which hath no wane
> Is cleped the gret Occeane,
> Out of the which arise and come
> The hyhe flodes alle and some;
> Is non so litel welle spring,
> Which ther ne takth his beginnyng,
> And lich a man that haleth breth
> Be weie of kinde, so it geth
> Out of the See and in ayein,
> The water, as the bokes sein.[62]

To cross the ocean, then, meant not only to challenge creation and the physical laws of the world, but also to mount an assault on the axioms of faith itself. The very creator who has 'ordered all things in measure, and number and weight' (Wisdom 11.21) has also erected an insuperable barrier, an infinite divide that would separate Paradise from the *oikumene*. For the writers of classical antiquity and for many early Christians this divide between life and death was the *oceanus dissociabilis*, an intractable (*inuium*) Styx. In his *Life of St Columba*, Adomnán (d. 704) describes the ocean into which Columba's monks journey as 'inremeabilis', where no return is possible.[63] He appears to borrow the term 'inremeabilis' from Virgil's *Aeneid*. Virgil calls Styx, the river separating the world of the living from Hades, 'inremeabilis unda', the waters which permit no return.[64] And there are other instances that show how Christian geography absorbed the classical *oceanus dissociabilis*.

The actual divide that separated the here from the Otherworld and symbol-

---

60 James McEvoy, *The Philosophy of Robert Grosseteste* (Oxford, 1982), p. 214.
61 *Isidori Hispalensis episcopi*, Book 13, Chapter 20.
62 *Confessio Amantis* in *The English Works of John Gower*, ed. G. C. Macaulay, 2 vols, EETS e.s. 81–2 (London, 1900–1), vol. 2, Book 7, lines 591–600.
63 Jacqueline Borsje, 'Zeemonsters en de mythische dimensie van de zee', *Madoc*: 13:4 (1999), 268–76 (270).
64 Borsje, 'Zeemonsters en de mythische dimensie van de zee', p. 270. Borsje, leaning on G. Brüning ('Adamnans *Vita Columbae* und ihre Ableitungen', *Zeitschrift für celtische Philologie* 11 (1917), 241–2), discusses the likelihood of Adomnán's familiarity with Virgil (p. 275, n. 10).

ised the final frontier of the *oceanus dissociabilis* is described in Benedeit's *Voyage* as a thick, almost impenetrable barrier of fog which takes Brendan three days to sail through (lines 1,649–58):

> E par l'otreid del rei divin
> Or aprisment vers le calin
> Qui tut aclot le paraïs
> Dunt Adam fud poësteïs.
> Nües grandes tenerge funt,
> Que li sun eir return n'i unt.
> Li granz calins tant aorbet,
> Qui i entret, tuz asorbet,
> Si de Deu n'at la veüe
> Qui poust passer cele nue.

> [But then, by the grace of the Divine King, they approached the fog which surrounded the Paradise over which Adam had held sway. Huge clouds created such darkness that the sons of Adam were helpless; the thick fog blinded every person who approached, with the result that he completely lost his sight unless God gave the vision required to penetrate the cloud.]

Benedeit elaborates the *caligo grandis* of the Latin *Navigatio* and emphasises that Brendan is granted safe passage through this barrier at God's express will, lines 1,649 and 1,657 above.[65] A less successful encounter with apparently the same frontier is narrated by Adam of Bremen (*fl.* late twelfth century) in his *History of the Archbishops of Hamburg-Bremen*. Adam tells of Archbishop Adalbert who (with hardly credible detail) reported an event that took place in the time of his predecessor: 'certain noble men of Frisia' attempted to sail toward the northern Atlantic beyond Iceland. This act of transgression turned swiftly into a tragic fiasco

> subito collapsi sunt in illam tenebrosam rigentis oceani caliginem, quae vix oculis penetrari valeret. Et ecce instabilis oceani euripus ad initia quaedam fontis sui archana recurrens infelices nautas iam desperatos, immo de morte sola cogitantes vehementissimo impetu traxit ad chaos – hanc dicunt esse voraginem abyssi – illud profundum, in quo fama est omnes recursus maris, qui decrescere videntur, absorberi et denuo revomi, quod fluctuatio crescens dici solet.

> [Of a sudden they fell into that numbing ocean's dark mist which could hardly be penetrated with the eyes. And, behold, the current of the fluctuating ocean whirled back to its mysterious fountainhead and with most furious impetuosity drew the unhappy sailors, who in their despair now thought only of death, on to chaos; this they say is the abysmal chasm – that deep in which report has it all the back flow of the sea, which appears to

---

[65] Selmer, ed., *Navigatio sancti Brendani*, p. 78.

decrease, is absorbed and in turn revomited, as the mounting fluctuation is usually described.][66]

Adam's sea invokes Alexander Neckham's (1157–1217) explanation of the tides, which are created either by the flexing and relaxing of Leviathan's coils or by the opening and closing of a cavity at the bottom of the ocean.[67] This extraordinary explanation of how the tides are generated creates a tangible idea of the ocean as a kind of temporal anti-matter that, at its farthest remove from the certainty of land, can refute the sequence of events that constitutes reality. Given the similarity of the circumstances, the dark mist is not so much the *caligo tenebrosa* of Genesis 15.17 as the translator of Adam's history suggests,[68] but the darkness of the *mare coagulatum* or Libersee that Brendan reports when he encounters a similar phenomenon.[69]

For a journey across the Christian *oceanus dissociabilis* to be successful and not to be perceived as an act of transgression, a strong spiritual desire, a divinely sanctioned expression of Providence, on the part of the voyager is necessary, and for Brendan this was his long-kept wish springing from his sincere love of God, a wish which enabled him to reach Paradise: 'Brandans, tu veis cest paraïs / Que tu a Deu mult requeïs' (lines 1,795–6) [Brendan, you can see this Paradise, for which you frequently besought God]. Where spiritual navigation makes all the difference, curiosity, or mere 'geographical desire' is insufficient.[70] Yet such was the wish of the Frisians:

> Item nobis retulit beatae memoriae pontifex Adalbertus in diebus anted-ecessoris sui quosdam nobiles de Fresia viros causa pervagandi maris in boream vela tetendisse, eo quod ab incolis eius populi dicitur ab ostio Wirrahae fluminis directo cursu in aquilonem nullam terram occurrere preter infinitum occeanum [preter illud mare quod Libersee dicitur].[71] Cuius rei novitate pervestiganda coniurati sodales.

---

66 *Adami Bremensis Gesta Hammaburgensis Ecclesiae Pontificum*, ed. W. Trillmich, Quellen des 9. und 11. Jahrhunderts zur Geschichte der Hamburgischen Kirche und des Reiches (Darmstadt, 2000), pp. 490 and 492. All translations are taken from Francis J. Tschan, trans., *Adam of Bremen: History of the Archbishops of Hamburg-Bremen, with a new introduction and selected bibliography by Timothy Reuter* (New York, 2002).

67 In the same passage Alexander famously discards the peasants' belief in the moon as causing the ebb and flow of the sea. Alexander Neckham, *De naturis rerum*, in *De naturis rerum libri duo, with the Poem of the Same Author, De laudibus divinæ sapientiæ*, ed. Thomas Wright, Rolls Series 34 (London, 1863), Book 2, Chapter 17, 'De accessu maris et recessu'.

68 *Adam of Bremen*, p. 220, n. 140.

69 On the Libersee or Liver sea, see Ad Putter, 'Walewein in the Otherworld and the Land of Prester John', *Arthurian Literature* 17 (1999), 79–99 (88). Putter points the reader to a number of works on this phenomenon (page 88, note 16).

70 The term is borrowed from Sylvia Tomasch and Sealy Gilles, eds, *Text and Territory: Geographical Imagination in the European Middle Ages* (Philadelphia, 1998), p. 2.

71 Not in all MSS. See *Adami Bremensis Gesta Hammaburgensis Ecclesiae Pontificum*, ed. W. Trillmich, Quellen des 9. und 11. Jahrhunderts zur Geschichte der Hamburgischen Kirche und des Reiches (Darmstadt, 2000), p. 490, note d.

[Archbishop Adalbert of blessed memory likewise told us that in the days of his predecessor certain noble men of Frisia spread sail to the north for the purpose of ranging through the sea, because the inhabitants claimed that by a direct course toward the north from the mouth of the Weser River one meets with no land [but only that sea called the Libersee.] The partners pledged themselves under oath to look into this novel claim][72]

With this in mind, it seems an ample reward for the Frisians' curiosity that the sailors, shortly after being hurled back from the end of the world, land on an exotic island where, at first, they take as much gold and precious jewels as they can carry but are then chased off the island by the native Cyclopes. Thus, their attempt to sail beyond the 'last clif of occean', that is, beyond the end of the world, takes them back in time to an uncivilised and wild place, much like Gogmagog's Britain in Geoffrey of Monmouth's *History of the Kings of Britain*.

To attempt circumnavigation was a sin punishable by divine wrath; even to *think* circumnavigation was possible was, as Augustine said, absurd. Infinity is the prerogative of the divine, as is Paradise, and it was Brendan's spiritual desire that empowered him to pierce the barrier of physical reality and transcend the paradoxical infinity of the ocean, perhaps best conveyed by the cyclical nature of his seven-year journey. For Christian writers, then, the great sea became a *limes* keeping Paradise pure and the *oikumene* at bay. As in antiquity, this border, the *oceanus dissociabilis*, continued to be viewed as sacred. The sea was a liminal 'territory', an anti-space which was confined to the edges of maps to render positive meaning to land only, and to provide a temporal, spatial and, most importantly, an anagogical barrier filled to the brim with fantastic and grotesque monsters. Only a handful of legendary mortals were able to cross this negative space and were granted a beatific vision of the terrestrial Paradise. But for lesser men the punishment for such a grave transgression as attempting a voyage to Paradise could very well be to drown in the wide ocean, which, technically speaking, carried the most dire consequences for the immortal soul: 'the greatest fear was that at the end of time the bodies of the shipwrecked would not be found for the general resurrection'.[73]

Burning Seas in the Chronicles of Matthew Paris

Over the skies of Britain an ominous red moon appeared on the first day of October 1250. During the following week, devastating storms wreaked

[72] *Gesta Hammaburgensis*, p. 490.
[73] Jacques Le Goff, quoted by Mollat du Jourdin, *Europe and the Sea*, p. 194. But there were also exceptions. James Peter Conlan, 'Marvellous Passages: English Nautical Piety in the Middle Ages and the Renaissance' (unpublished PhD thesis, University of California Riverside, 1999), shows how certain texts, most notably the Wakefield play *Processus Noe cum Filiis*, exceptionally question such prejudices (pp. 77–8).

havoc in England, and the catastrophic deluge that followed inspired some of Matthew Paris's most dramatic writing:

> Sub ejusdem temporis voluminibus, mense videlicet Octobris, luna existente prima, die mensis prima, apparuit novilunium turgens et rubicundum in signum futurarum tempestatum ... Cœpit igitur aer cotidie in prima incrementi lunaris septimana densa caligne et ventorum turbine vehementer commoveri ... Et quod dampnosius erat, mare perturbatum fines solitos, bis fluens sine refluxu, pertransiens, tam horribilem mugitum cum fremitu edidit, ut per remota terræ spatia, non sine stupore audientium, etiam senum, reboaret, quod nullus modernorum se meminit prævidisse.

> [In the course of this same time, namely in the month of October, the moon being in its first quarter, on the first day of the month the new moon appeared swollen and reddish in presage of future storms ... Daily in the first week of the waxing moon the air began to be much disturbed by dense mist and violent winds. ... And what was more damaging, the rough sea, rising above its usual level and the tide flowing twice in succession without any ebb, made such a horrible roaring noise that it resounded in places remote from it, to the amazement of the hearers, even old ones. No one living now could remember seeing this before.][74]

Matthew saw many floods in his lifetime if we are to trust his chronicles.[75] But none of his other descriptions renders anything nearly as comprehensive in the degree of its destruction as the flood of October 1250:

> Visum est etiam sub opaca nocte ipsum fretum quasi accensum ardere, et fluctus fluctibus conglomeratos dimicare, ita ut non posset nautarum peritia perituris navibus subvenire. Rates igitur magnæ ac solidæ submersæ perierunt.

> [In the darkness of night the sea seemed to burn as if set on fire and waves joined with waves as if in battle, so that the dexterity of the sailors could not come to the aid of their doomed ships. Even large and strongly-built vessels foundered and sank.][76]

The Benedictine monk is quick to point out that this flood did not come to a halt at church portals:

> Apud Winchelese autem quendam portum orientalem, exceptis tuguriis salinariis et piscatorum receptaculis et pontibus et molendinis, plusquam

[74] *Matthaei Parisiensis, monachi Sancti Albani, chronica majora*, ed. Henry Richards Luard (London, 1872–83), Rolls series, 7 vols, vol. 5, pp. 175–6 (henceforth: *Chronica majora*). Unless otherwise noted, all translation are taken from Richard Vaughan, trans., *The Illustrated Chronicles of Matthew Paris* (Stroud, 1993).
[75] See *Chronica majora*, for example: vol. 2, pp. 21, 410; vol. 3, pp. 242, 378, 519; vol. 5, pp. 30, 192, 175 ff., 263–4, 395, 453, 461, 561, 607.
[76] *Chronica majora*, vol. 5, p. 176.

trecentæ domus in ipso pago cum quibusdam ecclesiis per maris violentum ascensum sunt subversæ.

[At an eastern port called Winchelsea, apart from sheds for salt-making, fishermen's buildings, bridges and mills, more than three hundred houses and several churches were destroyed in that place by the violent rise of the sea.][77]

Quite predictably, his verdict is that the flood exacted divine retribution for transgressions committed on earth in a manner similar to the biblical flood of Genesis. Ever since God's storm caused Jonah to shipwreck, tempests, in particular, have been interpreted as vehicles of divine will:

ut manifeste ira Dei tam in mari quam in terra mortalibus appareret, secundum illud Abacuc vaticinium, vindicta videretur peccatorum imminere; *Nunquid in fluminibus iratus es, Domine? … Vel in mari indignatio tua?*

[So the anger of God was made clearly apparent to mortals both at sea and on the land and the punishment of sinners seemed imminent, as the prophecy of Habakkuk says: 'Was the lord displeased against the rivers? … Was thy wrath against the sea?'][78]

However, what is not so apparent is that England should be punished for sins committed at Rome, the *fons totius justitiæ*: 'Et quid mirum? a Romana enim curia, quæ fons esse totius justitiæ teneretur, enormitates irrecitabiles emanarunt' [And what wonder? For from the Roman curia, which is supposed to be the fount of all justice, unmentionable enormities emanated].[79] This interpretation of the storm itself as an instance of divine Providence becomes clear against the background of England's geographical and anagogical positioning at the 'last clif of occean' which brings with it tangible consequences. Here, where the end is closest, God's voice is more articulate. For Matthew and his pre-Newtonian understanding of time and history as figurative, it was unthinkable that any other reason could have caused the great flood of

---

[77] *Chronica majora*, vol. 5, p. 176.

[78] *Chronica majora*, vol. 5, pp. 176–7.

[79] *Chronica majora*, vol. 5, pp. 177. Others allegorically linked the clergy's fate to one of the Beasts of the Apocalypse that would emerge from the sea. In the apocalyptic poem *The Calamities of the Church of Liège* (*c*. 1090), Rupert of Deutz (*c*. 1070–1129) invokes Apocalypse 13.1 as a punishment for the disgraceful conduct of the diocese of Liège: 'Now the ancient enemy arises from the sea, / And rules as victor over the seven hills' (*Monumenta Germaniae Historica, Libelli de lite*, 3:624. Translation from Bernard McGinn, *Visions of the End – Apocalyptic Traditions in the Middle Ages* (New York, 1979), p. 97). Similarly, in 1147 Gerard of Poehlde wrote a letter to a certain Evermord, prior of the Norbertine house of Our Blessed Lady at Magdeburg at the beginning of the Crusade against the Wends. The troubled state of the Church is Gerard's greatest concern, and he likens the crucial unity of the Church to the last bulwark against the coming of the Apocalypse: 'The peace of the Church is the barrier against those evil ones whom John foretold as the beast coming out of the sea' (*Visions of the End*, p. 113).

1250.[80] The only thinkable possibility was that these meteorological signs were tokens of Providence. Besides being an established tradition that had a firm place in the spiritual topography of the known world, there is sufficient scriptural authority for Matthew's reading of the weather. Psalm 103.5–6 (KJV: 104) makes this perhaps clearest:

> 5   qui fundasti terram super stabilitatem suam non commovebitur in saeculum et in saeculum
> 6   abysso quasi vestimento operuisti eam super montes stabunt aquae
> 7   ab increpatione tua fugient a voce tonitrui tui formidabunt
>
> [5   Who hast founded the earth upon its own bases: it shall not be moved for ever and ever.
> 6   The deep like a garment is its clothing: above the mountains shall the waters stand.
> 7   At thy rebuke they shall flee: at the voice of thy thunder they shall fear.]

The interpretation of the past and the present as manifestations of divine truth will render historiography an applied typology of Providence. Weather is only a permutation of God's will:

> The notion that Providence, the will of God as it is exercised in history, can be illustrated by meteorogical events that occur at sea and influence the course of history inflected much of the English literature of the Middle Ages.[81]

One question remains to be addressed: why was Britain singled out for this punishment by deluge? The concept of the sea as an awesome instrument of God's wrath is an old one, and the reasoning behind this explanation runs deeper than Matthew's latent contempt for all things papal. What surfaces here is merely the peak of a long history of not always compatible views of the sea inherited from antiquity and from the Bible that, coupled with the liminal geographical positioning of Britain, not only reveal the cognitive categories of a thirteenth-century monk but also point to wider-held beliefs about the limits and limitations of the world.

In St Albans Matthew had at his hand one of the finest libraries in Europe, and hence access to the body of knowledge that would provide him with the tools to write histories of England and produce his maps of Britain and itineraries to Palestine. Naturally, his principal tool with which to classify reality was the Bible. In the passage quoted on page 93 Matthew cites Habakkuk's

---

[80] Matthew blames not only the flood of 1250 on God's wrath. In his entry for 1195, he makes a similar connection: 'Istam autem Dei iram aquarum diluvium praesignavit, quae segetes suffocans validam famem generavit', *Chronica majora*, vol. 2, p. 410.

[81] Conlan, *Marvellous Passages*, pp. 87 ff. Conlan goes on to discuss a string of such examples, including the *South English Legendary* and the *Siege of Jerusalem*.

canticle for the sins of his people (Habbakuk 3.8). Habbakuk praises God's omnipotence and strength and alludes to the miracles God worked on the sea in favour of the people of Israel. This is made clearer in verses 10–11 and particularly in verse 15 which recalls the parting of the Red Sea: 'viam fecisti in mari equis tuis in luto aquarum multarum' [Thou madest a way in the sea for thy horses, in the mud of many waters]. What Matthew cites is an instance of divine punishment delivered against the 'wrong justice' exercised on earth: 'propter hoc lacerata est lex et non pervenit usque ad finem iudicium quia impius praevalet adversus iustum propterea egreditur iudicium perversum' [Therefore the law is torn in pieces, and judgment cometh not to the end: because the wicked prevaileth against the just, therefore wrong justice goeth forth].[82] The failings of the Roman curia is yet another such instance at which God intervenes. That the form of punishment Habakkuk predicts to his people should be an invasion of the belligerent Chaldeans is of little significance here; it was obvious that the sea could punish too: 'dedit abyssus vocem suam altitudino manus suas levavit' [The deep put forth its voice: the deep lifted up its hands].[83]

Matthew Paris relies on Gildas for much of his knowledge of Britain. In his map of Britain in Corpus Christi College, Cambridge MS 16, fol. v verso, he includes a unique scale legend from Gildas, and in St Albans historical MS Roy. 13. D.V., fol. 152, he favours Gildas over other authorities: 'Hic est discordia inter hoc et Gildam de dimensione Anglie. Respice in principio Gilda' [At this point, there is disagreement between this and Gildas about the dimensions of England. Consult Gildas in the first place].[84] In his *Chronica majora* he evokes and intensifies the image of the ring of sea surrounding Britain and the giants dwelling there: Diana's prophecy of the events that will befall Brutus address the British protoplast with the words

> Brute, sub occasu solis, trans Gallica regna,
> Insula in occeano est, undique clausa mari,
> Insula in occeano est, habitata gigantibus olim.
>
> [Brutus, under the sunset, beyond the kingdom of Gaul, there is
> an island in the ocean, enclosed by the sea on all sides; there is
> an island in the ocean, in the past inhabited by giants.][85]

Matthew copies this passage verbatim from Geoffrey of Monmouth, who sets it in verse, which is unusual for the *Historia Regum Britannie* and is

---

82 Habakkuk 1.4.
83 Habakkuk 3.10.
84 Richard Vaughan, *Matthew Paris* (Cambridge, 1959; reissued 1979), pp. 239–40. Suzanne Lewis, *The Art of Matthew Paris in the Chronica Majora* (Aldershot, 1987) adds on page 509, note 108, that this memorandum is repeated in the *Abbreviatio Chronicorum*, British Library MS Cotton Claudius D. VI, fol. iv.
85 *Chronica majora*, p. 20. My translation.

reserved for moments of particular significance.[86] Albeit Brutus' preceding address to the goddess is also in verse, the use of anaphora emphasises the prophetic quality of Diana's words. He repeats the first phrase of line 2, 'Insula in occeano est', in the following line, stressing the importance of Britain's geographical positioning for the two subsequent relative clauses, 'undique clausa mari' and 'habitata gigantibus olim'. This emphasis on 'occeano' is cemented by 'occasu' in line 1, and although 'occasu' may not alliterate with 'occeano' in later Latin, it appears to hint at the etymological confusion surrounding the association of *occean* with the sunset (*occidentalis occeanum*).[87]

Elsewhere, Matthew tells of a battle of sea-monsters off the coast of Britain in 1240. He says that witnesses who lived by the sea saw miracles in the deep, amongst which was a war between fishes, whales and sea-monsters ('bellum … inter pisces, beluas, et monstra marina') so fierce that those beasts which perished were cast onto the shore ('ad litora sunt projecta').[88] The heading over this passage is, predictably enough, *Terribile pronosticum de piscibus in mari pugnantibus*, but Matthew does not offer any explanation of this sign. Suzanne Lewis notes that this sea battle represents 'the culmination of a whole series of natural and human disasters'.[89] Matthew appears to assume here that the natural habitat of sea-monsters is the *oceanus Britannicus*.[90] Together with the two battles of the sea-serpents in the Brendan-legend,[91] this presence of *belue marine*[92] in the sea surrounding Britain reasserts the pre-Christian idea that the northern ocean was particularly monster-infested, or, in Horace's words: 'te beluosus qui remotis / obstrepit Oceanus Britannis' [To you the beast-teeming Ocean that roars at the distant Britons].[93] Horace spells out the Romans' awe of the British sea which in its fierce, unpredictable nature seemed the mythical antithesis to their everyday *mare nostrum*, the almost tideless, benign Mediterranean.

Immediately before the passage quoted above, Matthew reminds the reader that it is the custom of the sea to vomit out objects: 'sicut natura maris est

86 *The Historia Regum Britannie*, ed. Wright, vol. 1, p. 9. A modified version ('Brute, sub occasu solis, trans Gallica regna, / Insula uasta [iacet] habitata gigantibus olim') appears in the verse chronicle *Gesta Regum Britannie*, Book 1, lines 279–80 (*The* Historia Regum Britannie *of Geoffrey of Monmouth*, ed. Neil Wright, vol. 5, *Gesta Regum Britannie* (Cambridge, 1991), p. 18).

87 See pp. 84–5.

88 *Chronica majora*, p. 81.

89 Lewis, *The Art of Matthew Paris*, pp. 295–7.

90 Using this scene from Matthew's entry for 1240 as a model, Daniel Birkholz speculates that the depiction of fighting sea-monsters in the North Sea area on the Gough Map may be similarly ominous in nature (*The King's Two Maps: Cartography and Culture in Thirteenth-Century England*, Studies in Medieval History and Culture 22 (London and New York, 2004), pp. 142–3).

91 Selmer, *Navigatio sancti Brendani*, Chapter 16 (pp. 45–6) and Chapter 19 (pp. 55–6); and *The Anglo-Norman Voyage of St Brendan by Benedeit*, ed. E. G. Waters (Oxford, 1928), lines 897–968 and 1,005–34.

92 Matthew uses this heading for his illumination of four sea-monsters in the margin of the above text, Corpus Christi College Cambridge MS 17, fol. 140.

93 Niall Kudd, ed. and trans, *Horace: Odes and Epocles*, LCB 33N (Cambridge, MA: 2004), Book 4, 15, lines 47–8, pp. 258–9.

morticiam ad aridam projecta evomere.'[94] This belief was shared by many writers before him, and it was held to be particularly true of the *oceanus Britannicus*. Commenting on the Viking incursions, Hariulf of Saint-Riquier (d. 1143) appears to pun on a similar notion when he says that 'the sea vomits upon its shores monsters which it feeds with its fish' and he admits that 'the Danes, those barbarians, from the middle of their raised masts appear to us as wild beasts in the forests'.[95]

That Britain's seas are so hospitable to serpents and monsters is largely the result of its proximity to the *oceanus infinitus*. Adam of Bremen, like Orosius and Bede before him, was also mindful of the fact that 'A tergo Britanniae, unde infinitus patet occeanus' [Beyond Britain ... the boundless ocean begins],[96] and the sea stretching there is hostile and utterly terrifying:

> Post Normanniam, quae est ultima aquilonis provintia, nihil invenies habitacionis humanae nisi terribilem visu et infinitum occeanum, qui totum mundum amplectitur.

> [Beyond Norway, which is the farthermost northern country, you will look and find no human habitation, nothing but the ocean, terrible to look upon and limitless, encircling the whole world.][97]

Together with the awe felt when facing infinity, this fear of the terrible northern seas produces the Libersee or *mare coagulatum*, a darkness of knowledge. And this is what Adam describes when he tells of Vinland: 'Post quam insulam, ait, terra non invenitur habitabilis in illo oceano, sed omnia, quae ultra sunt, glacie intolerabili ac caligine inmensa plena sunt' [Beyond that island, he said, no habitable land is found in that ocean, but every place beyond is full of impenetrable ice and intense darkness].[98] Adam adds the darkness to Martianus Capella's (*fl.* fifth century) frozen sea,[99] and he places the monsters – he chooses the classical Cyclopes – in the island of the ocean on which the Frisians land in the passage quoted on page 91 above.

When Matthew wrote of the floods of 1250, he had at his fingertips the Christian tradition of an unpredictable, infinite and intractable sea that was host to an army of monsters, waiting to become agents of Providence at God's command. The spiritual transgressions of the Roman curia, as well as the hubris of those who ventured into the sea and across the *oceanus dissociabilis*, were punishable by a disaster, executed by the sea, of course. Britain, lying unsheltered in the boundless ocean, had to endure these meteorological

---

94 *Chronica majora*, p. 81.
95 Quoted from Mollat du Jourdin, *Europe and the Sea*, p. 43.
96 *Gesta Hammaburgensis Ecclesiae Pontificum*, ed. Trillmich, p. 482.
97 *Gesta Hammaburgensis*, p. 482. Adam borrows here from Martianus Capella, *The Wedding of Philology and Mercury*, Book 6, paragraph 664, but the awe, though Virgilian in description (*Aeneid*, Book 6, lines 126–7, see Tschan, *Adam of Bremen*, p. 215) is Adam's addition.
98 *Gesta Hammaburgensis*, p. 490.
99 Martianus Capella, *The Wedding of Philology and Mercury*, Book 6, paragraph 666.

reprimands: some have observed that it is the nature of the ocean to rise higher in Britain. Coupled with Galenic theory, Ranulph Higden states that

> Þe hiȝe flood of ocean ariseþ vp þe costes of Bretaine foure score cubitis hiȝe. And þat risynge and depnesse is better i-knowe by þe cleues þan in the þe hiȝe see; for betynge of veynes is better i-knowe in þe vttre parties of bodies þan in þe myddel wiþynne.[100]

From this passage it emerges that being positioned at the end of the world means living on the outer edge of the infinite ocean, which, for the purpose of the tides and the occasional flooding, is one of the principal reasons why Britain, more than any other inhabited land, is affected by the fierceness of the sea. Perhaps no one has described the end of the world lying beyond Britain somewhere in the infinite ocean as fittingly as Adam of Bremen in his account of Harald of Norway's voyage into the ocean. At once, it becomes evident that the end of Adam's failing world was at the same time an impassable border marking the end of human knowledge and the beginning of divine infinity, to transgress which can only ignite God's wrath. Where Adam perceives the *ultimae fines*, the *abyssus* from Genesis 1 reappears, the primordial deep to which, according to Isidore, all water must return:[101]

> Temptavit hoc nuper experientissimus Nordmannorum princeps Haraldus. Qui latitudinem septentrionalis oceani perscrutatus navibus tandem caligantibus ante ora deficientis mundi finibus inmane baratrum abyssi retroactis vestigiis pene vix salvus evasit.

> [The very well-informed prince of the Norwegians, Harold, lately attempted this sea. After he had explored the expanse of the Northern Ocean in his ships, there lay before their eyes at length the darksome bounds of failing world, and by retracing his steps he barely escaped in safety the vast pit of the abyss.][102]

This October flood is not only the crowning catastrophe of Matthew's most disastrous year, but it was also supposed to conclude the entire chronicle and the world as he knew it: 'Thus, in the year [1250], unusual and dreadful disturbances were experienced, both by land and sea, which immediately threatened the end of the world.'[103]

The potent combination of the *translatio imperii*, Britain's fringe position at the end of the world and its spiritual geography was not only available to English writers. In his 2,000-line verse account of Edward III, *On Edward III, King of England*, the Flemish writer Jan van Boendale (1279–*c.* 1350)

---

[100] *Polychronicon Ranulphi Higden monachii Cestrensis*, vol. 1, p. 59. The translation is Trevisa's, taken from the same edition of Higden's work.
[101] *Isidori Hispalensis episcopi*, Book 13, Chapter 20, 'De Abysso'.
[102] *Gesta Hammaburgensis*, p. 490.
[103] Vaughan, *The Illustrated Chronicles*, entry for 1250, p. 196.

invokes Alexander the Great and the Trojan War as stations of the westward *translatio imperii* before he presents Edward as the scourge of God sent from the end of the world in the western ocean:

> Nu heeft God eenen verwect,
> Daer hi die sonden mede wrect,
> Des hi swaerlijc begint, te waren,
> Ende comt van over zee gevaren
> Van daer die zonne gaet onder,
> Daer hi gewracht heeft wonder
> Van manslachte, sekerlike,
> Ja ten einde van eerdrike
> (Dats in Scotlant) ende daer toe mee
> Neffens Vlaenderen op die zee,
> Des gelike men voir dien
> Herde selden heeft gesien.

[Now God has quickened one with whose help He punishes sins, on which he [Edward] truly embarks with force. And he came sailing across the sea from where the sun sets, where he slaughtered a vast number of people, indeed; yes, at the end of the world (that is in Scotland) and also on the sea near Flanders, the like of which has rarely been seen before].[104]

Boendale would later repeat some of these sentiments in his better-known *Deeds of the Dukes of Brabant*: 'Dat was Edewaert van Inghelant, / Die over zee vacht metter hant' [That was Edward of England who guards the sea with his person].[105]

Acts of transgression against God's law are, in the case of Britain, tied to the sea which can simultaneously serve as an allegory for the causes of sin and act as the retributive arm of Providence. The sea assumes a crucial role in the tradition of interpreting as moral and anagogical events resulting from Britain's position at the frontier of the spiritual topography of the Christian universe. This tradition, handed down from Gildas, reaches Matthew Paris, and is continued by John Wyclif whose sermons on storms preserve this theme for the fourteenth century and Protestant exegeses of meteorology.[106]

---

104 *Van den derden Edewaert, coninc van Engelant. Rymchronik geschreven omtrent het jaer 1347, door Jan de Klerk van Antwerpen*, ed. J. F. Willems (Ghent, 1840), lines 37–48.). I am grateful to Luuk Houwen for his help with the translation. The two battles Boendale refers to here are probably Halidon Hill (1333) and Sluys (1340).

105 *De Brabantsche yeesten, of Rymkronyk van Braband, door Jan de Klerk, van Antwerpen*, ed. J. F. Willems (Brussels, 1839), Chapter 11, lines 873–4. I would like to thank Luuk Houwen for his help.

106 Conlan dedicates an entire section to Wycliffite 'storm theology' in 'Marvellous Passages', Chapter 2, 'The Wind and God's Wrath', Part 1, pp. 192–228, in particular, pp. 202 ff.

4

Realms in Abeyance

The outraged law, like the bursting shells, had come to them, an insoluble mystery from the sea.

Joseph Conrad, *Heart of Darkness* (1902)

The barbarians push us back to the sea, the sea pushes us back to the barbarians; between these two kinds of death, we are either drowned or slaughtered.   Gildas (*c.* 504–70), *On the Ruin of Britain*[1]

The Matter of England: Land, Sea and Identity in the *Horn* Legend[2]

R omance tales are crowded with accounts of people who are exposed to the sea against their will, but the topos is of course much older.[3] In his groundbreaking study, 'Setting Adrift in Mediaeval Law and Literature', J. R. Reinhard discusses the custom of setting people adrift in (mostly) unsea-worthy boats, and he classifies the extant literary instances into a number of categories.[4] Reinhard concludes that in Celtic custom and, to a lesser extent, in some Germanic communities (as, indeed, was the case in Roman practice), there existed a code of punishing criminals and sometimes even presumed offenders by setting them adrift in a boat equipped with only the most necessary provisions, which, at most, amounted to providing them with only one oar.[5]

By the twelfth century it was no longer necessary for the culprit or suspect to share the same belief system as the group performing the ritual. As Thomas of England's *Romance d'Horn* (henceforth *RH*) opens *in medias res*, the

---

[1] *De Excidio Britonum*, ed. and trans. M. Winterbottom (London, 1978), pp. 23–4.

[2] An earlier version of this section has been published as 'Littorial Encounters: The Shore as Cultural Interface in *King Horn*', *Al-Masaq: Islam and the Medieval Mediterranean* 18:1 (2006), 79–86.

[3] See Carolyn Hares-Stryker, 'Adrift on the Seven Seas: The Medieval Topos of Exile at Sea', *Florilegium* 12 (1993), 79–98, passim, and Helen Cooper, *The English Romance in Time: Trans-forming Motifs from Geoffrey of Monmouth to the Death of Shakespeare* (Oxford, 2004), pp. 106–36.

[4] J. R. Reinhard, 'Setting Adrift in Mediaeval Law and Literature', *PMLA* 56 (1941), 33–68.

[5] The concept itself appears to be an ancient one. Reinhard acknowledges a cultural parallel with the Greek concept of the sea as an arbiter of justice and he links the origin of this notion to animistic beliefs (pp. 67–8).

Saracen king Rodmund has conquered Horn's native Suddene and killed Horn's father, King Aalof. A Saracen, Malbroin, finds Horn and fifteen other children hiding in a garden and is swayed by pity from his intention of killing them. Subsequently, he brings the children to King Rodmund who, too, is moved by pity and orders all the children to be cast adrift. Rodmund's actions are made all the more malicious as they simultaneously represent an act of challenging Christianity: 'Ja ne·s garrat lur deus, en ki il sunt creanz' [the god they believe in will never save them] (line 68).[6] Yet, in marked contrast to the one-dimensional portrayal of the Saracens in the thirteenth-century Middle English romance *King Horn*, the *RH* explicitly states that both Malbroin and Rodmund experience compassion at the sight of the young heir and shift the responsibility for Horn's fate to the elemental force of the sea (Chapters 2–3). It is tempting to view Horn's rescue from the sea as a vindication of God's control over the elements and, in the terms of the romance's civilisational dialectics, as a vindication of Christianity against the distorted Islam of the invaders: the fortunate outcome of the ensuing ordeal and the subsequent *felix naufragium* are tokens of God's judgement in favour of the Christian children whose faith is affirmed by Providence.[7] The *Romance of Merlin* tradition offers a haunting parallel. It had been prophesied to Arthur that his bastard son Mordred would one day cause his death. In order to prevent the prophecy from being fulfilled, Arthur sets newborn children adrift on the sea in a rudderless boat but the sea will not allow him to fool Providence (Figure 5). The topos of being set adrift in a rudderless or unseaworthy boat is a romance and, more importantly, an Insular commonplace. Besides the Horn-legend, it appears in many romance narratives, including the tale of Constance, *Sir Eglamour*, the *Quest of the Holy Grail* and the late-medieval favourite *Amadis de Gaule*, surviving well into the early-modern period in the works of Greene and Shakespeare.[8]

In the established redactions of the legends of Brendan and Tristan, as well as in the *immrama*, the examples of setting adrift or sailing into the dangerous unknown testify to the depth of the protagonist's faith as all journeys tend to emphasise the role of God as protector and arbiter of such enterprises. All those instances have in common as their starting point an active decision taken by the hero or the heroes to leave their native country, *exul patriae*. In contrast with these voluntary journeys, Horn's forced setting adrift is an undeserved penitence. Not only is he unjustly punished, but the method of his punishment is usually reserved for criminals whose guilt cannot be proved

---

6 All citations from *RH* are taken from *The Romance of Horn by Thomas*, ed. Mildred K. Pope, 2 vols, Anglo-Norman Text Society 9–10, 12–13 (Oxford, 1955). The translations are from Judith Weiss, *The Birth of Birth of Romance – An Anthology* (London, 1992).

7 Survival *against the odds*, especially at sea, is a mark of being favoured by God or the gods, as Helen Cooper observes (*The English Romance in Time*, p. 110).

8 The topos has been magisterially covered by Cooper, *The English Romance in Time*, pp. 106–36 (in particular, pp. 106–13). Cooper adds that the *Golden Legend* contains an account of Judas being set adrift as a child (pp. 375–6). This would make Mordred and Judas the only two 'deserving' recipients of this treatment. See also Hares-Stryker, 'Adrift on the Seven Seas', passim.

Figure 5. Arthur sets the children adrift (British Library, MS Add. 38,117, fol. 97v).

beyond doubt.[9] What Horn's setting adrift has in common with Brendan's and Tristan's decisions to set out onto the sea is that it passes on a complex moral judgement to a higher force: it is an appeal to a superior form of justice, to Providence. Hence, in the best Insular fashion, all traces of apparent human bias are removed as the boat is hardly furnished: 'N'i ot tres n'avirum, guvernail ne struman' [It had neither sail, oar, rudder nor steersman] (line 74). The literary experience created by this instance of setting adrift comes to a climax once the ropes that tied Horn's sea-battered vessel to his Saracen escort are cut:

> Al palagre de mer sunt sil venu najant,
> Ne lur pert nule part de terre tant ne quant.
> La corde unt trenché, dunt tret unt le chalant,
> As venz erent posé tuit li noble enfant
> E il sunt senz cunseil; as undes vunt walcrant. (lines 91–5)

---

9   Reinhard, 'Setting Adrift, pp. 47 ff.

[They rowed towards the open sea; no land was to be seen anywhere. They cut the ropes pulling the boat, abandoning all the noble children to the winds. They were helpless, tossing on the waves.]

'Noble' implies emotional refinement and elegance, and paired with the help-less and small 'enfant', the contrast with the overwhelming force of the sea and its waves, 'undes', further exaggerates the pathos of the situation. The resulting image of helpless yet precious Christian souls in a small boat tossed by violent waves is compelling as well as reminiscent of *ecclesia* sailing on the sea of the world and helps exacerbate the cruelty the children are forced to endure. This image of helpless souls adrift on the sea of the world will return in Chaucer's and Gower's tale of Custance/Constance, who, on one occasion, is even set adrift with her child.[10]

But the children in the *RH* are not entirely 'senz cunseil': 'Deus lur est cunseilliers ki salveres est puissant. / Si iert il, si li plest' [God was their helper, our powerful Saviour. And it will turn out as He wishes] (lines 96–7). The narrative reminder of God's impending help arrives together with a sudden turn of events, as the 'senz cunseil' of the previous line is promptly invalidated by 'cunseilliers'. In a way, this shift is reminiscent of the monks' horror in Benedeit's *Voyage* at the sight of the sea-monsters and the strange creatures on the ocean floor.[11] In both instances Brendan's assurance of God's help was as immediate as the narrative intercession in line 97: 'Seignurs, n'entrez en dutance: / Deus vus en ferat la venjance' [Lords, do not be afraid; God will avenge you] (lines 923–4) and:

> 'Seignurs, de rien pur quei dutez?
> Voz creances cum debutez!
> Perilz avez suffert plus granz,
> Vers tuz vus fud Deus bons guaranz.' (lines 1,055–8)

[Lords, why are you afraid of anything? How quickly you give up your faith! You have survived much greater perils, against all of which God has been a good defence to you.]

Horn's first voyage marks a substantial change of paradigms in Insular sea-writing. The established tradition of the Irish *peregrinatio pro amore Dei* that had been so successfully transformed by Benedeit into a quasi-secular sea-pilgrimage towards the unknown is replaced by the brief crossings of *RH* characteristic of so much of later English literature, ranging from the pragmatic travels of Havelok, and the fateful but mainly brief journeys of the

---

[10] For a bold reading of *The Man of Law's Tale* in conjunction with *ecclesia* and the sea of the world, see V. A. Kolve, 'The Man of Law's Tale: The Rudderless Ship and the Sea', in *Chaucer and the Imagery of Narrative* (London, 1984), Chapter 7, pp. 297–358.

[11] See p. 55 on the passage from the *Voyage*, and p. 126, n. 18, on the restlessness on the ocean floor.

Tristan-legend to the abrupt channel-hopping in Laȝamon's *Brut*. The spiritually inspiring sea of the *immrama* and the Brendan-legend passed through
intermediate stages of symbolic significance (it was still an option for Tristan
to seek healing on the sea) until it had been reduced to being the marginalised
peril of later English narratives. What was a choice for Brendan and a last
solution for Tristan has become Horn's nemesis against which he fashions
himself as a Christian king. A noteworthy exception is perhaps Constance
who, like Brendan, spends years on the sea.[12]

To a large extent, this first exile of Horn is also the final exile of the sea
from the poem. From this point onwards, the presence of the sea dwindles
until it is gradually withdrawn from the narrative. Horn's next passage
assigns less space to an increasingly feeble sea, both quantitatively if meas-
ured in lines and qualitatively as it no longer poses a perceivable threat to
the maturing hero (lines 2,164–77). The crossing is safe and swift; instead of
acknowledging the presence of the sea the narrator concentrates on the skill
of the sailors.

Horn's next crossing aims at preventing the wedding of Rigmel and King
Modin. From the very outset, there is no question of the sea even indirectly
interfering with Horn's ambitions. In the quickest possible fashion the sea is
disregarded and the journey is confined to the barest ingredients essential for
successful sea-travel:

> E quant del rei fud pris del aler li cungiez,
> Tost sunt as nefs venuz e tost sunt eschipez.
> Les veilz traient amunt kar bon fud li orez,
> Ja ne fineront mais, si seront arivez. (lines 3,921–4)

> [And when they had taken leave of the king they swiftly came
> to the ships and swiftly embarked. They hoisted the sails, for
> the breeze was good. They would not stop till they arrived.]

It takes Thomas less than seven lines to deal with Horn's crossing, and not
all of these are even necessary from a structural point of view. Line 3,924,
for example, conveys a mere tautology, yet it appears to transmit an autho-
rial perception that offers an answer to the relative absence of the sea from
the poem. Of course, there is no point in stopping a sea-voyage if one wants
to complete one's journey in the shortest time possible. The sea is clearly
not a place, rather, it is a temporal function of the space that separates two
shores.

Unfortunately, the crossing that takes Horn back to his private *reconquista* in Suddene cannot be reconstructed from the extant three manuscripts,
but there is no reason to assume that the text suddenly alters its pattern of

---

12 On two occasions Gower even adds that Constance dwells on the sea with her child: 'And thus
upon the flod thei wone, / This ladi with hire yonge Sone' (Book 2, lines 1,053–4) and 'that I forth
with my litel Sone / Upon the wawes scholden wone' (Book 2, lines 1,151–2). The references are
to G. C. Macaulay's edition, EETS e.s. 81–2 (London, 1900–1), 2 vols.

ever-diminishing sea-voyages. In fact, the subsequent crossing demonstrates that Thomas can reduce Horn's sea-passages to only two lines: 'En ses nefs est entrez, oret ad e bon vent. / Ore le cunduie Deus, li reis omnipotent!' [He embarked, and they had good breezes and wind. Now God, the Lord Almighty, guide them!] (lines 5,028–9). The text separates Horn's departure from his arrival in an almost montage-like fashion, and the scene moves to Wikele's mischief; then, 137 lines later, Wothere, Wikele's brother and loyal servant to Horn, on descrying Horn's sails, frantically leaps into the sea to greet the hero: 'Ne se poet atenir e pur els plus haster / Si est mis enz al noer' [He could not stop himself and, to hasten their arrival, he began swimming] (lines 5,143–4). Yet, despite Wothere's heroic effort, the sea remains a marginalised element of the narrative after Horn's pivotal setting adrift.

However, although exiled from the gravitational centre of the romance, the sea continues to present a threat to political and social stability throughout the poem. The two episodes in which Saracen fleets casually land and challenge the kings of Westir and Brittany reveal just how vulnerable insular communities are. A fleet can be far quicker and more easily moved over the sea than an army by land. Without any warning a Saracen fleet arrives at the port of Costance (lines 1,323–5). Neither is the *regne preisez* Westir safe from the peril of a hostile fleet landing. Ports in particular are soft spots:

> A un jor sunt venu dui mut felun tirant
> El regne de Westir od lur flote siglant.
> …
> A terre s'en issent (fors) grant orgoil demenant,
> E al port sunt remis e buces e chalant
> Od cables afermez e od ancres tenant. (lines 2,905–6 and 2,920–2)

> [One day two wicked princes came sailing with their fleet to the kingdom of Westir. … They disembarked with great arrogance, leaving the ships and boats behind in harbour moored with ropes and held by anchors.]

This particular aspect of the sea returns in the Middle English *King Horn* where the ease with which the dangerous sea flows up to king Hunlaf's throne shows how the unknown can all of a sudden issue challenges, not unlike the realm of *fayerie* that sends its agents into King Arthur's hall in later romances such as *Sir Gawain and the Green Knight*.[13]

The threat posed by the sea in a maritime narrative like the *Voyage* or, to a lesser extent, in the Tristan-legend, comes mainly from storms. In *RH* the

---

[13] In the Middle English *King Horn* the Saracen challenge to King Thurston is issued by a 'geaunt' from 'paynyme' (lines 802–3). Like this giant from 'paynyme', the oversized Morholt fights Tristan on the Cornish beach (in some versions of the legend). In both instances, the conflict is a contest to determine Cornwall's political future. Intriguingly, D. J. Shirt, 'A Note on the Etymology of Le Morholt', *Tristania* 1 (1975), 21–8, argues that Morholt was a sea-monster in an *Ur*-version of the tale since the name 'Morholt' is said to be derived from such a creature.

danger is not strictly maritime but must be located on the shore, and consequently, much of the poem's action takes place along coastlines. Hunlaf's seneschal Herland finds the shipwrecked children on the shore: 'Cist veneit chevauchant par la rive de mer' [He came riding along the sea-shore] (line 132). Later, the description of Horn's shoreline battle against the invading Saracens reminds the reader that the sea is not far off when the noise of a trumpet could be heard 'par la marine' [over the sea] (line 1,662). Similarly, Gudmod, alias Horn, leads Westir's host on the shore into a massacre of Rollac's Saracen army: 'Gudmod les cunduit bien par [mut] grant vasselage / Vers [les] paiens tut dreit ki sunt en cel rivage' [Gudmod led them, bravely and well, straight towards the infidels on the shore] (lines 3,234–5). And as has been mentioned above, Wothere is awaiting Horn's landing on the shore: 'Sis freres s'en isseit, ki ne·s poet asgarder, / Sur un cheval curant s'en alad a la mer' [His brother went out, he could not watch them, and on a swift horse went towards the sea] (lines 5,137–8). This littoral and, hence, transitional nature of the tale is even more prominent in the Middle English *King Horn* which will be scrutinised below.

RH constitutes the most advanced stage of the sea's transformation in early Anglo-Norman romance. Whereas the *Voyage* is still very much a seaborne tale celebrating the maritime culture of the Irish and, to some extent, also that of the Anglo-Saxons, the Tristan-legend, although its familiarity with the sea pervades the fabric of the poem, moves towards acknowledging greater space to the negative aspects of seafaring, expressed in the structural significance of the storm during Ysolt's final journey. In Thomas's *Tristan* much of the action takes place on land yet the sea remains a vital force, unconquered yet not entirely hostile. In the face of the storm, Ysolt's thoughts bear witness to the degree of entrelacement the characters' lives have experienced with the sea. The *RH*, on the other hand, remains largely shore-centred. The sea is a potentially dangerous and often foreboding presence. Nothing good comes from it. Not only does it mark Horn's manifold exiles, as it does for Tristan, but it also grants the hated enemy safe passage, failing the islanders.

The Normans were very much part of the same spiritual geography as their Anglo-Saxon predecessors, and, like them, their concept of history was a non-linear one. As a result, the *RH* is a part of the great Norman mythographic attempt at rereading and justifying their presence by seeking out meaningful typologies in the Insular past.[14] But with the *RH*, the literary evidence begins to tilt towards a narrative ambivalence to the sea. The Irish sea, romanticised and empowered by Benedeit, has been assigned a place

---

[14] The Norman tendency to create English ancestors for themselves has been observed by many scholars. See, for example, Robert M. Stein, 'Making History English: Cultural Identity and Historical Explanation in William of Malmesbury and Laȝamon's *Brut*', in *Text and Territory: Geographical Imagination in the European Middle Ages*, ed. Sealy Gilles and Sylvia Tomasch (Philadelphia, 1998), pp. 97–115 (p. 106). The tale of Horn, as the protagonist's Germanic name documents, may well have existed in an English version that preceded the Anglo-Norman text (Cooper, *The English Romance in Time*, p. 117).

among the external threats to the protagonist in the *RH*, thus further disconnecting the perception of the sea from its pre-Conquest Insular tradition. This semantic demotion of the sea's place in the Anglo-Norman cultural topography appears to record the political and cultural changes that have occurred on its shores during the eleventh and twelfth centuries. This change has not much to do with the 'coming of chivalry' or a 'Continental fear of the sea'; rather, apart from fishing rights (which were largely unregulated), water was difficult to inherit and of only little value as a bargaining unit.

Readers have observed that *King Horn*'s simple prosodic structure, reliant on a short, two- or three-stress line, is more akin to Old English than to syllabic French models.[15] At the same time, its vocabulary does not rely on a substantial stock of Anglo-Norman borrowings, and Susan Crane claims that 'a conservative faith in established social patterns is appropriately embodied in a verbal style that connotes the same conservative faith'.[16] *King Horn* is often described as bare and skeletal compared to the *RH* and it lacks the elaborate descriptions of courtly life found in the Anglo-Norman poem. All this, together with the fact it has been written in Middle English, suggests that the poem has been conceived for an audience that had very different expectations from those who listened to the Anglo-Norman version.

Half a century after the *RH* the English vernacular reclaims the sea as a territory for literature. *King Horn* stands at the beginning of this literary renaissance, and, despite its indebtedness to the Anglo-Norman *RH*, assigns far greater prominence and hence significance to the sea. From the outset, the land in *King Horn* is associated with the native Christian inhabitants of Suddene and the sea becomes the no-place from which the Saracens materialise. The land, rightfully held by King Muri ('He fond bi the stronde, / Arived on *his* londe' [my emphasis]; lines 35–6), is frequently used as an attribute of its inhabitants: 'Thi lond folk we schulle slon, / And alle that Christ luveth upon' (lines 43–4).[17] This 'lond folk', to which Horn belongs and whose future ruler he will be, defines itself against the marauding Sara-

---

[15] Jennifer Fellows, ed., *Of Love and Chivalry: An Anthology of Middle English Romance* (London, 1993), Introduction, p. x. Usually dated *c.* 1225, this early date has been challenged by Rosamund Allen, 'The Date and Provenance of *King Horn*: Some Interim Reassessments', in *Medieval English Studies Presented to George Kane*, ed. Edward Donald Kennedy, Ronald Waldron, and Joseph S. Wittig (Cambridge, 1988), pp. 99–125. The hitherto established composition date of 1225 rested on the belief that Cambridge University Library MS Gg.4.27 (C) was composed in the middle of the thirteenth century. The date of this MS has now shifted nearer to 1300 (Rosamond Allen, *King Horn: An Edition Based on Cambridge University Library MS Gg.4.27 (2)* (New York, 1984), pp. 3, 101). As a result, Bodleian Library MS Laud Misc 108, which is thought to have been produced in the late thirteenth century, is considered to be the earliest MS containing the poem (Allen, *King Horn*, pp. 13, 105). However, the dating of the manuscripts does not necessarily have to impact on the dating of the poem's composition. All citations from *King Horn* refer to Fellows, *Of Love and Chivalry*, but I have consulted Allen's *King Horn* where necessary.

[16] Susan Crane, *Insular Romance: Politics, Faith, and Culture in Anglo-Norman and Middle English Literature* (Berkeley and Los Angeles, 1986), p. 30.

[17] 'Lond' can of course mean both 'country' and 'land' in a more general sense.

cens. Horn's description of King Ailmair's people of Westernesse as 'londisse men', relies on this antithesis:

> 'I fond o schup rowe,
> Mid watere al byflowe,[18]
> Al with Sarazines kyn,
> And none londisse men.' (lines 631–4)

What these lines suggest is that the inhabitants of Westernesse, Horn's first exile, are 'londisse' men like those dwelling in his native Suddene. As *landish* men, the Christians, then, share among them the values and kinship 'of the land' as opposed to the out*landish* and alien 'Sarazines kyn'. In very much the same way lines 81–2 contrast 'paynes' with the natives: 'Horn was in paynes honde, / With his feren of the londe.'

When the deceitful Fikenhild schemes against Horn in Westernesse, he persuades King Ailmar to 'do [Horn] ut of londe, / Other he doth the schonde!' (lines 701–2). A few lines later Ailmar repeats these words nearly verbatim to Horn, exiling the protagonist from his exile: 'Wend ut of my londe, / Other thu schalt have schonde' (lines 713–14). An aristocratic exile is punished two-fold since banishment from land (in the sense of 'realm' or 'country') carries with it the loss of one's land (i.e. possessions) which diminishes the value of certain derivative concepts such as title, reputation and identity. To some extent, this will also be the case in Gower's and Chaucer's setting adrift of Constance/Custance, although her suffering is aggravated by the fact that she experiences multiple exiles, including one with her child. But in both cases prolonged (aristocratic) exile sustains the entire narrative.

Conservative and aristocratic, *King Horn*'s value system pivots around land. The following passage gives us an insight into the kind of joy felt by Horn and his associates on reaching land after their initial setting adrift: 'Blithe beo we on lyve –/ Ure schup is on ryve' (lines 131–2). 'On lyve' [alive] rhymes with 'on ryve' [on shore], and the association of reaching land with being alive renders the sea a place of death. This implied juxtaposition of the dangerous and death-bringing sea with stable, Christian land dyes the fabric of the entire poem. Thus, moving from the sea to land is always an ascending movement as the latter is superior to the former: 'And up he yede to londe' (line 1,302).[19] The supremacy of land over sea is temporarily called into question with the Saracens' invasion of Suddene, and so Horn, the prince without land, is repeatedly associated with land to uphold his claim and his social identity: 'Lord he is of londe' (line 511). It is therefore unsurprising that the polysemantics of 'londe' work in Horn's favour as the word confers

---

[18] I follow Oxford, Bodleian Library, MS Laud Misc. 108 rather than Cambridge University Library, MS Gg.4.27. (2), which has 'Tho hit gan to flowe'. See also Fellows, *Of Love and Chivalry*, p. 274, note to line 632.

[19] There are many more instances of where land is poised against the sea: lines 753–4, 785, 788, 1,274, 1,285, 1,302, 1,416, 1,450.

kinship and *kynde*, authority, religious values and, to some extent, linguistic identity throughout the poem. The Saracens' land-taking is visualised in lines 59–60: 'The pains come to londe, / And name hit in here honde.' By figuratively seizing the land with their hands, an act of sacrilege is committed against Christian territory. When Pope Urban II called the First Crusade at a council in Clermont in 1095, one of the accounts of his rally urging Europe's Christian rulers to evict the infidel from the Holy Land relied on the same association of 'londisse men': 'a race utterly alienated from God ... has invaded the lands of those Christians [of Jerusalem and Constantinople] and has depopulated them by the sword, pillage and fire.'[20] Written in celebration of the First Crusade, the anonymous late twelfth-century *Chanson d'Antioche* even inverts the land/sea dichotomy as Christ, hanging on the Cross, speaks from *Outremer* about the Franks who will come to liberate his land:

> 'Amis', dist Nostre Sire, 'sachiés tout vraiement
> Que de là outre mer venront novele gent,
> Qui de la mort lor père penront le vengement:
> Ne demora Paiens des ci qu'en Orient.
> Li Franc auront la terre tote delivrement.'

> [Friends, said Our Lord, know
> That from across the sea a new people will come
> They will exact vengeance for the death of their Father
> No pagans shall remain from here to the East
> The Franks will liberate all the earth.][21]

Horn's identity is shaped by his borderline existence, as he is, in much the same way as the language with which his name is etymologically linked, chronically landless yet 'londisse' by birth and cultural affinity. Even the poem's topography expresses the transitional nature of the tale; virtually the entire plot is set along the shore, the meeting point of land and sea. In this, the poem foreshadows the similarly littoral Digby MS play *Mary Magdalen* (*c.* 1500) where much of the narrative consists of boarding ships and disembarking, with stage directions frequently referring to coasts.[22] In *King Horn* the fate of every 'londisse' person and every Saracen is determined along a narrow strip of land.[23] And we can see how the littoral setting of the poem heightens the acuteness of danger coming from the sea:

---

[20] Cited from Victoria O'Donnell and Garth S. Jowett, *Propaganda and Persuasion* (San Francisco, 1992), p. 45.

[21] *Chanson d'Antioche*, ed. Suzanne Duparc-Quioc (Paris, 1977), lines 205–11 (pp. 27–8). The translation is taken from John V. Tolan, *Saracens: Islam in the Medieval European Imagination* (New York, 2000), p. 121.

[22] Digby *Mary Magdalen*, in *Late Medieval Religious Plays of Bodleian MSS Digby 133 and E Museo 160*, ed. Donald C. Baker, John L. Murphy and Louis P. Hall, Jr., EETS o.s. 283 (Oxford, 1982).

[23] A distant but intriguing analogy is offered by the last episode of the Tristan-legend, where the dying protagonist has his bed set up on a beach in Brittany. Here, Tristan lingers between life and death as he tries to make out the colour of the ship's sails from a distance.

Muri, the god king,
Rod on his pleing,
Bi the se side,
Ase he was woned ride.
He fond bi the stronde,
Arived on his londe,
Schipes fiftene,
With Sarazins kene. (lines 31–8)

The shore emerges as the main theatre of conflict. All battles and skirmishes are fought on the shore, kings meet their nemeses there, Horn encounters his foes, and rescues Rimenhild from a castle enclosed by the sea. And the setting hardly changes throughout the poem: 'And setten fout to grounde; / Bi the se side' (lines 134–5), 'Bi the se brinke' (line 141), 'Icomen ut of the bote, / Fram the se side' (lines 202–3), and 'Ihc habbe walke wide, / Bi the se side' (lines 955–6). In addition, when Athulf is looking out for Horn from the tower, he can see 'the se flowe' (line 1,097), which appears to indicate that he must be in or near a littoral location. Gradually, it transpires that the shore is not the end of the land but the beginning of the sea.

Unlike the cognate Anglo-Norman *RH*, the Middle English poem assigns far greater prominence and hence significance to the sea. Writing on *King Horn*, Susan Crane observes that

> the strongest natural force in *King Horn* is the sea. The sea's power, to which the pagans originally confer the execution of Horn and his followers, dominates all but Horn himself: it terrifies the children, drowns Rimenhild's messenger and casts him up at her feet, makes Fikenhild's castle impregnable – but Horn can row his followers to safety, travel over the sea just as he likes, and arrive by boat at Fikenhild's castle at precisely the crucial moment.[24]

This 'natural force' becomes an attribute of the sea-borne Saracens who set Horn and his friends adrift in a 'galeie' ('Us he dude lede / Into a galeie', lines 184–5). Here, the 'galeie' is a Saracen vessel, an aspect of their territory – hostile and deliberately ill-equipped to surrender to the hazards of the open sea.[25] Having been set adrift by the Saracens, Horn promptly battles with the waves:

Ofte hadde Horn beo wo,
A[c] nevre wurs than him was tho.
The se bigan to flowe,
And Horn child to rowe. (lines 115–18)

---

[24] Crane, *Insular Romance*, pp. 31–2.
[25] Most boats are referred to as 'schip'/ 'schup' (e.g.: lines 37, 139, 752 etc.) and receive no nearer description. With one exception (line 1,010), no further references to 'galeie' are made throughout the poem.

The short, three-stress couplets give the verse a truncated and almost jagged quality by frequently reducing it to essentials. Yet it is this plain, paratactic syntax that pronounces Horn's achievement so clearly. The force of the sea, registered in the word 'flowe', is matched by the protagonist's physical response, 'rowe'. Every blow the sea deals Horn's life, the protagonist shakes off. Although the 'galeie' in *King Horn* is symbolically equipped with at least one oar, the 'flowe/rowe' rhyme articulates Horn's considerable ability to live up to the physical challenges posed to him by the sea.

'Galeie' appears only once more, when the military balance in the tale shifts in favour of Horn who now decides to win Rimenhild back. As he does so, he reclaims Saracen territory and embarks on a 'god galeie' (line 1,010):

> Horn dude him in the weie,
> On a god galeie.
> The [wynd] him gan to blowe,
> In a litel throghe. (lines 1,009–12)

All the more complete, then, is Horn's transformation as he assumes command of a 'god galeie' to set out on the *reconquista* of what is his by birthright and merit: his usurped land and his promised wife. The controlling of the 'galeie' is also a powerful token of Horn's need first to take Saracen territory – the formidable warship at sea – before he can win back his own native land.[26]

That the sea is associated with death, unhappiness and the 'Sarazins blake' (line 1,321) is made clear as Fikenhild – in all but name a Saracen – has a castle built for himself which he foolishly surrounds with the sea, trusting that it will protect him in times of danger:

> Ston he dude lede,
> Ther he hopede spede.
> Strong castel he let sette,
> Mid see him biflette,
> Ther ne mighte lighte
> Bute foghel with flighte;
> Bute whanne the se withdroghe,
> Mighte come men ynoghe. (lines 1,395–1,402)

Fikenhild's castle is well fortified by the sea and can be reached by low ebb only ('whanne the se withdroghe'). But he backs the wrong horse and his plan misfires. The sea's fickleness tricks him, too, and Horn enters the sea precisely during low ebb:

---

[26] I discuss the size of the 'galeie' and its historical relevance at the time of the poem's composition in 'The 2,000 Saracens of *King Horn*', *Notes and Queries* 52:4 (2005), 443–45.

> And [Horn] tok felaghes fewe,
> Of knightes suithe snelle,
> That schrudde hem at wille.
> Hi yeden bi the gravel
> Toward the castel. (lines 1,465–8)

The Saracens, moreover, can bring the sea's uncertainty and changeability to the land.[27] In fact, their presence can threaten the certainty of land itself:

> There cam in at none
> A geaunt suthe sone,
> Iarmed, fram paynyme,
> And seide thes ryme:
> 'Site stille, sire kyng,
> And herkne this tything!
> Her buth paens arived –
> Wel mo thane five
> Her beoth on the sonde,
> King, upon thi londe.
> On of hem wile fighte
> Ayen thre knightes:
> Yef o[w]er thre slen ure,
> Al this lond beo youre;
> Yef ure on overcometh your threo,
> Al this lond schall ure beo.' (lines 801–16)

All of a sudden, King Thurston's rule in Ireland is no longer certain. His possession of his own land is being suspended by the subjunctive mood of the pagan challenge as 'beo youre' and 'ure beo' become the two possible outcomes of the seemingly unequal contest: he can win his land back or lose it. What is even more interesting is the invaders' beguiling presence: there is no point in negotiating with those who come from the sea as the King accepts the challenge without any ado.

The final vanquishing of the Saracens coincides with the final overcoming of the sea, and both are accomplished by Horn's last voyage:

> Horn tok Rymenhild bi the honde,
> And ladde hure to the stronde;
> And ladde with him Athelbrus,
> The gode stuard of his hus.
> The se bigan to flowe,
> And Horn gan to rowe. (lines 1,501–6)

---

27 Diane Speed, 'The Saracens of *King Horn*', *Speculum* 65:3 (1990), 564–95, passim, argues convincingly against previous theories of reading the Saracens of *King Horn* as echoes of Viking invaders.

This last journey exactly mirrors the memorable couplets of his first, unwanted sea-journey. As lines 1,505–6 almost exactly match lines 117–18, Horn's reconquest of his homeland and his culture is complete. The striking difference is the absence of 'child' in line 1,506. In between these two couplets, the protagonist has attained the maturity for which the challenging of the still powerful sea is a necessary condition: when the sea begins to 'flowe' the seasoned hero still needs to 'rowe'.

Horn's triumphant return to his reconquered homeland is accompanied by an assertion of the sea's undiminished vigour, but, in the end, the constant trials and exiles have allowed Horn to grow into a kingmaker who restores the cultural balance as the Saracens and his enemies are quietly replaced by Christian kings: 'Hi gunne for arrive / Ther King Modi was sire / Athelbrus he makede ther king' (lines 1,507–9). Horn has finally conquered the equilibrium which regulates the balance of land and sea, asserting his birthright to the insular land he had previously been robbed of. Without this control of the sea and its littoral border, Horn's entitlement to Suddene is reduced to a claim. Delivered by the sea, the Saracen invader becomes the negation of Horn's 'londisse' identity and dynastic purpose, and forces his existence to be a littoral one, oscillating between the two opposing poles of land and sea. Until Horn establishes his authority over the shore, his insular realm remains a title, and his *landish*ness a possibility.

The *Kyndness* of Strangers in Gower's Tale of Apollonius

It is hard to overlook the parallels between Odysseus and Apollonius of Tyre. Both are Mediterranean rulers, living in a politically fragmented sea-world of scattered principalities. Both experience long separation from their families, and both find themselves pitted against an almighty Neptune/Poseidon. This is by no means an exhaustive list; many more similarities could be added. But when it comes to the role of the sea, there is a marked difference between these two narrative traditions: nominally, Odysseus appears to be spending a great deal more time at sea than Apollonius does, but despite the Aegean general's decade-long incarceration on the Mediterranean, the sea never really comes close to him. Odysseus' Poseidon is a predictable adversary, sworn to avenge the blinding of his son Polyphemus. In his attempt to delay Odysseus' homecoming, the god of the sea masterminds an elaborate game, involving island temptations and maritime snares, to protract the hero's misery at sea. Motivated by the parity of give and take that underlies the economics of vendetta, Poseidon wishes to exact the same pain on Odysseus that his son Polyphemus had experienced: just as the Cyclops is no longer able to see his father, so will Telemachus not be able to see Odysseus for another ten years, rendering both blind to their own kin, a circumstance that is accentuated by the celebrated recognition scene between father and son when Odysseus returns to Ithaca.[28] Poseidon does not desire Odysseus' death; it is his life he wishes to make more difficult.

Now, much of this would also hold true for the tale of Apollonius in its various redactions. Separation, recognition and vision are certainly powerful themes in the tale, all being direct results of the sea's interference with Apollonius' life. But the link between the sea and Neptune in the various Latin redactions and in the Old English translation of the tale is not nearly as strong, nor as personal, as in *The Odyssey*. In the Latin *Historia Apollonii Regis Tyri* (before the tenth century) and in Godfrey of Viterbo's *Pantheon* there are only a handful of references to Neptune. Most significantly, there is Apollonius' tirade against Neptune when he suffers his first shipwreck. In most versions of the legend this is a vital element; it appears in the *Historia Apollonii*, in the *Pantheon* and in the Old English version, for instance.[29] Godfrey's adaptation includes two further instances of Neptune, whereas the *Historia Apollonii* adds the detail that Apollonius arrives in Mitelene during the Neptunalia, the festivities in honour of the god of the sea.[30] In the tale of Apollonius, as in so much of patristic and later Christian writings about the classical period, 'fortune' stands for the whimsical, moody tyranny of fate that seemed to hold the world of pagan antiquity hostage and against which the dependability of Christian values looks so attractive. In other words, the delineation of the sea in these two tales, *The Odyssey* and the Apollonius-legend, both of which share a similar pre-Christian setting, is informed by the starkly differing worldviews of the cultures that generated these narratives: one, at home with its own value system; the other, by definition unsympathetic to the worldview in opposition to which it emerged.

Although the rehabiliation of the classical pantheon may not have been on Gower's agenda, the fourteenth-century poet makes very different choices from his predecessors. On the one hand, the tale, which forms the bulk of Book 8 of the *Confessio Amantis*, strengthens the association of the sea with a Neptune who assumes the neo-Platonic guise of fortune. This becomes particularly apparent during Apollonius' first shipwreck. Gower breaks with the tradition of the address to Neptune, which, in the *Historia Apollonii* is even set in verse, and inserts the laconic but assertive observation that

---

[28] One need only think of Joyce's *Ulysses*, where this scene is elevated to the rank of chapter.

[29] The respective passages are as follows: for the *Pantheon*, see S. Singer, *Apollonius von Tyrus: Untersuchung über das Fortleben des antiken Romans in späteren Zeiten* (Halle an der Saale, 1895), p. 155; for the *Historia Apollonii*, see Elizabeth Archibald, *Apollonius of Tyre: Medieval and Renaissance Themes and Variations* (Cambridge, 1991), pp. 123–4; and for the Old English translation, Benjamin Thorpe, ed. and trans., *The Anglo-Saxon Version of the Story of Apollonius of Tyre* (London, 1834), Chapter 17.

[30] Archibald, *Apollonius of Tyre*, p. 157. A large section of the Old English text, including Apollonius' arrival in Mitelene, is missing.

> he which hath the see on honde,
> Neptunus, wolde noght acorde,
> Bot al tobroke cable and corde. (Book 8, lines 622–4)[31]

Despite the seeming demotion of this passage, Gower asserts Neptune's sway over the sea, which he 'hath on honde'. In addition, much detail is added to the storm description, with the effect that the shipwreck does not fail to leave a mark on the reader as a significant event in the narrative.

A comparative reading of Apollonius' chance landing in the harbour of Mitelene during the Neptunalia proves revealing. Gower's alleged source, Godfrey of Viterbo's *Pantheon*, omits any references to the feast of Neptune. Godfrey only mentions that the Tyrean arrives during certain festivities in the port city.[32] The *Historia Apollonii*, however, makes clear that 'the feast of Neptune was being celebrated there'.[33] Not only does Gower incorporate this detail, adding further evidence for the poet's access to a version of the tale other than the *Pantheon*, but he also prefaces Apollonius' landing with a reference to Neptune that would appear to be his own invention:

> Bot sodeinly the wynd and reyn
> Begonne upon the see debate,
> So that he soffre mot algate
> The lawe which Neptune ordeigneth;
> Wherof ful ofte time he pleigneth,
> And hield him wel the more esmaied
> Of that he hath tofore assaied.
> So that for pure sorwe and care,
> Of that he seth his world so fare,
> The reste he lefte of his caban,
> That for the conseil of no man
> Agein therinne he nolde come,
> Bot hath benethe his place nome,
> Wher he wepende al one lay,
> Ther as he sih no lyht of day.
> And thus tofor the wynd thei dryve,
> Til longe and late thei aryve
> With gret distresce, as it was sene,
> Upon this toun of Mittelene,
> Which was a noble cité tho.
> And hapneth thilke time so

[31] All references to the *Confessio Amantis* are to *The English Works of John Gower*, ed. G. C. Macaulay, EETS e.s. 81–2 (London, 1900–1), 2 vols. The fifteenth-century Brussels Redaction and a fifteenth-century French edition replace Neptune with Fortune in Apollonius' tirade (Archibald, *Apollonius*, p. 103).

[32] Singer, *Apollonius von Tyrus*, p. 168.

[33] 'Ibique Neptunalia festa celebrantur', Archibald, *Apollonius*, pp. 156 and 157. Another version of the *Historia Apollonii* embeds this detail in a brief exchange with the helmsman, who concludes the dialogue with 'Rejoice, lord, today is the feast of Neptune!' [Gaude, domine, hodie Neptunalia esse!], Archibald, pp. 156 and 157, note to line 52.

> The lordes bothe and the comune
> The hihe festes of Neptune
> Upon the stronde at the rivage,
> As it was custumme and usage,
> Sollempneliche thei besihe. (lines 1,592–1,617)

I quote the passage in full because it cuts to the heart of the function Neptune and the sea perform in Gower's tale. It is not so much Thaise's assumed murder that causes Apollonius to slide into depression; rather, it is the realisation that he is subject to the laws of Neptune that triggers his psychological demise. This is a rare glimpse of a romance protagonist simply giving up 'for pure sorwe and care' (line 1,599). With the allegorical acumen of a pre-modern mindset, Apollonius interprets the wind and rain 'debating' at sea not only as Neptune's law in action but also as reminiscent of his own world falling apart: 'he seth his world so fare' (line 1,600). In Gower's tale the sea, more so than Neptune or Fortune (who is not even mentioned in this passage), acts both as a catalyst for Apollonius' darkest hour and a metaphor for the ruinous course his life seems to have taken.

Apollonius' grief contrasts starkly with the joyful celebrations that await him in Mitelene, where the 'hihe festes' of Neptune is under way. It is only in Gower's version that Neptune appears, within only a few lines' space, as the cause of unhappiness and as the reason for joy, thus encapsulating, perhaps more articulately than in any of the sources, the seemingly arbitrary power of Fortune to give and to take. But to stop here would mean to ignore that Apollonius will very soon have cause to partake in the celebrations, since he is about to recognise his daughter. What is more, Gower shows that it is Neptune's storm that brings the protagonist nearer to his happiness in Mitelene. This circumstance, it must be admitted, substantially diminishes the arbitrariness of Neptune's actions and, hence, the association of the god with Fortune. On the contrary, the storm and the emotional pain it causes Apollonius operate more along the Christian dynamics of *felix culpa*, the 'happy sin', where unhappiness and misery are temporary (and temporal) phenomena, instrumental in a grander design of happiness.

Peter Nicholson is certainly correct in stating that 'the narrative metaphor for the nature of life in the world, in this tale and others like it, is the sea-voyage', but the associative chain of Fortune, Neptune and the sea is an altogether more complex one, so that one cannot talk of the sea 'as the domain where "Fortune doth the lawe" [line 600]'.[34] The passage in question ('His cours he nam with seil updrawe, / Where as fortune doth the lawe', lines 599–600) does not have to refer to 'the sea' as the object of the second line; it is equally if not not more plausible to read line 600 closer to the sense of 'wherever Fortune would care to take him'. By the same token, it does

---

[34] Peter Nicholson, *Love and Ethics in Gower's* 'Confessio Amantis' (Ann Arbor, MI, 2005), p. 374.

not do the tale justice to talk of 'the simple arbitrariness of Neptune'.[35] In fact, Fortune is a much bigger phenomenon in this tale than Neptune or the sea; and whilst Neptune is in agreement with Fortune during the first shipwreck, he nevertheless appears as a distinct force. It would almost appear as if Neptune manages to appease Fortune: just before the longer extract quoted above, at lines 1,584–5 Apollonius rails against Fortune before thanking an apparently neo-Platonic God ahead of his ill-fated voyage for Tyre. It is then than Neptune's storm takes him to Mitelene, where his arrival coincides with the Neptunalia. The recognition scene follows, ending with Gower's assertion that 'for this day forth fortune hath sworn / To sette him upward on the whiel' (lines 1,736–7). But since Neptune's storm that took him to Mittelene in the first place was a happy circumstance, it would seem that either Fortune responds to Neptune's restitutive impulse or that Neptune is an entity quite independent of Fortune. Otherwise, Gower's comment on Fortune having changed its mind ought to precede Apollonius' landing in Mitelene.

In Gower's tale the sea is a real place. The most momentous events in Apollonius' life occur at sea or are facilitated by the sea: the apparent death of his wife and the reunion with his daughter. Given that his wife does not really die, it does not seem evident to me that the sea should be put on a par with the whims of Fortune, for most if not all of the sea's actions are positive. The first shipwreck takes him to Pentapolis, where he meets his wife. Then the sea carries his wife's coffin to safety, preserving her body intact. Later, a shipwreck forces the pirates toward Mitelene, laying the foundations for Thaise's safety and eventual happiness. And, finally, a last effort by Neptune steers Apollonius' ship toward Mitelene to reunite him with his daughter. In fact, the sea, or Neptune, arranges one *felix naufragium* after another. So, rather than being an instrument of Fortune, the sea illustrates the more constructive and reconciliatory actions of fate. Even more so: its keeping safe and reuniting Apollonius' family aligns it more with 'kynde' than with Fortune. It is in this sense that an observation made by two recent editors of *Pericles* about the sea in Shakespeare's play also holds true for Gower's version of the legend:

> The journey of the hero through the archetypal rhythms of birth, life, death
> and rebirth, in a sea which is not merely a body of water under his ship but
> the fecundating emblem of these rhythms.[36]

As a final comment on the sea's at least partial independence of Fortune, the following lines, probably elaborated by Gower from his Latin source, reveal an idiosyncratic law regulating the sea. Here, the master shipman observes that

---

35 Nicholson, *Love and Ethics*, p. 374.
36 William Shakespeare, *Pericles, Prince of Tyre*, ed. Doreen DelVecchio and Antony Hammond, The New Cambridge Shakespeare (Cambridge, 1998), p. 6.

the see be weie of his nature
Receive mai no creature
Withinne himself as for to holde
The which is ded. (lines 1,089–92)

Macaulay regarded these lines as a crux, offering the far-fetched explanation that 'apparently the meaning is that the sea will necessarily cast a dead body up on the shore, and therefore they must throw it out of the ship, otherwise the ship itself will be cast ashore with it'.[37] As a closer paraphrase of these lines, I would like to offer the following: 'because of its nature, the sea may not grant passage to anyone [receive … withinne himselfe] who carries a corpse on board [as for to holde / The which is ded]'. Unlike Fortune, the sea can be understood by some of the more experienced sailors, pointing to an altogether more predictable nature as an entity that can be appeased by certain behaviours.

Gower was clearly interested in the narrative possibilities of the sea, as my brief exploration shows. In contrast to some of the legend's earlier redactions, Gower's sea obeys Neptune who is associated with but nevertheless distinct from Fortune. Narratively the sea differs from Fortune in its relative predictability and its restitutive actions. Remotely psychologised, it even offers Apollonius a metaphorical mirror image of his own life. And while it drives the protagonist from one place to another, the sea sustains, supports and shelters both him and his family, to which the reunion with Thaise – taking place aboard his ship during the high feast of Neptune – literally testifies. The fact that the two longest tales in the *Confessio Amantis*, the tales of Apollonius and of Constance, are both maritime tales, points to a structural role of the sea as a facet of Fortune that is neither altogether arbitrary nor entirely predictable.

---

[37] Macaulay, ed., *The English Works*, vol. 2, note to Book 8, lines 1,089 ff.

5

Between the Devil and the Deep Blue Sea

> May ocean waves engulf me and I fall
> Headlong into the depths of hell below,
> Ere I shall any secret trusts betray,
> Or evil word find exit from my mouth.[1]
> > *Speculum Stultorum* (twelfth century),
> > spoken by the Cock, lines 3,157–60

> So wode were the waghes & þe wilde ythes,
> All was like to be lost, þat no lond hade.
> The ship ay shot furth o þe shire waghes,
> As qwo clymbe at a clyffe, or a clent hille, –
> Eft dump in the depe as all drowne wolde.
> > *The Gest Hystoriale of the Destruction of Troy*
> > (fourteenth century), Book 5, lines 1,992–6

A Cold Embrace: Jonah in the Belly of the Whale

When God charges Jonah to proselytise among the gentile Ninevites, the prophet shies away from this task. The Bible is silent about the rationale for Jonah's conduct: 'et surrexit Iona ut fugeret in Tharsis a facie Domini' (Jonah 1.3) [And Jonah rose up to flee into Tharsis from the face of the Lord]. In the fourteenth-century alliterative poem *Patience* the causal relationship between the prospect of obedience to the divine will and the promise of suffering is made explicit: 'If I bowe to His bode and bryng hem þis tale, / And I be nummen in Nuniue, my nyes begynes' (lines 75–6).[2] Subsequently, after weighing the implications of God's command, Jonah visualises his likely ordeal at the hands of the Ninevites with unsettling acumen:

> 'He telles me þose traytoures arn typped schrewes;
> I com with þose typþinges, þay ta me bylyue,

---

[1] The translation is taken from G. W. Regenos, *The Book of Daun Burnel the Ass* (Austin, TX, 1959).

[2] *The Poems of the Pearl Manuscript: Pearl, Cleanness, Patience, Sir Gawain and the Green Knight*, ed. Malcolm Andrew and Ronald Waldron, fourth edn (Exeter, 1987; originally published 1978). All references to *Patience* draw on this edition.

Pynez me in prysoun, put me in stokes,
Wryþe me in a warlock, wrast out myn yȝen.' (lines 77–80)

Instead of accepting God's will unconditionally, Jonah attempts to rationalise the divine motivation for his near-certain suffering: 'Þis is a meruayl message a man for to preche / Amonge enmyes so mony and mansed fendes' (lines 81–2). He trembles at God's apparent intentions: 'Bot if me gaynlych God such gref to me wolde, / For desert of sum sake þat I slayn were' (lines 83–4).[3] Much of the acerbity of Jonah's tone hinges on the conjunction 'bot if', perhaps best approximated by modern 'unless', which propels his musings into sacrilegious territory: 'Unless … God wished for me to come to such grief / so that I were slain to settle some score.' Even though Jonah fails to discern a reasoned design ('Þis is a meruayl message'), it dawns on him that God may have an ulterior motive ('sum sake') for sacrificing him, and he finds in bitterness the idiom that expresses his bewilderment.

By long tradition, Jonah was conceived of as a type of Christ.[4] And although Jonah had been demoted by the Fourth Lateran Council in 1215 to the rank of minor prophet, the prefiguring of Christ by Jonah persisted in eschatological commentary.[5] Exegetes took Jonah's three days and nights in the whale's belly to foreshadow Christ's Harrowing of Hell: 'So in a bouel of þat best he bidez on lyue, / Þre dayes and þre nyȝt, ay þenkande on Dryȝtyn' (lines 293–4). Jonah's acrimonious refusal to subject himself joyfully to suffering clashes sharply with the Synoptics' account of Christ's self-sacrificial perseverance in the garden of Gethsemane: 'Abba pater omnia possibilia tibi sunt / transfer calicem hunc a me / Sed non quod ego volo sed quod tu' [Abba, Father, all things are possible to thee: remove this chalice from me; but not what I will, but what thou wilt] (Mark 14.36; compare Matthew 26.39 and Luke 22.41). This contrast is strengthened by the dependence of 'slayn' on 'sake', a causal relationship to which Jonah rebelliously vows physical defiance: ' "At alle peryles," quoþ þe prophete, "I aproche hit no nerre" ' (line 85). Besides, the semantic hierarchy is cemented by the syntactic inversion of conventional word order where the verb 'slayn' follows the noun 'sake'. Christ, on the other hand, endorses physical martyrdom for the highest spiritual prize, humankind's salvation ('sed non quod ego volo sed quod tu').

---

3   Jonah's bitter tone has been noticed by Andrew and Waldron, note to lines 83–8, p. 189. A more literal translation of line 84 would be 'in recompense for some fault/offence'. I consider the phrase 'to settle some score' as sufficiently forceful to convey the bitterness of Jonah's sneer.

4   Malcolm Andrew discusses the typological juxtaposition of Jonah and Christ in this poem in 'Jonah and Christ in *Patience*', *Modern Philology* 70 (1977), pp. 230–3. The differentiated typological tradition of Jonah as Christ has also been treated by John B. Friedman, 'Figural Typology in the Middle English *Patience*', in *The Alliterative Tradition in the Fourteenth Century*, ed. Bernard S. Levy and Paul E. Szarmach (Kent, OH, 1981), pp. 99–129. Friedman shows that it was likely that the *Gawain*-poet had been influenced by visual representations of the scene. The ultimate sources for this typological tradition are Luke 11.29–30, 32 and Matthew 12.40–1, where Matthew likens Jonah's stay in the whale's belly to Christ's Harrowing of Hell.

5   R. H. Bowers, *The Legend of Jonah* (The Hague, 1972), pp. 51–4. It was not until the Council of Constance in 1414 that Jonah's theological rank was restored.

What to Christ is the *calix*, or the bitter cup, is to Jonah his petrifyingly likely death for 'sum sake'.

It is emblematic of Jonah's ignorant misreading of God's attributes – a misreading underpinned by a puerile relationship with his God – that he does not entrust himself to God's Providence. The purpose of his own suffering appears unfathomable to him ('sum sake') and the compliment 'gaynlych' [gracious; kindly] looks suspiciously out of place and insincere in a grammatical construction that ends in Jonah reaching the conclusion that he is in trouble.[6] Jonah's belief in God is confined by the limitations of his experience of the physical world he knows. His imagination centres upon the violation of his own body as he fears the 'prysoun', 'stokes', 'warlock' and the loss of sight: 'wrast out myn yȝen' (lines 81–2). Jonah's knowledge of the geography of his world sharply diverges from his muddled topography of the spiritual world: God's motivation is compressed into 'sum sake' and he believes that God soars 'so hyȝe' in Heaven above that He cares 'ful lyttel' what fate may befall His prophet in Nineveh (lines 93–4).

Jonah's cardinal error springs from confusing 'presence' with 'notice'. He tries to flee God's presence ('I wyl me sum oþer waye', line 86), thinking he will thus escape His notice ('þat He ne wayte after', line 86). By transferring the emphasis from the place of hiding – the Vulgate has 'ut fugeret in Tharsis a facie Domini' (Jonah 1.3) – to the mode of passage ('sum oþer *waye* þat He ne wayte after' [my emphasis]), *Patience* initiates a process that will lead to a theologically momentous alteration of the source material. Jonah is not going to Tarsus to hide from God, but he is going *by sea* because he believes that God has no power over the sea. This significant break with established exegetical practice is reinforced by the extraordinary claim in lines 111–12: 'He wende wel þat þat Wyȝ þat al þe world planted/Hade no maȝt in þat mere no man for to greue.'

Jonah's God is a land-dwelling God. He is the God of the Israelites, an agricultural not a seafaring people. Consequently, Jonah's God is a farming God, a *cultor*: 'þat Wyȝ þat al þe world planted'. A landlubber, Jonah naively supposes that the changeable nature of the sea will wash away the footprints of his ill-fated flight from Providence. And, in his partial, supercilious presumption ('wende' designates 'knew', 'supposed' and 'believed'), Jonah fails to comprehend how his God could possibly wield power beyond his own microspatial experience. The constant, land-based God of the Israelites cannot possibly restrain the moving, fickle sea. The contrast with God's sway over the elements during Custance's maritime ordeals as asserted by the Man of Law could not be greater:

> Who kepte hire from the drenchyng in the see?
> Who kepte Jonas in the fisshes mawe

---

[6] The *MED* offers two meanings for 'gaynlych' (also 'gaynly', 'gainly(-i)' and 'geinli(-y): (a) gracious, kindly, and (b) suitable, fitting.

Til he was spouted up at Nynyvee?
Wel may men knowe it was no wight but he
That kepte peple Ebrayk from hir drenchynge,
With dry feet thurghout the see passynge.

Who bad the foure spirites of tempest
That power han t'anoyen lond and see,
Both north and south, and also west and est,
'Anoyeth neither see, ne land, ne tree?'
Soothly, the comandour of that was he
That fro the tempest ay this womman kepte
As wel whan she wook as whan she slepte.[7]

But perhaps the singularity of *Patience*'s Jonah is best demonstrated by a comparison with the obedient willingness with which a saint accepts such a challenge in the remarkable Digby *Mary Magdalen* (*c.* 1500). Mary, like Jonah, receives an order from God to convert the pagan King of Marcylle:

ANGELUS: Abasse þe novtt, Mary, in þis place!
Ower Lordys preceptt þou must fullfyll.
To passe þe see in shortt space,
Onto þe lond of Marcyll.

Kyng and quene converte xall 3e,
And byn amyttyd as an holy apostylesse.
Alle þe lond xall be techyd alonly be the,
Goddys lawys onto hem 3e xall expresse.
þerfore hast yow forth wyth gladnesse,
Goddys commav[n]ddement for to fullfylle.[8]

The angel's request is virtually identical to that of God in the Book of Jonah and *Patience*, yet Mary's reaction is marked by an enthusiasm that finds its counterpoint in Jonah's flinching:

MARY MAGDALEN: He þat from my person seuen dewllys mad to fle,
Be vertu of hym alle thyng was wrowth;
To seke thoys pepyll I woll rydy be.
As þou hast commavnddytt, in vertv þey xall be browth.

Wyth þi grace, good Lord in Deite,
Now to þe see I wyll me hy,
Sum sheppyng to asspy.
Now spede me, Lord in eternall glory!
Now be my spede, allmyty Trenite![9]

---

7   *The Riverside Chaucer*, gen. ed. Larry D. Benson (Boston, 1987), II, lines 485–97.

8   Digby *Mary Magdalen*, lines 1,376–85, in *Late Medieval Religious Plays of Bodleian MSS Digby 133 and E Museo 160*, ed., Donald C. Baker, John L. Murphy and Louis P. Hall, Jr., EETS o.s. 283 (Oxford, 1982).

9   Digby *Mary Magdalen*, lines 1,386–94.

As some of Mary's phrases seem to echo and complete Jonah's imperfection in *Patience* (compare, for example, 'I wyl me sum oþer waye' in *Patience* and 'Now to þe see I wyll me hy' in the Digby play), the text creates the impression that it has been written with *Patience* in mind. This impression, it seems to me, gains in clarity when one compares those passages in both texts that mention the sea in connection with creation.

Again, in a marked departure from the Vulgate and later treatments of the narrative, the text of *Patience* redefines the sea's function in Jonah's emphatic affirmation of his creed to the mariners. Here, the sea is clearly omitted from God's creation:

> 'I am an Ebru,' quoþ he, 'of Israyl borne;
> Þat Wyʒe I worchyp, iwysse, þat wroʒt alle þynges,
> Alle þe worlde with þe welkyn, þe wynde and þe sternes,
> And alle þat wonez withinne, at a worde one.' (lines 205–8)

In comparison, the Vulgate explicitly states that Jonah is aware of God's creation of both land and sea: 'Hebraeus ego sum et Dominum Deum caeli ego timeo qui fecit mare et aridam' (Jonah 1.9) [And he said to them: I am a Hebrew, and I fear the Lord the God of heaven, who made both the sea and the dry land]. As indicated above, in the Digby play Mary emphatically affirms this point twice in the space of only 26 lines: 'He mad hevyn and erth, lond and see' (line 1,475) and 'þat tyme he made both see and lond' (line 1,501).

This considerable semantic intervention cuts right through the nerve-centre of the alliterative poem, sending out extensive signals for the continual debate about likely sources for *Patience*. None of the proposed source texts appears to provide an analogous accentuation of the sea by *omitting* it.[10] This is not to say that the *Gawain*-poet did not rely on sources, but I would like to suggest the poet's reading of the Book of Jonah is characterised by innovation rather than tradition. The two most frequently advocated influences on *Patience*, Marbod of Rennes's (*c.* 1035–1123) *Naufragium Ionae Prophetae* and Prudentius's (348–after 405) *Hymnus Ieiunantium*, provide no precedent for *Patience*'s changes.[11] Jonah's decision to leave for Tarsus is dealt with in the context of escaping divine will in the leonine hexameters of the *Naufragium Ionae Prophetae*:

---

[10] On the protracted debate on the poem's sources and analogues, see O. F. Emerson, 'A Parallel between the Middle English Poem *Patience* and an Early Latin Poem Attributed to Tertullian', *PMLA* 10 (1895), 242–8; S. B. Liljegren, 'Has the Poet of *Patience* Read *De Jona*?', *Englische Studien* 48 (1914), 337–41; Ordelle G. Hill, 'The Late-Latin *De Jona* as a Source for *Patience*', *Journal of English and Germanic Philology*, 66 (1967), 21–5; Ellin M. Kelly, 'Parallels Between the Middle English *Patience* and *Hymnus Ieiunantium* of Prudentius', *ELN* 4 (1966–67), 244–7; Francis Cairns, 'Latin Sources and Analogues to ME *Patience*', *Studia Neophilologica* 59:1 (1987), 7–18; and Kathryn Wall, 'Saint Gregory's *Moralia* as a Possible Source for the Middle English *Patience*', *Notes and Queries* n.s. 39:4 (1992), 436–8.

[11] Marbod of Rennes, *Naufragium Ionae Prophetae*, *PL* 171, col. 1,675, and Prudentius, *Hymnus Ieiunantium* in *Aurelii Prudentii Clementis Carmina*, CCSL 126.

Jonas surrexit; sed iter per devia flexit,
Ad mare descendit, dum Tharsum pergere tendit.
Non erat hoc jussum, tamen optat pergere Tharsum;
Sed profugum Domini fluctus tenuere marini.

[Jonah arose, but he turned his journey paths off the track. He went down to the sea, while he tried to make for Tarsus. This was not the order, but he chooses to head for Tarsus. But the waves of the sea held on to the Lord's exile.][12]

Similarly, at no point does Prudentius suggest that God's governance fails at sea:

sed nosset ille [Jonah] cum minacem iudicem
seruare malle quam ferire ac plectere,
tectam latenter uertit in Tharsos fugam.

celsam paratis pontibus scandit ratem,
udo reuincta fune puppis soluitur.
Itur per altum. Fit procellosum mare.

[But Jonah, who knew that the threatening judge preferred to save, rather than strike and punish, made his flight to Tarsus secret in hidden ways.

He boarded the lofty ship after the gangways had been made ready. Untied from the damp rope, the ship is let loose. They make their way through the deep. The sea becomes stormy.][13]

These two accounts of Jonah also fall short of offering a parallel for lines 111–12 ('He wende wel þat þat Wyȝ þat al þe world planted / Hade no maȝt in þat mere no man for to greue'), and, consequently, both pay little attention to Jonah's remarkable creed to the mariners.

Given the centrality of the sea to *Patience* – corroborated by the extraordinarily meticulous description of the ship's parts as well as the lively storm passage[14] – and its apparent divorce from the narrative focus in all identified treatments of the story of Jonah, the debate concerning whether or not the poet of *Patience* read and elaborated patristic and later treatments of the tale of Jonah is of limited consequence. Much of the evidence is coincidental and,

---

12 *Liber cathemerinon*, hymnus 7, *Naufragium Ionae Prophetae*, lines 103–8. Quoted from *PL* 171, col. 1676. I am very grateful to Andrew Doe for his assistance with the passages from Marbod of Rennes and Prudentius. I also thank Otto Zwierlein for the suggestion to emend 'qui' to 'cum' in the first line of the quotation from Prudentius.

13 *Aurelii Prudentii Clementis Carmina*, CCSL 126, *Hymnus Ieiunantium*, lines 103–8.

14 Robin M. Ward argues convincingly that the *Gawain*-poet had in all likelihood experienced the sea directly on the basis of the amount of maritime detail in the poem ('An Elucidation of Certain Maritime Passages in English Alliterative Poetry of the Fourteenth Century' (unpublished MA thesis, University of Keele, 1991), p. 79). See also Nicholas Jacobs, 'Alliterative Storms: A Topos in Middle English', *Speculum* 47:4 (1972), 695–719; for *Patience*, see 708–12.

in its expressive mode and content, the poem communicates, as far as the Jonah-tradition is concerned, an idiosyncratic view of the sea which appears to be connected with the tradition that the sea existed before creation.

Thus, Jonah's tactical calculations in *Patience* gain a theological dimension: the sea, covering the abyss and assuming some of its hostile traits, is a place at the greatest possible distance from God; it is the exile to which the demons have been banished (Luke 8.31); it is the eternal storehouse of all sins (Micah 7.19), and the domain from which the Beast itself will ascend (Apocalypse 11.7; 17.8). Jonah desires to flee God's presence ('a facie' in the Vulgate) and he conceives of the sea as a sphere over which God's rule (and, hence, Providence) does not extend. The unprecedented frequency and quality of the word 'abyme' in *Patience* appears to corroborate Jonah's understanding of the sea in this poem.

'Abyssus' is mentioned only once in the Book of Jonah. When the luckless prophet is snatched by the whale and taken to the depths of the sea, the word 'abyssus' captures Jonah's despair. Physically and spiritually, Jonah is drowning: 'circumdederunt me aquae usque ad animam abyssus vallavit me pelagus operuit caput meum' [The waters compassed me about even to the soul: the deep hath closed me round about, the sea hath covered my head] (Jonah 2.6). Here, 'abyssus' is not so much applied to the physical depths as to the metaphorical abyss denoting the spiritual state of sinking into sin (Micah 7.19), an image that influenced Augustine's view of the abyss.[15]

Jonah's spiritual confinement is complemented by his physical imprisonment in *Patience*. Unsurprisingly, the waters exercise restraint when the prophet is 'wrapped in water' and the 'abyme byndes' the 'body' which he inhabits ('byde').[16] Ingeniously, the text imposes a two-layered custody on Jonah's soul: the abyss 'byndes' Jonah's body in which he himself is confined ('byde'). The absolute incarceration he experiences matches that of his worst fears. Not by accident does this form of punishment mirror Jonah's anticipated suffering at the hands of the Ninevites in lines 77–80, proving beyond any reasonable doubt to the renegade prophet that God's will cannot be tricked, not even at sea. That the sea does not lie outside God's jurisdiction is evident by now.

Later, following a moment of despair, Jonah submits to God's control over the waters and the abyss: 'Þe grete flem of *Þy flod* folded me vmbe;/ Alle þe gotez of *Þy guferes* and groundelez powlez' [my emphases] (lines 309–10).[17] But Jonah's deference to the sea's strength is not entirely unwarranted. Even

---

[15] *De Civitate Dei* 20, 7: 'Here, the bottomless pit signifies the innumerable multitude of the ungodly', *The City of God Against the Pagans*, ed. and trans. R. W. Dyson (Cambridge, 1998), p. 981.

[16] Lines 317–18.

[17] 'Flod' are the diluvian waters of the abyss that surround him and the 'guferes' are rendered in the *MED* as 'whirlpool'. 'Gufere', however, is only mentioned in *Patience* but Lewis and Short translate the Latin cognate *gurges* as 'raging abyss, whirlpool, gulf', which appears more fitting in this circumstance. Randle Cotgrave's *A dictionarie of the French and English tongues* (1611) still maintains this meaning for 'gouffre' in the seventeenth century: '*Gouffreux: m. euse: f.*

here, the text maintains an element of the sea's primordial autonomy. After it is pacified by Jonah's sacrifice, the sea does obey God's wish ('Þe se saȝtled þerwith', line 232), albeit not immediately ('as sone as ho moȝt', line 232). The sea's obedience to God's commands is subject to its own overriding dynamic, a dynamic that still preserves some of the ungovernable qualities of the primeval *abyssus*.

It would appear possible to treat the frequency of 'abyme' in *Patience* as an outcome of the alliterative text's shortage of synonyms at these particular instances. Certainly, in some circumstances that view may appear defensible, but the three other instances in which the word 'abyme' is employed are all of structural significance to the theological meaning of 'abyme'. The first use of the word in the poem suggests an awareness of the sea's life-giving role in God's creation. Like the soil that gives birth to plants, the 'abyme' becomes the terrifying womb of all marine life: 'Þe abyme, Þat breed fysches' (line 143). According to Genesis 1.20–1, it is the waters that first give birth to living beings: 'dixit etiam Deus producant aquae reptile animae viventis et volatile super terram sub firmamento caeli' [God also said: Let the waters bring forth the creeping creature having life, and the fowl that may fly over the Earth under the firmament of Heaven].

Chapter 1 has shown that the terms *abyssus*/'abyme' and *aquae*/'depthe' have been conflated by the fourteenth century, and, hence, when the text of *Patience* employs the word 'abyme' in line 143, it is already synonymous with the *aquae* of Genesis 1.20, the well-spring of all life. It is only logical, then, that the womb of life should be characterised by movement, perhaps most vividly expressed by restlessness, or, in the idiom of *Patience*, the 'roȝ' that boils at the 'bothem' of the sea (line 144). The 'wawes', having raged 'ful wode' on the stormy surface (line 142), return to the seat of all life (line 143) where the turmoil they cause prevents the fishes from remaining on the floor of the abyss. The primeval waters, conflated with the pre-creation abyss and the sea, designate, at the same time, what John Trevisa translates as 'firste matere' from which all creation is fashioned and from which, consequently, all animate life springs. Uncreated, merely governed, the sea's heart must remain in constant movement since animate life is defined by the ability to propel itself, to maintain movement.[18] To the fugitive prophet Jonah, it is this violent matter of invention that antedates God's rule and lures with the promise of shelter. The sea is simultaneously the beginning of life and the executor of God's disciplinary will.

    Gulfie, full of gulfes; infinitely deepe; (vnsatiably) deuouring, or swallowing vp whatsoeuer approaches, or comes into, it.'

[18] The restlessness at the bottom of the sea may be indebted to Job 41.22 and, even more clearly, to the description of the whale in the *Physiologus*/Bestiary tradition: 'Ne mai it [the whale] wunen ðerinne, / So droui is te sees grund' (Hanneke Wirtjes, *The Middle English Physiologus*, EETS o.s. 299 (Oxford, 1991), p. 14, lines 358–9). Similar passages can be found in Latin versions of the *Physiologus* and in many Bestiaries. It is possible that the *Gawain*-poet drew on this tradition. In lines 247–8, for example, the whale is said to have been 'beten fro þe abyme', which lies at the bottom of the sea.

And it is only consistent with this corrective repositioning of the sea as the narrative background to God's judgement-in-action in *Patience* that the whale, the instrument of divine exaction, emerges not from the sea as such, but precisely from the abyss, the seat of all life: 'A wylde walterande whal, as Wyrde þen schaped, / Þat watz beten fro þe abyme, bi þat bot flotte' (lines 247–8). The untamed, primal whale, ordained ('schaped') by God's unbending decree ('Wyrde') to act on His behalf, is driven from the abyss.[19] 'As Wyrde þen shaped' naturally points directly to 'creavitque Deus cete grandia' [And God created the great whales] (Genesis 1.20) but it is important to note here that *cete* or *cete grandia* can mean either 'whale' or 'sea-monster', as opposed to *balaena* or *balena* which is restricted to 'whale'.[20] R. E. Latham's *Revised Medieval Latin Word-List* offers as a translation of *cete* (from *c.* 1200 the later Latin alternative to *cetus*) the meaning 'whale' and examples of the plural form *coetia* [sea monsters] from as early as *c.* 550.[21] This is corroborated by Lewis and Short who list the following meanings for *cetus* (also *cetos* and *cete*): 'any large sea-animal, a sea-monster; particularly a species of whale, a shark, dog-fish, seal, dolphin, etc.'. The Vulgate does not refer to a whale or *balaena* and the whale in the Book of Jonah is referred to as a great *pisces* (e.g. Jonah 2.1–2). Lewis and Short give the Greek *kete* as the source for *cete/cetus/cetos*. *Kete*, even more clearly than its Latin cognate, denotes a sea-monster and never a whale.[22] Intriguingly, the Septuagint provides *kete* both for the Genesis and Jonah passages, making Jonah's whale not so much a whale (*phallaina*, the Greek equivalent to *balaena*), but the same sea-monster as that of Genesis 1.20. It is noteworthy here that *kete* has a secondary meaning, denoting 'abyss'.[23] Hence, the *abyssos* of Jonah 2.6 is already conveyed by the *kete* swallowing Jonah: the abyss has swallowed the prophet with the whale acting as its arm.

Patience does not require the Septuagint to propose this reading. Isidore of Seville distinguishes unmistakably between *ballena* and *cete*:

> 7. Ballenae autem sunt inmensae magnitudinis bestiae, ab emittendo et fundendo aquas vocatae; ceteris enim bestiis maris altius iaciunt undas; *ballein* enim Graece emittere dicitur. 8. Cete dicta *to ketos kai ta kete*, hoc est ob inmanitatem. Sunt enim ingentia genera beluarum et aequalia montium corpora; qualis cetus excepit Ionam, cuius alvus tantae magnitudinis fuit ut instar obtineret inferni, dicente Propheta (2, 3): 'Exaudivit me de ventre inferni'.

> [7. Whales (*ballena*) are beasts of enormous size, named from casting forth and spraying water, for they throw waves higher than the other sea animals;

---

[19] Cf. Andrew and Waldron, *The Poems of the Pearl Manuscript*, p. 196, note to line 247.

[20] Charlton T. Lewis and Charles Short, *A Latin Dictionary* (Oxford, 1879).

[21] *Revised Medieval Latin World-List: From British and Irish Sources* (Oxford, 1999; first published 1965), fascicle C (1988).

[22] Henry George Liddell and Robert Scott, *A Greek-English Lexicon*, rev. by H. Stuart-Jones et al. (ninth edn, Oxford, 1949): '1. any sea-monster or huge fish.'

[23] Liddell and Scott: '2. an abyss, hollow.'

in Greek *ballein* means 'cast forth'. 8. The sea monster (*cetus*, plural *cete*) is named *ketos*, plural *kete*, that is, on account of its vastness. These are huge types of sea monsters (*bellua*), and their bodies are the same size as mountains. Such a *cetus* swallowed Jonah; its belly was so big that it resembled hell, as the prophet says (cf. Jonah 2.3): 'He heard me from the belly of hell.']²⁴

Given this longstanding tradition of adorning the description of whales with attributes of sea-monsters, *Patience* imagines a whale complete with the primeval and infernal characteristics of the abyss: 'Warded þis wrech man in warlowes guttez' (line 258).

Andrew and Waldron note that the 'symbolic connection between the whale and Hell was commonplace in the Middle Ages'.²⁵ As a source for this tradition, they suggest three sources: Isaiah 5.14, the passage from Isidore quoted above and the Middle English *Bestiary*, 'where it is stated that the whale stands for the devil'.²⁶ The *Physiologus*/Bestiary genre interprets the whale as the Devil, and in the Middle English version the name for the whale is, in fact, 'cethegrande' which harks back to Genesis and the tradition that furnished Isidore's discussion of the whale.²⁷ In this tradition, the whale/sea-monster compound is a tempter who pretends to be an island, luring unknowing sailors and emitting a sweet smell from its mouth to attract marine animals.²⁸ Isaiah 5.14 does not associate Hell with a whale; it merely mentions Hell-mouth. Isidore's *Etymologies* are, as demonstrated above, a more persuasive source, yet Isidore clearly distinguishes between a whale and a sea-monster. And although it is certainly very likely that the poet had been influenced by the *Physiologus*/Bestiary tradition, as his noting of the turbulence at the bottom of the sea suggests (see page 126, note 18), a further, biblical undercurrent appears to inform and direct the whale's characterisation in *Patience*.

The 'wylde walterande whal' resides at the 'abyme', which is, as we have seen above, the seat of Hell in an accepted and influential strain of patristic

24 *Isidori Hispalensis episcopi etymologiarum sive originum*, ed. W. M. Lindsay, 2 vols (Oxford, 1911), Book 12, Chapter 6, 'De Piscibus', pp. 7–8.
25 Andrew and Waldron, *The Poems of the Pearl Manuscript*, p. 196, note to line 258. On the medieval Hell-mouth convention, see Ernst Guldon, 'Das Monster-Portal am Palazzo Zuccari in Rom', *Zeitschrift für Kunstgeschichte* 32 (1969), 229–61.
26 Andrew and Waldron, *The Poems of the Pearl Manuscript*, p. 196, note to line 258.
27 Although this is often the case, there are notable exceptions. The Latin *Aberdeen Bestiary* (Aberdeen University Library MS 24), for example, confers the same guileful attributes on the whale and compares it to the Devil, yet it refers to the whale as *balena* throughout (e.g.: fol. 73r).
28 The whale-as-island (*iascanius*) appears in the various redactions of the Brendan-legend. Parallels can be found in a number of ancient and medieval stories, including the tales of Sinbad's voyages. See Albert S. Cook, 'The Old English "Whale"', *MLN* 9:3 (1894), 65–8, Cornelia Catlin Coulter, 'The "Great Fish" in Ancient and Medieval Story', *Transactions and Proceedings of the American Philological Association* 57 (1926), 32–50, Florence McCulloch, 'Pierre de Beauvais' *Lacovie*', *MLN* 71:2 (1956), 100–1, and Mary Allyson Armistead, 'The Middle English *Physiologus*: A Critical Translation and Commentary' (unpublished MA thesis, Virginia Polytechnic Institute and University, 2001), pp. 104–5.

and later pre-modern exegesis. Furthermore, according to the Book of Job, the abyss is inhabited by the ancient sea-serpent Leviathan. Gregory the Great makes it abundantly clear in his immensely popular *Moralia* that Satan, the serpent, lived in this abyss.[29] Rahner states that Leviathan had been identified with the Devil from earliest times.[30] This interpretation is strengthened by the dragon of the Apocalypse (Apocalypse 12.3–4, 7, 9; and 13.4), who, as Rahner notes, is clearly identified with Leviathan in Apocalypse 20.2.[31] In patristic exegesis, the Leviathan is understood to be a great fish, the *cetus* of Genesis, and, hence, becomes a whale.[32] Origen, in his *Homilies on Genesis*, muses why God should have created the whale and other terrifying monsters, and arrives at the conclusion that these evils, signifying the Devil and his demons, are necessary tests for the Christian soul on its journey to salvation (Origen's theodicean explanation of the existence of the whale is important to this argument and will be revisited below).[33]

By specifying that the whale was beaten from the abyss, *Patience* strengthens the association of the whale with the abyss, and therefore with Leviathan. In fact, the whale of *Patience* shares a number of features with Job's extensive description of Leviathan. For instance, the mouth of the whale is likened to a cathedral door: 'As mote in at a munster dor' (line 268).[34] This seems to echo Job 41.5: 'portas vultus eius quis aperiet per gyrum dentium eius formido' [Who can open the doors of his face? His teeth are terrible round about]. Similarly, Job appears to provide a distant source for the concept of the turbulence at the bottom of the sea: 'fervescere faciet quasi ollam profundum mare ponet quasi cum unguenta bulliunt' (Job 41.22) [He shall make the deep sea to boil like a pot, and shall make it as when ointments boil].[35] Moreover, both reside in the abyss, where so many exegetes understood the *sedem inferni* to be: 'post eum lucebit semita aestimabit abyssum quasi senescentem' (Job 41.23) [A path shall shine after him, he shall esteem the deep as growing old].

This association of the whale with the abyss has also been understood by the illuminator. The illumination of the whale in the manuscript containing *Patience* (British Library Cotton Nero A.X Art. 3, fol. 86r) shows the sailors

---

29 *S. Gregorii Magni Moralia in Job*, ed. M. Adraien, CCSL 143, 3 vols (Turnhout, 1979 and 1985), p. 933.

30 Hugo Rahner, *Symbole der Kirche* (Salzburg, 1964), p. 290. Augustine's exegesis of Psalm 103 is outspoken in identifying the Devil with Leviathan (*Enarrationes in Psalmos*, CCSL 39 (Turnhout: 1956), p. 1529). The Church Father quotes a Latin version of the Septuagint translation of Job 41.25.

31 Rahner, *Symbole der Kirche*, p. 291.

32 The gradual conflation of *cetus/cete* and *baleana* appears to have been influenced by this exegesis.

33 For Origen, see Rahner, *Symbole der Kirche*, p. 291. Jerome captures the exegetic equation Leviathan=great whale=Satan in his influential commentary on Isaiah (*S. Hieronymi Presbyteri Commentariorum in Esaiam*, ed. M. Adraien, 2 vols, CCSL 73 (Turnhout, 1963), p. 10).

34 On the *munster dor* image, consult Malcolm Andrew, 'Patience: the *munster dor*', *ELN* 14:3 (1977), 164–7.

35 However, in Job, Leviathan causes the bottom of the sea to boil as opposed to the turbulent ocean-floor which forces the whale to move up. See n. 18.

Figure 6. Jonah being thrown into the whale's mouth (British Library Cotton Nero A.X Art. 3, fol. 86r).

inserting Jonah directly into the whale's mouth (Figure 6). The whale's head is visible in the left-hand corner whereas his tail fin can be seen in the bottom right hand of the illumination, suggesting a circle-shaped whale. This circular shape is also hinted at by the movement of the waves. John B. Friedman, in his analysis of the illumination on fol. 86r argues that the miniature in the manuscript of *Patience* was 'inspired by Bible illustrations' and he lists a number of these. However, none of these contain a circular Leviathan.[36] Leviathan, surrounding the world and inhabiting the abyss, often features in Jewish manuscripts, and by the thirteenth-century, it was common to depict Leviathan as a circle to show that he inhabited the entire world ocean, or abyss (Figures 7 and 8).[37] Although only a remote possibility, it is not inconceivable that the illumination on fol. 86r had been inspired by illuminated Jewish manuscripts.[38]

As we have seen, in one exegetical tradition the abyss and the waters were regarded as primeval and therefore nearly deified forces that could be regarded as capable of compromising God's sovereignty over the sea. Job 41.24 attributes a similar potency to Leviathan/the whale: 'non est super terram potestas quae conparetur ei qui factus est ut nullum timeret' [There is no power upon Earth that can be compared with him who was made to fear no one]. Taken literally, this line could be interpreted to mean that God could not contend with Leviathan on Earth, and it would appear that Jonah applies precisely such a literal and ultimately misguided understanding of the sea at the beginning of *Patience*.

But the centrality of the sea does not stop with the whale episode in the Middle English poem. What may be one of the most original innovations in the story of Jonah and the whale occurs when the prophet arrives in Nineveh and begins to preach to the Gentiles. Warning the Ninevites, Jonah proclaims that the following misery may befall them:

> '3et schal forty dayez fully fare to an ende,
> And þenne schal Niniue be nomen and to no3t worþe;
> Truly þis ilk toun schal tylte to grounde;
> Vp-so-doun schal 3e dumpe depe to þe abyme,
> To be swol3ed swyftly wyth þe swart erþe,
> And alle þat lyuyes hereinne lose þe swete.' (lines 359–64)

36 John B. Friedman, 'Figural Typology in the Middle English *Patience*', in *The Alliterative Tradition in the Fourteenth Century*, ed. Bernard S. Levy and Paul E. Szarmach (Kent, OH, 1981), pp. 99–129, p. 122 (cf. plates on pp. 110–21).

37 Jacqueline Borsje, 'Zeemonsters en de mythische dimensie van de see' *Madoc* 13:4 (1999), 271–3.

38 Lois Drewer, 'Leviathan, Behemoth, and Ziz: A Christian Adaptation', *Journal of the Warburg and Courtauld Institutes* 44 (1981), 148–56, shows that Jewish teaching on Leviathan may have influenced representation in Christian art. See also Cecil Roth, 'Jewish Antecedents of Christian Art', *Journal of the Warburg and Courtauld Institutes* 16:1/2 (1953), 24–44.

Figure 7. Leviathan from the thirteenth-century Ambrosian Bible, South Germany (Biblioteca Ambrosiana B. 32 inf., fol. 136r).

Figure 8. Image of the world-encircling Leviathan from the North French Miscellany (British Library MS Add 11,639, fol. 518v).

It is striking that Jonah should threaten the Ninevites with the abyss swallowing their town.[39] Even more surprising is the absence of the sea from this passage despite the mentioning of the abyss. *Patience* appears to merge two traditions of the *abyssus*, the Augustinian, which places the abyss at the bottom of the sea, and Tertullian's view which locates it in the nether regions of the Earth.[40]

From whichever angle the abyss is viewed in *Patience*, its theological significance is by now undeniable: the *abyssus*, the primeval seat of disorder, and by extension of evil, is organically connected to God's power to punish. The harsh yet corrective punishment that has struck Jonah at sea threatens to be visited upon the Ninevites. Jonah has fallen 'depe in to þe abime' and has emerged unscathed, like Within, an English fisherman who also enjoyed God's protection in a poem by the tenth-century monk Letaldus.[41] By analogy, the Ninevites, although likely to experience God's relentless judgement-in-action, can still hope for deliverance from the abyss.

In her bold new reading of the fourteenth-century dream vision *Piers Plowman*, Nicolette Zeeman views Will's cognitive movement not in terms of a linear and accretive development but as a cyclical sequence of failure, rebuke and renewal.[42] Above all, Zeeman's approach emphasises the didactic function suffering performs in the poem as well as in the Augustinian tradition underlying this cycle of failure, rebuke and renewal. *Patience*, much more so than its biblical source, appears to be informed by the very same principle. Besides the formal aspects of alliteration and, roughly speaking, geographic provenance, *Patience* offers a number of internal parallels with the Vision of Kynde in *Piers Plowman* B XI. Both Jonah and Will misunderstand nature, thereby undermining creation's perfection, and they both come to appreciate suffering 'by ensaumples'.[43] The virtue in which Jonah is being instructed, patience, corresponds to Will's initial lack of 'suffraunce', the patient enduring of hardship. In *Piers Plowman* 'suffraunce' forms the focus of Reson's elaborate rebuke of Will (B XI, lines 375–84), which culminates in a French proverb that stresses the virtue of suffering: 'bien dire et bien suffrir fait lui suffrant a bien venir'.[44] Like Will, Jonah moves through the cycle of failure, rebuke and renewal, and, like Will, he learns through suffering.

---

[39] The Vulgate has only a general warning in this place: 'adhuc quadraginta dies et Nineve subvertetur' (Jonah 3.4) [Yet forty days, and Nineveh shall be destroyed].
[40] Cf. Chapter 1. I am grateful to Ad Putter for pointing out to me that 'abyme' is being employed in a similar sense in *Cleanness*, lines 960 ff.
[41] On Letaldus's poem, see Jan Ziolkowski, 'Folklore and Learned Lore in Letaldus's Whale Poem', *Viator* 15 (1984), 107–18.
[42] Nicolette Zeeman, *Piers Plowman and the Medieval Discourse of Desire* (Cambridge, 2006), p. 248 and passim.
[43] William Langland, *The Vision of Piers Plowman: A Critical Edition of the B-Text*, ed. A. V. C. Schmidt (London, 1995), Passus XI, line 324.
[44] *The Vision of Piers Plowman*, XI, line 384.

Margery's Flight to Dansk

We owe our knowledge of the pseudo-autobiography of the entrepreneur-turned-mystic Margery Kempe to a chance find of the sole surviving manuscript in 1934.[45] *The Book of Margery Kempe*, as it is known to modern readers, was most likely composed between 1436 and 1438. The work is divided into two sections, referred to as 'books'. The first book takes up the vast majority of the manuscript and is an account of Margery's conversion to the spiritual life and of her tribulations in England and on the Contintent. By contrast, the second book is a brief account of her journey to Dansk (the modern Gdańsk), Prussia and eastern Germany. The striking differences between the two books have been frequently noted and, in a recent publication, David Wallace comes close to suggesting that Book 2 approaches a different genre:

> The writing of Book 2, however, comes very much sooner after the *aventure* of its living out; and it observes a temporality more ordered and sequenced than the more random memorialisations of Book 1. This forward drive of Book 2 is thus much more akin to the narrativity of romance than to the more static forms of contemplative literature; the trajectory of Book 2 in fact models a basic structure of romance, what Susan Wittig termed (in the structuralist 1970s) the 'exile-and-return motifeme'.[46]

A close reading of Margery's sea-voyage in its immediate textual context shows that whilst the exile-and-return motifeme is certainly present in Book 2, the actual journey draws equally on the by now time-honoured *peregrinatio pro amore Dei* topos and appears to be modelled on the Brendan-legend in particular.

Even at the beginning of Book 2 there is a hint that the sea will play a significant role in the ensuing adventure. When Margery hears that her son, who lives in Dansk, has become father to a baby girl, she expresses to God the wish to see him and his family. Instantaneously, she is answered that 'sche schulde seen hem alle er than sche deyid',[47] yet she wonders how this 'schulde be so', since her son lives abroad and she 'on this half of the see' (p. 388). After all, she had planned never 'to passyn the see whil sche levyd' (p. 388). This sentiment, however, is quickly dismissed by her trust in God to whom 'was nothyng impossibyl' (p. 388), including the sudden alteration of her plans. Soon afterward, her son makes preparations for his family to join

---

[45] Now kept in the British Library as Additional MS 61,823.

[46] David Wallace, *Margery in Dansk: The Middle Ages Catch Us Up*, William Matthews Lecture 2005 (London, 2006), p. 3. On the differences between the two books, see Barry Windeatt, 'Introduction: Reading and Re-reading *The Book of Margery Kempe*', in *A Companion to the Book of Margery Kempe*, ed. John H. Arnold and Katherine J. Lewis (Cambridge, 2004), pp. 1–16 (esp. pp. 7 ff).

[47] *The Book of Margery Kempe*, ed. Barry Windeatt (London, 2000; repr. Cambridge, 2004), p. 388. All references to the text are taken from this edition.

him on a voyage to Lynn. But the sea will prevent the reunion: 'Whan thei weryn in the schip, there resyn swech tempestys that thei durstyn not takyn the see, and so thei comyn on lond ageyn, bothyn he, hys wife, and her childe' (p. 390). Having realised that the sea cannot be altogether trusted, they decide to leave their daughter with friends and, after having opted for the arduous overland route, arrive safely in England. But their joy quickly turns to tears when Margery's son suddenly falls ill and dies, leaving his wife, who cannot speak English, alone in the company of her mother-in-law.

After receiving letters from home, the daughter-in-law requests permission to return home to her child and family. Margery realises that it might be God's desire for her to accompany her daughter-in-law and wonders whether she ought to consult her confessor in this matter: 'Lord, yyf it wer thi wille, I wolde takyn leve of my confessowr and gon wyth hir ovyr the see' (p. 391). Since she is unwilling to break her pledge never to go by sea, she is relieved when God tells her to abandon the thought:

> Than was sche ryth glad and mery, trustyng sche schulde not gon ovyr the see, for sche had ben in gret perell on the see afortyme and was in purpos nevyr to comyn theron mor be hir owyn wille.[48]

Nevertheless, after much to-and-fro, Margery finds herself compelled to accompany the daughter-in-law on this voyage, however unwillingly: 'but evyr was labowryd and comawndyd to gon ovyr the see' (p. 392). In her very own manner she tries to convince God that this would not be such a good idea after all. Her negotiations fail, of course, and Margery resolves to go by sea. But since she refuses to return to Lynn before the journey or to make any preparations, the text casts Margery in the role of an unwilling *peregrina* 'for the lofe of hir dowtyr-in-lawe':

> Sum seyd it was a womanys witte and a gret foly, for the lofe of hir dowtyr-in-lawe, to putte herself, a woman in gret age, to perellys of the see, and for to gon into a strawnge cuntre where sche had not ben beforn, ne not wist how sche schulde come ageyn.[49]

The text's insistence on including passages that reflect how Margery and her actions are being perceived by her environment has the quality of inserting an audience into the narrative that operates as a first readership of this life. In an interpretative context, this has the added benefit of validating Margery's remarkable experiences by inserting the voice of a witness. Here, it is this voice that reads her resolution to go to Dansk in the terms of a literary *peregrinatio pro amore Dei*: Margery spontaneously abandons hearth and home for a strange country, not knowing how and whether she will be able to return. The only modification lies in the formula 'for the lofe of hir dowtyr-

48 *The Book of Margery Kempe*, p. 391.
49 *The Book of Margery Kempe*, p. 395.

in-lawe' where 'dowytyr-in-lawe' replaces *Deus* in *pro amore Dei*. Naturally the text is very selective about admitting readers' voices, so that the only truly critical witness, Margery's daughter-in-law, is muted as much by her own inability to speak English as by the focus on Margery's musings.

And the similarities between the Brendan-legend and Margery's sea-voyage do not stop here. One of the most salient features of the Latin *Navigatio* and, to a lesser extent, of the vernacular versions of the Brendan-legend is the structural role assumed by the liturgical year. The major feasts serve as points of orientation for Brendan's journey and particular holidays are repeatedly associated with the same locations. Margery's brief but eventful voyage echoes this principle of building the itinerary around the *temporale*:

> The sayd creatur [Margery] and hir felawschip entryd her schip on the Thursday in Passyon Weke, and God sent hem fayr wynde and wedyr that day and the Fryday, but on the Satirday owr Lord, turnyng hys hand as hym likyd, and the Palme Sonday also, prevyng her feith and her pacyens, wyth the ii nyghtys, sent hem swech stormys and tempestys that thei wendyn alle to a ben perischyd.[50]

The first holiday that is mentioned in the Brendan-legend, Maundy Thursday, also falls in Holy Week. Brendan and his monks celebrate Maundy Thursday to Holy Saturday on the Isle of Sheep, before hastening to spend Easter on Jascanius, as they will do for the coming six years (*Navigatio*, Chapter 9). This detail would remain a part of the versions of the legend available in England until Caxton's adaptation.[51] Margery's voyage, also firmly set in Holy Week, moves to the next station, Norway or Easter, depending on whether one reads her journey literally or spiritually. It would be perfectly sufficient to mention that Margery spends three days there. Instead, with the same liturgical precision as the Latin *Navigatio*, we are told that the crew landed in Norway on Good Friday and remained there during 'Ester Evyn, and Estern Day and the Monday after Estern' (p. 397). Besides serving to authorise Margery's journey as ordained by divine will, all this must put a considerable question mark over the reliability of Book 2 and one wonders how authentic these dates really are.

The strongest and perhaps most obvious parallel with Brendan's voyage and the *peregrinatio* tradition occurs during the storm:

---

[50] *The Book of Margery Kempe*, p. 396.
[51] The *temporale* as an organising principle of maritime voyages became a feature of other romances, such as Philippe de Rémi's thirteenth-century *Roman de la Manekine*, which is partly set in the British Isles. For a summary and a mapping of the religious feasts in the romance, see Helen Cooper, *The English Romance in Time: Transforming Motifs from Geoffrey of Monmouth to the Death of Shakespeare* (Oxford, 2004), pp. 125–6.

The tempestys weryn so grevows and hedows that thei myth not rewlyn ne governe her schip. Thei cowde no bettyr chefsyawns than comendyn hemself and her schip to the governawns of owr Lord.[52]

'Governawns' puns of course, as David Wallace points out, on *gubernator*, 'steersman' or 'helmsman'.[53] But the allusion runs much deeper: this is an almost literal invocation of the *deus gubernator* phrase that is an essential part of the *peregrinatio pro amore Dei* pattern, according to Angenendt. Ultmately, its source is Brendan's reaction to the first time his crew face trouble at sea: 'God is our helper, our helmsman and our captain'.[54] A vital element of the *deus gubernator* is 'the shipping of the oars': 'Put down all your oars and the rudder. And leave the sails and let God do as He wishes with His servants and His ship.'[55] Nor is such a passage missing from Margery's voyage: 'thei left her craft and her cunnyng and leet owr Lord dryvyn hem where he wolde' (p. 396). And yet, despite all this, Margery is no Brendan. Like Jonah, she seems to doubt God's power over the sea, as God's words to her imply: 'why dredist the? Why art thu so aferd? I am as mythy her in the see as on the londe' (p. 397).

Wallace is right in identifying the chaotic manner of Margery's departure as 'semi-sanctioned exile or romantic flight' and her crossing as an instance of being set adrift in the manner of Chaucer's Custance.[56] His observation gains strength when one reads Margery's reflections on her social status during the tempest:

The pepil hath many tyme bannyd me, cursyd me and wariid me for the grace that thu hast wrowt in me, desiryng that I schulde deyin in myschef and gret disese, and now, Lord it is lyke that her bannyng comyth to effect.[57]

Here, Margery herself talks of her exile or 'bannyng' coming into effect as she fashions her plight into a spectacular tale about exile and return. But it is similarly valid, as I have attempted to show, that the manner of her leaving, her motivation, the liturgical references, the reference to God as helmsman and the 'shipping of the oars' all point to a narrative indebtedness to the *peregrinatio pro amore Dei* and the Brendan-legend. What makes this passage unique, then, is that the writer of Margery's life combines the motifs of exile-by-sea and pilgrimage-by-sea in a text whose generic boundaries

---

52 *The Book of Margery Kempe*, p. 396.
53 Wallace, *Margery in Dansk*, p. 7.
54 'Deus ... adiutor noster est et nautor et gubernator atque gubernator', *Navigatio Sancti Brendani Abbatis*, ed. Carl Selmer (South Bend, IN, 1959), Chapter 6.
55 'Mittite intus omnes remiges et gubernaculum. Tantum dimitte uela extensa et faciat Deus sicut uult de seruis suis et de sua naui', Selmer, ed., *Navigatio*, Chapter 6.
56 Wallace, *Margery in Dansk*, pp. 6–7.
57 *The Book of Margery Kempe*, p. 396.

remain in flux. It also tells us that, by the mid-1430s, Brendan's sea-voyage had not gone out of fashion. The *South English Legendary* with its version of the Brendan voyage was still being copied and some fifty years later Caxton would include his account of Brendan in the *Golden Legend*.

6

A Thousand Furlongs of Sea

What, they lived once thus at Venice where the merchants were the kings,
Where Saint Mark's is, where the Doges used to wed the sea with rings?
Robert Browning, *A Toccata of Galuppi's* (1855)

La puissance des armes requiert non seulement que le roi soit plutôt fort
sur la terre, mais elle veut en outre qu'il soit puissant sur la mer.
Cardinal Richelieu (1585–1642), *Testament politique*

Territorial Waters: The Origin of a Contradiction

At first glance, the concept of territorial waters must be a paradox. 'Territory', with its etymology rooted in *terra*, denotes ground, firm land, which contrasts sharply with the fluidity of 'waters'. The term 'territorial waters' denotes the theoretical and, at times, practical imposition of political claims on spaces that seem ill-equipped to meet them, with the result of yielding, at best, a mixed metaphor (one only has to think of Xerxes' whipping of the sea). And yet, wars have been fought for the strategic or economic value of water territory, and even to this day there exists no universally accepted agreement on the precise extent and definition of 'territorial waters'.[1] The term belongs to the world of legal taxonomy, and its exact demarcation in early fifteenth-century England is vital for the development of the sea's perception in political thought and literature.

Following the Roman understanding of the sea as land, the proto-egalitarian concept of the natural freedom of the seas was first challenged as a legal notion by the Glossators working in the University of Bologna

---

[1] In 1982, the United Nations Convention on the Law of the Sea (UNCLOS) addressed ocean law issues, including rights of navigation and overflight, fishing, marine scientific research, seabed minerals development and marine environmental protection. Its outcome, the Law of the Sea Treaty, went into effect only in 1994. However, some states, most prominently the United States, have modified the treaty or follow a different practice. The result is that custom and tradition remain – as in the Middle Ages – the guiding principles for solving maritime disputes. See R. P. Anand, 'Non-European Sources of Law of the Sea', in Susan Rolston, ed, *Pacem in maribus 2000* (Halifax, Canada, 2002), pp. 9–20, and R. R. Churchill and A. V. Lowe, *The Law of the Sea* (Manchester, 1985; third edn 1999).

during the twelfth century.[2] The Glossators provided extensive commentaries on Justinian's sixth-century *Corpus Iuris Civilis*. As concerns maritime law, they agreed on the communality of the sea. One particular gloss, however, introduces a consequential amendment by stating that whereas use of the sea is common to all, jurisdiction of the same resides with the Emperor:

> Mare est commune, quo ad usus: sed proprietas est nullius: sicut aër est communis usu: proprietas tamen est nullius ... sed iurisdictio est Caesaris.
>
> [The sea is common to all, as concerns use: but it is no-one's property: just as air is of common use: yet it is no-one's property ... but the jurisdiction is Caesar's.][3]

One historian attributes this considerable modification of the ancient freedom of the seas to the equally ancient need to suppress piracy at sea. Rome's legal administrators considered action against pirates an Imperial prerogative and, consequently, the state assumed a juridical role over the sea: 'Celsus had attributed to the *populus Romanus* the position of *arbiter* of the seashore.'[4] It is important to note here that these legal approaches to the sea are transferable outside the strict confines of the Mediterranean since the definition of the sea employed by the Glossators is universal throughout pre-modern Europe. It is consistent with the Bible and with the universally authoritative Isidore: 'mare [est] congregatio aquarum multarum' [the sea [is] a gathering of many waters].[5]

Various barbarian and Christian rulers began to claim some form of jurisdiction over the sea, mainly to protect their 'firm' territories against piratical

---

[2]   The standard works on historical and current maritime law are R. P. Anand, *Origin and Development of the Law of the Sea* (London, 1982) and Churchill and Lowe, *The Law of the Sea*. On territorial waters and the freedom of the seas, see Thomas Wemyss Fulton, *The Sovereignty of the Sea: An Historical Account of the Claims of England to the Dominion of the British Seas* (Edinburgh and London, 1911); Pitman B. Potter, *The Freedom of the Seas in History, Law and Politics* (New York, 1924; repr. Buffalo 2002); Percy Thomas Fenn, Jr, 'Origins of the Theory of Territorial Waters', *American Journal of International Law* 20:3 (1926), 465–82; and, most recently, Edda Frankot, 'Medieval Maritime Law and its Practice in the Towns of Northern Europe: a Comparison by the Example of Shipwreck, Jettison and Ship Collision' (unpublished PhD thesis, University of Aberdeen, 2004). I am grateful to Edda Frankot for her comments on the history of legal claims to the sea.

[3]   Gloss on Dig. 1.8.2.[1]. Unless otherwise noted, all translations are my own.

[4]   Fenn, 'Origins of the Theory of Territorial Waters', p. 465. Dig. 43.8.3: 'Litora, in quae populus Romanus imperium habet, populi Romani esse arbitror' [The shores over which the Roman people has dominion I consider to belong to the Roman people]. The translation is taken from *The Digest of Justinian*, ed. T. Mommsen and P. Krueger, trans. Alan Watson, 4 vols (Philadelphia, 1985) vol. 4, facing page 576.

[5]   Gloss on Dig. 48.9.9.1, 'alioquin' (see Fenn, 'Origins of the Theory of Territorial Waters', p. 465). For the biblical similarities: 'Et congregationes aquarum vocavit maria' [And He called the gathering of the waters 'sea'] (Genesis 1.10) and 'viam fecisti in mari equis tuis in luto aquarum multarum' [Thou madest a way in the sea for thy horses, in the mud of many waters] (Habakkuk 3.15). Isidore defines the sea as following: 'Mare est aquarum generalis collectio' [A sea is a general gathering of waters] (*Isidori Hispalensis episcopi etymologiarum sive originum*, ed. W. M. Lindsay, 2 vols (Oxford, 1911), Book 13, Chapter 14). On the study of Glossators and Post-Glossators in England, where, in most courts, common law was practised, see p. 145, n. 21.

activity, but also to control trade and regulate access to land during times of war. However, for the most part, these claims had neither a basis in classical legal thought nor any justification in contemporaneous legal theory. The twelfth-century Glossators were the first to offer a strictly legal justification for any claims to the sea. In a gloss on the doctrine of the Roman jurist Paulus (Dig. 47.10.14), the glossator Azo states that there are two ways in which claims to the sea can be justified: *per privilegium* and *per longam consuetudinem*, that is by grant of privilege or through long-established custom.[6] This legal justification did not initially have sufficient weight for claims to the sea to be accepted in practice. The pre-modern prince, argues Percy Thomas Fenn, Jr, 'was restricted by the *ius divina* (transformed into the terms of ecclesiastical law) and probably by the *ius naturale*'.[7] Because canon law could not provide any basis for appropriating the sea as territory, rulers and their legal counsels had to look toward natural law. An examination of the sea in natural law quickly led to the realisation that the sea was considered by nature ineligible to be private property (Ovid's exclamatory assertion of the public nature of water comes to mind, page 33). As a result, no legislation to challenge the public nature of the sea could be found. It must be added here that pre-modern law, like historiography, was judicial and not legislative: 'law was interpreted, not created; discovered not made'.[8] Furthermore, a ruler's ambitions could be thwarted by the law of custom, the *ius gentium*, which – ironically – Azo chooses as one of the foundations for justifying claims to the sea. On closer inspection, the *ius gentium* undeniably revealed that fishermen had been exercising free access to seashores for generations (*per longam consuetudinem*). This realisation secured the sea's freedom for a little longer. Once discovered, law could not be easily altered. Thus, a change of the sea's legal status was dependent on a change of the nature of law.

Whereas the pre-ordained nature of law prevented rulers from arbitrarily seizing sea as land other than by means of customs duties and coastal fishing and harbour rights, some have proposed that it was feudal practice that gradually led to the creation of territorial waters.[9] In feudal or quasi-feudal contexts, it was customary for monarchs to grant exclusive use of a particular territory to a vassal although, nominally, the territory would remain an immutable constituent of the crown.[10] In practice this often meant that the territory in question passed into the hands of a particular family or dynasty for generations. Nevertheless, the sovereign remained the titular landowner. The contractual process of granting land to a baron, often *de facto*, subjected the sea to some form of regulation. When land was conferred, certain rights of use pertaining to the adjacent waters, such as 'exclusive' fishing rights, could be appended. Furthermore, it was also practice to grant sea fisheries to

---

[6]   Fenn, 'Origins of the Theory of Territorial Waters', p. 466.
[7]   Fenn, 'Origins of the Theory of Territorial Waters', p. 466.
[8]   Fenn, 'Origins of the Theory of Territorial Waters', p. 466.
[9]   Fenn, 'Origins of the Theory of Territorial Waters', pp. 467 ff.
[10] I define my use of the term 'feudal' on p. 17, n. 50.

private persons, to exempt people from paying port or harbour dues and to permit freedom of commerce or travel in certain waters.[11] While, on the one hand, this development signalled the legal and, at times, exclusive 'appropriation' of coastal parts of the sea for private use, it still fell short of rulers claiming sea as their territory. This custom of appending coastal portions of the sea to fiefs soon filtered into the *ius gentium*, and the next step towards seizing the sea as territory had been taken.

The birth of territorial waters and, with it, the legal war over (and political recognition of) the sea as territory were made possible by two factors. The first is the pre-modern concept of the *regalium*, that is, an a priori legal and political privilege bestowed on a ruler. The second factor is the fundamental change observed in lawmaking during the thirteenth century, which enabled new legislation. The former, *regalia*, allowed the sovereign to assert certain privileges for himself. Typical *regalia* granted the king prerogatives related to towns, markets, coinage, mining, land, etc., but no such privileges relating to the sea were automatically conferred and there was no recognised process for 'crafting' these, despite the fact that the sovereign's supreme authority, manifest in the various royal *regalia*, provided a tentative basis on which legally vindicated claims to territorial waters could, in principle, be erected.[12]

Change came with the Post-Glossators. This fourteenth-century school of jurists did not content itself with merely commenting on Justinian's *Corpus Iuris Civilis*, but began to provide detailed advice, *consilia*, on the desirable applications of Roman law to contemporary practice. It was here, in these *consilia*, that law would regain its legislative potency. The founder of this school was also the father of territorial waters in legal history: the Italian jurist Bartolus of Sassoferrato (1313/14–57). Bartolus was a professor of law at the universities of Bologna, Pisa and Perugia, and a counsellor to Emperor Charles IV. Commenting on the *Corpus Iuris Civilis*, he supplies a groundbreaking definition of the sea: 'Mare dicitur illius Domini, sub cuius territorio comprehenditur' [It is said the sea of this lord, under whose territory it [the sea] is understood].[13] Bartolus's justification for the treatment of the sea as territory rests upon an analogy with the policing of land. Bartolus assigned this task to the *praeses*. By the time Bartolus was writing, the office of the *Amiratus*, the admiral, the equivalent of the Roman *praeses* on the sea, had already been established in a number of European countries, most

---

[11] Fenn, 'Origins of the Theory of Territorial Waters', p. 467.

[12] An interesting exception, overlooked by many medieval authorities, appears in the Captitulary of Louis the Pious as early as 816: 'siquidem cuiuscumque potestatis sint littora, nostra tamen est regalis aqua' (Regesta Imperii I, 628, 30 August 816; consulted at http://regesta-imperii.uni-giessen.de), see also Vilho Niitemaa, *Das Strandrecht in Nordeuropa im Mittelalter* (Helsinki, 1955). I am grateful to Edda Frankot for pointing this out to me.

[13] *Gemma legalium seu Compendium aureum* (Venice, 1602), entry under *mare*. See also *Omnium Iuris Commentaria*, ed. P. Mangrelia, 10 vols (Venice, 1602), *Ad decimem lb. Codicis, de Classicis, Additio, Alix. Quidem Habent*, vol. 8, p. 33.

notably – for the purpose of this argument – in France and England.[14] One of the Admiral's principal tasks was to 'guarder la mere', that is, to combat piracy.

In a state's claim to its territory Bartolus also includes those islands that are nearest its coast: 'tamen ego dico, quod illa insula est pars illius provinciae, qui adhaeret' [I however say that this island is a part of that province which is adjacent].[15] In the case of islands, the state extends its authority to include islands near its coast, thereby appropriating the sea lying in between. Thus, the sea becomes 'collateral' property in a state's attempt to lay hold upon an island. As a result, the mainland's relationship to an island overrides the Roman doctrine that the sea is common to all. This aspect of Bartolus's justification for (limited) territorial waters is only bound by his understanding of how far these islands must be from the mainland in order for the state to express a valid claim. In his tract on rivers, *De Fluminibus*, Bartolus argues that islands that are separated from the mainland by 'modico spacio' [a moderate distance] are the rightful property of the nearest state. According to Bartolus, a 'moderate distance' amounts to 100 miles [185 km].[16]

Bartolus's favourite pupil, Baldus of Ubaldi (*c.* 1327–1400), later professor of law in Bologna, Pavia, Perugia and Florence, went a step further in his commentary on 'feudal' or fief law, *Usus Feudorum Commentario*. Baldus defines the validity of a sovereign's *regalia* and considers these to be legitimate in both the sovereign's territory and the *mare adiacens*, the sea that is adjacent to his territory. He calls the sea not *territorium* but *districtus*.[17] Only six years after Baldus's death, in 1406, England's Henry IV refers to the sea in the same breath as dominions and districts of the Crown: 'ubicumque supra mare, per et infra dominia, juridictiones, et districtus nostra' [wherever on the sea, across and below our dominions, jurisdictions and districts].[18] This distinction renders the sea an area under someone's authority and supervision without sharing all the properties of a territory. It seals the sea's attachment to land, making it a territorial and, if needs be, administrative appendix to land. The sea thus becomes a political buffer zone into which certain states may venture to enforce a particular decree or regulation.

And so, by 1400, the first inroads into claiming parts of the sea as territory have been made. The Post-Glossators' changes represent a partial 'closure' of the Roman *mare liberum*, but the concept of the *mare clausum*, the exclusive territorial waters, has not yet been reached.[19] From a legal point of view,

---

14 Originally from the Arabic (*amir-al* [*bahr*] or 'king of [the sea]'), the office was first introduced in France in 1249 (Fulton, *Sovereignty of the Sea*, pp. 31–2, identifies the first 'Admiral of all France' in 1280, followed by admirals appointed by the King of Castile and Leon). The first English Admiral was appointed in 1297 (Fulton, *Sovereignty of the Sea*, p. 31).

15 *Opera*, ed. P. C. Brederodius, 10 vols (Basle, 1589), vol. 1, p. 492 (vol. 1, p. 151 in the Venetian edition of 1602).

16 Fenn, 'Origins of the Theory of Territorial Waters', p. 477.

17 Fenn, 'Origins of the Theory of Territorial Waters', p. 472.

18 Fulton, *The Sovereignty of the Sea*, p. 16, note 1. The translation is mine.

19 *Mare clausum*, or 'closed sea', is the title of John Selden's 1635 response to Hugo Grotius's *Mare*

the sea can be viewed as territory for the purposes of policing it or if it falls in between the mainland and an island lying not more than 100 miles away. Furthermore, Baldus states that the entire adjacent sea (again, not more than 100 miles away from the coast) can be administered as a *districtus*. It is another 200 years before Albericus Gentilis (1550–1608) completes this legal process when he unconditionally speaks of the sea as territory: 'Mare adiacens pars ditionis est, et territorium de terris dicitur et de aquis' [The adjacent sea is part of the dominion and is called a territory of both lands and waters].[20] It must be noted here that, although these authorities have first been presented to an English audience as part of a complete argument on the sea in John Selden's *Mare Clausum* (1636), the work of the Glossators and Post-Glossators was read throughout Europe, including England.[21] Besides, as will be shown below, the arguments used by the Post-Glossators correspond to existing practices in England.

England Reaches for the Sea: *The Libelle of Englyshe Polycye*

One of the most important early political poems written in English, the *Libelle of Englyshe Polycye* (1436/7) makes a fervent case for England to govern the seas surrounding its coast and build a strong navy to exercise control over trade.[22] Although the *Libelle of Englyshe Polycye* (henceforth *Libelle*) did not succeed in swaying English policy toward achieving these objectives, it appears to have circulated among influential Englishmen during

---

Liberum, a spirited defence of the freedom of the seas, published in 1609. Grotius (1583–1645) was a Dutch lawyer, diplomat, and philosopher who published *Mare Liberum* to justify the claims of the Dutch East India Company to trade in the Far East. His work is considered the beginning of modern international law.

[20] *De Iure Belli*, ed. T. E. Holland, 3 vols, (Oxford, 1877), vol. 3, p. 369. My translation.

[21] There is evidence, well into the seventeenth century, that Bartolus of Sassoferrato exercised considerable influence on English ecclesiastical law (Walter Ullmann, 'Bartolus and English Jurisprudence' in *Bartolo da Sassoferrato: Studi e documenti per il VI centenario*, ed. D. Segolini, 2 vols (Milan, 1962), vol. 1, pp. 49–73 (p. 62)). Civil law and, thus, the thought of the Glossators and Post-Glossators, was taught in English universities, and Walter Ullmann argues that 'like the ecclesiastical courts this court [the court of the Constable and Marshall, the so-called *Curia militaris sub conestabili et marescallo Angliae*] too was composed entirely by [sic] graduates and must therefore be presumed to have become acquainted with Bartolus's teachings during their legal education' (Ullmann, 'Bartolus and English Jurisprudence', p. 62). Furthermore, the Bodleian Library holds a fifteenth-century copy of Bartolus's *Tractatus* in the original Latin, as well as a translation into English, and the British Museum owns a copy made before 1426.

[22] The most recent edition of the poem is George Warner's *The Libelle of Englyshe Polycye – A Poem on the Use of Sea Power, 1436* (Oxford, 1926). Since Warner's edition the number of known manuscripts of the work has nearly doubled. See Frank Taylor, 'Some Manuscripts of the *Libelle of Englyshe Polycye*', *Bulletin of the John Rylands Library* 24 (1940), 376–418; C. M. Meale, '*The Libelle of Englyshe Polycye* and Mercantile Literary Culture in Late-Medieval London', in *London and Europe in the Later Middle Ages*, ed. Julia Boffey and Pamela King (London, 1995), pp. 181–228 (pp. 226–7); and A. S. G. Edwards, 'A New Manuscript of *The Libelle of English Policy*', *Notes and Queries*, n.s. 46:4 (1999), 444–5). Warner's dating of the poem, hingeing on the Duke of Burgundy's abortive siege of Calais in July 1436 and Emperor's Sigismund's death in December 1437, has been widely accepted.

the subsequent two centuries.[23] The famous early editor of voyage narratives Richard Hakluyt, for example, deemed the poem sufficiently important to print it in his *Principall Navigations*.

Interest in the poem has been growing in recent years, and John Scattergood's reading of the *Libelle* as an attempt to define the English nation and its place in Europe from the perspective of an emerging merchant class marks only the most recent chapter in the discussion of the *Libelle*.[24] It has been argued that the *Libelle* is driven by mercantile interests which, when forming the basis of a nationally coordinated policy towards the sea, often diverge sharply from the interests of the established aristocratic classes: 'Though the poem purports to speak for the whole of England, it is very much a redefinition of the nation by reference to a specific sectional interest.'[25] This infiltration of the political and economic spheres by the land/sea dialectic need not be surprising: the sectional interest of merchants involved in long-distance trade is strongly linked to the sea just as that of the aristocracy is tied to land, and the poem infuses the elemental antithesis of 'land' and 'sea' with a political and economic dimension. To some extent, then, the *Libelle* offers a reorientation of politics away from the land and towards the sea, or, rather, towards an Insular (and therefore English) understanding of the sea as territory.

'Nothing is ours which another may deprive us of', writes Thomas Jefferson about the liberating value of intellectual pleasures.[26] It may seem anachronistic to preface a discussion of a fifteenth-century poem with this adage, but it succinctly makes the fine but crucial point that a right which is not enforced or enforceable is, essentially, reduced to a claim. This principle extends to both land and sea in a territorial sense, although one may grant that it is more difficult, if not impossible in accord with the Roman doctrine of the *mare liberum*, to hold or 'kepe' the sea in the same way in which land can be 'kept'.

Almost overconfidently, the *Libelle* makes the unconditional 'keeping' of England's entire adjacent sea its objective from the outset: 'to exhortynge alle Englande to kepe the see enviroun and namelye the narowe see'.[27] 'Enviroun' denotes 'all around', that is, the *mare adiacens*, and 'narowe see' appears to refer specifically to the Straits of Dover.[28] Although the poem erects its

---

23 See p. 22, n. 73.

24 John Scattergood, 'The *Libelle of Englyshe Polycye*: the Nation and Its Place', in Helen Cooney, ed., *Nation, Court and Culture: New Essays on Fifteenth-Century English Poetry* (Dublin, 2001), pp. 28–49 (p. 33). Scattergood articulates a similar if less developed view in *Politics and Poetry in the Fifteenth Century* (London, 1971), pp. 37–8, 45–6, 90–5, 101, 327–30, 334–6.

25 Scattergood, 'The *Libelle of Englyshe Polycye*', p. 33.

26 'Letter to Mrs Cosway', Paris, 1786 in *The Works of Thomas Jefferson*, ed. P. L. Ford, 10 vols (New York, 1905), vol. 4, p. 317.

27 Proem (the proem is written in prose and has therefore no lineation). All citations from the *Libelle* are taken from Warner's edition.

28 Warner, note to the proem, p. 59, understands 'narowe see' to denote the 'straits between Dover and Calais' although it is equally plausible that it refers to the wider English Channel. This second, wider understanding does not apply throughout as lines 813–14 document.

argument mainly on a number of immediate tactical and long-term strategic justifications for maintaining control over the Straits of Dover, the *Libelle*'s holistic claim not only to 'hold' this specific part of the Channel nominally but also to 'kepe' the 'see enviroun' is tantamount to asserting England's unlimited and exclusive sovereignty over its adjacent seas. The primary meaning of 'kepe' is 'to guard', but I will show that the *Libelle* appears to use the word throughout, and most likely here, too, in the sense of 'to keep' or 'possess.

To this day, the standard work on the history of England's claims to sovereignty over the British seas is Thomas Wemyss Fulton's *The Sovereignty of the Sea* (1911). In the preface, Fulton advances the theory that the claim to a special sovereignty over the British seas was introduced by the Stuarts.[29] However, in the light of the development of territorial waters in mind, as outlined above, an analysis of England's historical claims to its territorial waters will demonstrate how progressive and vital a role the *Libelle* played in advancing this claim.

The earliest English demands for sovereignty over the British seas can be traced to William of Malmesbury's *Gesta Regum Anglorum*. William, as a historiographer, was also eager to carve out spiritual privileges for England based on its proximity to the realm of Providence.[30] In William's account of King Edgar's charter of 964, Edgar styles himself 'Emperor of all Albion, and also of maritime or insular kings dwelling about'.[31] In effect, Edgar's title renders him Emperor over islands, i.e. territories, in the sea and over other rulers who are merely 'kings'. However, Fulton observes that this preamble to the charter may not be authentic, and, at any rate, the claim limits itself exclusively to land in the sea and land adjacent to the sea (this is certainly the way in which William's translators understand the passage) rather than to the sea itself. Evidence for more assertive and comprehensive claims to the sovereignty over England's adjacent seas does not begin to emerge before the Conquest and, in particular, the Plantagenets' reign.[32] During the twelfth and thirteenth centuries, England's possession of both shores of the Channel, possibly conveyed by the 'narowe see' in the *Libelle*, rendered the Channel virtually a water highway between the parts of the royal domain. The Channel itself was of paramount significance in a number of ways: culturally, militarily and commercially. A significant volume of trade passed through the

---

[29] Fulton, *The Sovereignty of the Sea*, p. viii.

[30] See Chapter 3, in particular, pp. 78–9.

[31] 'Ego Edgarus totius Albionis basileus, necnon maritimorum seu insulanorum regum circumhabitantium (adeo ut nullus progenitorum meorum)' [I Edgar, monarch of all Albion, who by the subjection of neighbouring kings of coasts and islands am raised higher than were any of my forbears], *Gesta Regum Anglorum*, ed. and trans. R. A. B. Mynors with R. M. Thomson and M. Winterbottom, 2 vols (Oxford, 1998), vol. 1, pp. 248–9. The distinction between 'maritimorum' and 'insulanorum' probably refers to different sizes of islands.

[32] However, the establishment of the Cinque Ports organisation during the reign of Edward the Confessor could be viewed as one such step towards expressing an active interest in the sea. The guarding of the coasts was one of the reasons for the development of the Cinque Ports. See K. M. E. Murray, *The Constitutional History of the Cinque Ports* (Manchester, 1935).

Channel, which merchants and other sectional interest groups began to regard as permanent English territory by virtue of their prolonged use of it (*per longam consuetudinem*), thus instituting a right rooted in ancient practice and custom, not unlike the *ius gentium*. And it would appear that the *Libelle* is clearly aware of this when it exhorts its audience to do its best to 'kepe' the narrow sea and Calais:

> And chefely kepe sharply the narowe see
> Betwene Dover and Caleise, and as thus
> That foes passe not wythought godewyll of us,
> And they abyde oure daunger in the lenghte,
> What for oure costis and Caleise in oure strenghte. (lines 813–17)

Clearly, the text advocates a resolute defence of Calais for strategic purposes. At the time of the *Libelle*'s composition, the Hundred Years War was still under way and these hostilities rendered the monitoring of exactly who sailed through the Straits of Dover vital for the successful protection of 'oure costis'. By placing emphasis on guarding the narrow sea at all costs ('kepe sharply'), the *Libelle* draws on the extended and prolonged custom of English kings *de facto* governing parts of the sea, a custom that started 300 hundred years earlier during the Angevin Empire of the twelfth century. This argument of prolonged use, *per longam consuetudinem*, is articulated in the list of precedents set by Edgar, Edward III and Henry V, and will be discussed in greater detail below.

Besides prolonged use, the text advances a further authority for its advocacy of laying a territorial claim to these waters, as Edgar did by styling himself Emperor among insular kings. Although in practice not always regarded as such, in political theory, the Emperor represented the highest secular authority, being king among kings or father of an imperial family of *reges* (*primus inter pares*).[33] More importantly, the Emperor inherited by right what were thought to be Roman *regalia* amongst which was the indubitably Imperial prerogative to crown kings. The person of the Emperor symbolised at the same time the highest authority for judicial disputes. By invoking the Emperor Sigismund, who came to Canterbury in 1416, the *Libelle* adduces the foremost legal authority to voice his opinion on the strategic importance of the Straits of Dover and adjudicate in the internal dispute over the most desirable policy towards policing the sea.[34] Crucially, the text foregrounds the Emperor – depicted as a friend and ally of Henry V – by placing this account of his solemn meeting with the King at the very beginning of the poem:

---

[33] The phrase *primus inter pares* is attributed to the Emperor Augustus who styled himself 'citizen with special powers' when 'restoring' the Republic in AD 27.

[34] It does not matter here, I think, that the Emperor represented civil law. The *Libelle*'s exploitation of his visit to Canterbury is motivated by pragmatic concerns. Besides, ecclesiastical and admiralty courts in England employed civil law, and English lawyers were acquainted with Continental writings on civil law, which formed part of their training. See p. 145, n. 21.

For Sigesmonde the grete Emperoure,
Whyche yet regneth, whan he was in this londe
Wyth kynge Henry the v^te, prince of honoure,
Here moche glorye, as hym thought, he founde,
A myghty londe, whyche hadde take on honde
To werre in Fraunce and make mortalite,
And ever well kept rounde aboute the see. (lines 8–14)

The fact that the text insists on restoring the Roman imperial hierarchy of Christian rulers – Sigismund is the 'grete Emperoure' whereas Henry is only a 'prince of honoure' – acquires extraordinary significance when Sigismund addresses Henry with 'my brothere', permitting the text to bestow, at least by implication, quasi-Imperial *regalia* and prerogatives on Henry. A further purpose of this address is that it allows the poem to lay the groundwork for the subsequent stressing of the 'justness' of England's claims (based on the territorial use of 'kepe') to the 'narowe' sea:

And to the kynge thus he seyde, 'My brothere',
Whan he perceyved too townes, Calys and Dovere,
'Of alle youre townes to chese of one and other
To kepe the see and sone for to come overe,
To werre oughtwardes and youre regne to recovere,
Kepe these too townes sure to youre mageste
As youre tweyne eyne to kepe the narowe see.' (lines 15–21)

The Emperor appears to suggest here that Calais and Dover are indispensable for the keeping of the sea in between these two ports as well as for providing Henry with bridgeheads for his Continental campaign to recover his 'regne' in France. Imperial authority signals ultimate sanction not only for Henry's Continental claims ('youre regne to recovere') but also 'to kepe the see'. The importance of Imperial authority and justification for the poem's defence of England's sovereignty over the British Sea is again accentuated by reminding the audience of Sigismund's presence and authority later in the poem: 'well conceyved the emperoure Sigesmounde, / That of all joyes made it one the moste / That Caleise was soget unto Englyssh coste' (lines 829–31).

From a historical, customary perspective, the *Libelle*'s unrelenting insistence on the Straits of Dover as the vital element in the poem's defence of England's claim to the sea appears to be, even by the standards of the influential Italian jurists mentioned above, a legitimate one. Incidentally, Parliament presented a proposal to Henry V in 1420 to claim the Channel as English dominion.[35] Henry politely refused this invitation to execute his sovereignty over the sea with the formula *soit avise par le Roy*, but, and this is significant for the inclusion of the legal evolution of the claim to territorial waters in this chapter, Parliament drafted the proposal in harmony with the opinions of

---

[35] *Rot. Parl.*, vol. 4, p. 126, entry for 1420.

Italian lawyers and justified its claim on the grounds that England possessed both shores.[36]

But the history of English claims to the sovereignty over the *mare adiacens* is not exhausted with the historical possessions in France. It was under Plantagenet rule that the phrase *guarder la mere* entered usage.[37] The term, later translated into English as 'kepe the se[e]', denoted primarily the countering of piracy or, more accurately, privateering along a country's adjacent coasts and, later, seas.[38] This latter distinction is brought to prominence by the fact that most early titles for the office that would later become known as 'Admiral' referred to coast-guarding rather than sea-guarding.[39] And so, following a French precedent, the first 'Admiral of the Sea of the King of England' was appointed in 1297, at first to keep the coasts and sea clear of pirates. The title seems to suggest that the sea was personally attached, through a royal prerogative (*regalium*), to the King because it was the King's peace which was being kept on the seas.[40] Later, the admiral was entrusted with naval warfare, but the initial justification was to reduce and prevent widespread piratical activity – in very much the same way in which Pompey acted as the Roman Republic's Admiral or *praeses*. As has been mentioned above, Bartolus argued that the sea be understood as territory because one would drive *homines males* off the sea just as one would drive criminals off one's land, referring to the established practice of appointing admirals in France and England.

A comparable treatment of the sea as territory, as far as pirates are concerned, can be found in the oldest collection of documents pertaining to maritime law in England, the *Black Book of the Admiralty*.[41] In the earliest part of the *Black Book*, a law on the banishing of felons (attributed by the text

36 'Par la grace de Dieu est venuz que nostre dit seignour le Roy est seignur des costes d'ambeparties del meer', *Rot. Parl.* vol. 4, p. 126.
37 Fulton, *Sovereignty of the Sea*, p. 31, n. 3.
38 Piracy, as understood between the twelfth and fifteenth centuries, is an elusive term. Whether a privateer was a pirate or operated under the sanction of, for instance, a hostile power, depended on the political circumstances and on the victim's perception. Privateers were regularly hired by states to perform piratical activities against an enemy, to police the sea or to participate in 'regular' military operations. I employ the term 'piracy' to denote privateers who rob at their own will without explicit or implicit sanction from a state. On the ambiguous nature of piracy in the fifteenth century, see C. J. Ford's article 'Piracy or Policy? Crisis in the Channel, 1400–1403', *Transactions of the Royal Historical Society* 29 (1979), 63–78.
39 Fulton, *Sovereignty of the Sea*, p. 31.
40 On the etymology of the title 'Admiral', see n. 14.
41 The *Black Book of the Admiralty*, a mysterious collection of documents that had been 'lost' for half a century before it was found at the bottom of a chest in 1873, was compiled in the fourteenth and fifteenth centuries and contains the earliest documents regulating maritime law. Amongst these are the influential Rolls of Oleron, which also form the beginning of French maritime law. The *Black Book* has been edited by Travers Twiss, *The Black Book of the Admiralty*, 4 vols (London, 1871–6) and there are a number of discussions of the history of the Rolls of Oleron: Karl-Friedrich Krieger, *Ursprung und Wurzeln der Rôles d'Oléron* (Cologne, 1970), Timothy J. Runyan, 'The Rolls of Oleron and the Admiralty Courts in Fourteenth-Century England', *American Journal of Legal History* 19:2 (1975), 95–111, and Georges Peyronnet, 'Un document capital de l'histoire du droit maritime: les rôles d'Oléron, XII-XVII siècles', *Sources, Travaux Historiques* 8 (1986), 3–10.

to Henry I but written in the thirteenth century) expressly banishes perpetrators from both land and sea:

> Et adonceques sera crie quil soit certain jour et lieu devant ladmiral a respondre au roy de certaine felonnie dont il est endite ou autrement il sera banny hors dAngleterre et de mer appartenant au roi dAngleterre par quarante ans ou plus ou moins.

> [and then it shall be cryed (or proclaymed) that hee come at some certaine ffelony whereof hee is indicted, otherwise hee shal be banished out of England and from the sea belonging to the king of England for forty yeares more or lesse.][42]

Two aspects of this passage are central for an understanding of the sea's growing territoriality. First, the sea, albeit not considered under the law to be similar in its nature to land, is nevertheless mentioned in the same breath as land, for the perpetrator is banished from England *and* from the sea belonging to the King of England. The second and equally important point is that the sea is attached to the King of England and *not* to England itself, just as the title of the Admiral reveals that the sea belongs to the King.

With the opinions and *consilia* of the Glossators and Post-Glossators in mind, the following legal argument appears plausible: claiming sovereignty over the sea is a royal prerogative, a *regalium*, a claim supported by extending the King's law to the sea (Bartolus's argument for the sea's territoriality). The quasi-feudal genesis of this concept is betrayed by not attaching it organically to the territory of the country but to the person of the King as *seignur*, reflecting the precedence of law over geography. During the fourteenth century, for example, English kings bore the title 'Lords of the English Sea'.[43] The titles 'Lord of the Sea' and 'King of the Sea' proved popular throughout the fourteenth and fifteenth centuries, providing evidence for the lasting appending of the sea to the person of the King.[44]

The following passage shows that the *Libelle* is aware of this tradition and insists on the sea being directly subject to the King (using custom – *per longam consuetudinem* – as the source of authority):

> And thus conclude I by auctorite
> Of cronicle that environ the see
> Shulde bene oures subjecte unto the kynge,
> And he be lorde therof for ony thynge (lines 944–7)

---

[42] Twiss, *The Black Book of the Admiralty*, vol. 1, pp. 58 and 59.
[43] AD 1336, *Rotuli Scotiae*, ed. D. Macpherson, 2 vols (London, 1814–19), vol. 1, p. 442 ('Domini Maris Anglicani').
[44] The *Foedera* (ed. Thomas Rymer and Robert Sanderson, 3 vols (London, 1816–69)) refer to the King as *seigneur de la mer* in 1320 (vol. 2, p. 434). The *Rot. Parl.* address the King as 'le roi de la mier' in 1372 (vol. 2, p. 311) and claim the title 'seignurs del meer' for English kings in 1420 (vol. 4, p. 126). See also the title of the admiral: 'Admiral of the Sea of the King of England' (p. 150).

A slight semantic shift, however, reveals the *Libelle*'s pivotal and hitherto unappreciated role in the history of the concept of territorial waters. The text states that the sea should be '*oures* subjecte unto the kynge' [my emphasis]. The possessive pronoun advances the view that the sea's territoriality is not so much vested in royal *regalia* alone, but is commonly owned by the King's subjects, 'oures' (perhaps a faint yet undoubtedly learned echo of the Roman doctrine *mare nostrum/mare est commune*). This collective ownership of the sea by England is stated even more directly in line 617: 'to make this lande have lordeshyp of the sea,' and lines 328 and 343 both have 'oure stremes'. Legal historians, driven by the objective of tracing and charting the development of territorial waters mainly in legal and administrative documents, appear to have overlooked this innovation. The communal, mercantile colonialism articulated in line 617 stems from a disappointment with Henry VI's failure to 'kepe the see', and the *Libelle* passionately puts forward the claim that the sea ought to be a possession ('have lordeshyp of the sea') of England, imbuing the body politic with sovereign *regalia* that allow for the seizing of the sea as territory.[45] The unruliness of the sea is captured in the anthropomorphic nature of contractual terminology: it is made a subject (line 946) and a vassal (line 617). But there is further evidence for the proposition that the *Libelle*, in a pioneering manner, advocates the concept of territorial waters.

Piracy forms a pressing concern for the *Libelle*. With mercantile interests prominent, the *Libelle* dedicates much space to the fight against piracy as a justification for the forceful keeping of the sea. When naming the notorious Flemish pirate Hankyn de Lyons, the *Libelle* adduces another argument to vindicate the sovereignty over the sea:

> Thane Hankyn Lyons shulde not be so bolde
> To stoppe us and oure shippes for to holde[46]
> Unto oure shame; he hadde be betene thens. (lines 602–4)

The text invites the reader to subscribe to its aim of purging 'the see unto oure grete avayle' (line 612) so that the prosperity of the nation be no longer compromised by pirates. Guarding the sea against piracy is also adduced by the *Libelle* as a vindication for integrating the sea with England's territory.

This emancipation of the sea as fully fledged territory is expressed in a

---

45 Under meaning 1(c) of 'lordeshype', the *MED* gives the following: 'ownership (of lands, wealth, etc.), possession'. Furthermore, senses 2(b) and (c) have 'the land or territory belonging to a king or ruler' and 'a district or province in a country', respectively. There are a number of other relevant senses. Most revealing, perharps, is sense 4 as well as the example adduced by the *MED*: '(a) A feudal estate or an aggregate of such estates; manor; demesne land; an estate held by the sovereign; ~ royal; ~ of Irlond, Ireland considered as the holding of the English kings; also *fig.*; (b) the power, authority, or rule of a feudal lord; also *fig.*'

46 The marginal gloss has: 'This tyme anno regni regis Henrici VI. xiiij. was Hankyne Lyons archer[o]bere on the see, and afore Pety Pynson. Allas, allas.' The anxiety about the disastrous consequences of piracy expressed in this comment ('Allas, allas') shows that merchants were not only well informed as far as Flemish pirates were concerned ('afore Pety Pynson'), but that piracy was a lasting concern for merchants as well as for coastal communities.

Figure 9. Henry VI's noble, struck 1422–61. The obverse side shows Henry VI on board a ship.

number of instances that underline the territorial equivalence of land and sea. From the outset, the poem refers to the centrality of keeping the sea. Derived from the French *guarder la mere*, to 'kepe the see' refers to the defence and the policing of coastal and adjacent waters.[47] The *Libelle*, however, uses the same term to express the perceived political need to 'keep' land, suggesting that 'kepe' means more than just protecting and policing. Line 700 has 'To kepen Yrelond that it be not loste', stating that Ireland could be won or lost. By analogy, this would imply that the sea can also be an object in these territorial negotiations and quarrels. In the same way, Wales and Calais must be 'kepte' (line 783: 'An exhortacione to the kepynge of Walys', and line 817: 'An exortacion of the sure kepynge of Calise'). If the sea can be kept (and lost) just as land, then the territoriality of the sea and land must have similar properties. Indeed, ships are said to 'ryde' into ports (line 678), and, perhaps most memorably, the text resorts to the King's seal to express this unprecedented parity of land and sea. Earlier, the text reminds the reader, the English noble features four items: 'Kyng, shype and swerde and pouer of the see' (line 35). The obverse side of the noble shows the King with sword in hand on a ship, representing the King's claims to the sea (Figure 9).[48] This idea of the two-sided medallion returns when the *Libelle* introduces the King's great seal:

---

[47] Colin Richmond discusses sea-keeping in the early fifteenth century in 'The Keeping of the Seas during the Hundred Years War: 1422–1440', *History*, n.s. 49 (1964), 283–98, and 'English Naval Power in the Fifteenth Century', *History*, n.s. 52 (1967), 1–15.

[48] In a cynical and punning manoeuvre the text goes on to suggest replacing the ship with a sheep, alluding to a contemporary insult repeatedly hurled against the English in Brittany and Flanders. The larger context of this reference, it would seem, could have been the selling of Henry V's great armada: 'Where bene oure shippes, where bene oure swerdes become?' (line 36).

> Liche as the seale, the grettest of thys londe,
> On the one syde hathe, as I understonde,
> Aprince rydynge wyth hys swerde idrawe,
> In the other syde sittynge (lines 588–91)

The seal shows a riding knight on one side, symbolising control of the land, and the other depicts the enthroned King 'by sceptre and swerde', as the marginal gloss states. By analogy, the *Libelle* claims that there should also be a great seal for the sea:

> So one lychewysse I wolde were on the see.
> By the noble that swerde schulde have powere
> And the shippes one the see aboute us here. (lines 595–7)

Drawing on the noble's motif to express the sea's territorial emancipation, the poem proposes that the King should have a second great seal dedicated to the sea and the keeping of the sea ('swerde schulde have powere') to match the existing seal. This juxtaposition of land and sea, together with the emphasis on territoriality in the context of piracy, is perhaps the most forceful argument for the *Libelle*'s groundbreaking contribution to the development of the notion of territorial waters.

The pretensions of the Kings of England to sovereignty over the sea are also expressed in a document, which, some historians argue, is a draft never intended for circulation. Apart from styling himself 'Lord of the Sea' and acting as a determined sea-keeper, Edward III may have been responsible for producing a roll with the title *De Superioritate Maris Angliae et Jure Officii Admirallatus in eodem* [On the Supremacy of the Sea of England and the Right of the Office of Admiralty in the Same].[49] The most important feature of this document is a memorandum on the allegedly ancient supremacy of the Kings of England over the sea.[50] The memorandum summons the historical authority of Edward I as a token of his achievement in providing the legal framework to maintain the 'ancient supremacy of the crown in the sea of England' [antiquam Superioritatem Maris Angliae].[51] It also states that the basic maritime laws which were in place at the time were the Rolls of Oleron, supposedly instituted by Richard I on his return from the Holy Land.[52] This roll is, amongst other evidence, the best *prima facie* indication of Edward's

---

[49] *Chancery Rolls*, Miscellaneous Inquisitions, Treatises and Diplomatic, Bundle 14, No. 15, membrane 4.

[50] Edward also expressed this claim in a mandate to his admirals in 1336: 'We, calling to mind that our progenitors ... were Lords of the English Sea' (Fulton, *The Sovereignty of the Sea*, p. 36).

[51] *Chancery Rolls*, Miscellaneous Inquisitions etc.

[52] *Chancery Rolls*, Miscellaneous Inquisitions etc. There are numerous circumstantial reasons why this is not more than a ceremonial attribution to Richard. First, after being shipwrecked in 1192 on his return from the Holy Land, Richard was captured and handed over to Emperor Henry VI, who only set him free in 1194. Richard then went back to England, travelling through Flanders and therefore cannot have written the laws at Oléron before taking them to England. Second, the Rolls show no sign that somebody as important as a king had anything to do with their 'codi-

reputation as a King of England committed to the sea's cause. Yet it is important not to forget that, despite his significant role in the history of England's claim to the sea, Edward believed in the *mare liberum*.[53] Foreign fishermen and merchants were readily permitted free use of England's sea, the extent of which was never defined, and, in consistence with other English sovereigns, Edward did not alter the fact that England never exercised a 'right to exclude others from an equal use of a particular sea'.[54]

Before the *Libelle*'s contribution to the theory of territorial waters can be assessed, one adjustment to the current understanding of the development of this concept in England must be made, namely the observation that the notion of the sea as 'territory' was further advanced in England than has hitherto been admitted. On the one hand, there is the quasi-feudal/contractual basis for the titles English kings relied on to express and vindicate their claims to the sea. On the other hand, there is the circumstantial evidence for an exclusive claim to the sea in certain regulations of the admiralty. The earliest maritime regulation appears to be the so-called 'striking of the sail'. This naval ordinance is accredited to King John who is said to have issued it in 1201 although the earliest manuscript containing this ordinance dates from the fifteenth century.[55] The ordinance requires all foreign vessels to lower their sails when sighted by one of the King's ships, thereby paying homage to England's territorial claims over the sea. That this regulation was in force during the fifteenth century lies beyond doubt. The first recorded incident involving the 'right to the flag' occurred in 1402 (antedating the oldest MS containing the ordinance) and, curiously, concerned a ship not in the Channel but in the North Sea.[56] In a letter to Thomas Daniel, dated 25 May 1449, Robert Wennington describes an incident that occurred near the coast and involved 'a flote of a c grete schyppys of Pruse, Lubycke, Campe, Rastocke, Holond, Selond *and* Flandres' refusing to strike their sails. Wennington was rebuked and he complains that he could not enforce the King's laws because he 'had so fewe schyppys *and* so smale, that they scornyd w*yth* [him]'.[57]

According to the doctrine of the *mare liberum*, the sea is common to all just as everything that is in the sea is common to all. Bartolus argues that islands actually do not belong to the sea but to the nearest coast (provided the distance does not exceed 100 miles), thus leaving this aspect of Roman teaching on the *mare liberum* intact. The thirteenth-century 'Rules and

fication' (Krieger, *Ursprung und Wurzeln der Rôles d'Oléron*, p. 43). Third, the laws were not recorded until *c.* 1286. I am grateful to Edda Frankot for these insights.

53 Although not mentioned directly in the poem as this would contradict its argumentative thrust, Edward backed the freedom of the seas. In the *Libelle* he is presented as a defender of mercantile interests: 'For he hadde a manere gelozye / To hys marchauntes' (lines 186–7).

54 Fulton, *The Sovereignty of the Sea*, p. 33.

55 Twiss dates the oldest MS containing this ordinance as having been completed before 1422 and most probably in 1420 (*The Black Book of the Admiralty*, vol. 1, Introduction, p. xix).

56 Fulton, *The Sovereignty of the Sea*, p. 43.

57 I am grateful to Richard Beadle for making accessible to me this re-edited letter from a forthcoming edition of the Paston Letters by Richard Beadle and Colin Richmond.

Orders about Admiralty Matters' in the *Black Book of the Admiralty* explain in painstaking detail the implications for those who conceal flotsam from the Admiral. Flotsam, the regulation states, belongs to the Admiral, who is acting on behalf of the *seignur* of the sea:

> Item soit enquiz de tous ceulx qui ont trouve sur la mer tonnel ou pippe de vin flotants balles de marchandises ou autre chose quelconque comme *floteson*, cest assavoir quant la mer a eut plus grant maistrie que la terre, et contelent hors de la possession de ladmiral, se aucun est endite et ce convicte par douze il paiera la value de ce quil a ainsi trouve.

> [Item, lett inquiry be made of all those whoe have found at sea caske or pipe of wine floating, bales of goods, or any other thing whatsover, as ffloatson, (that is to say) when the sea hath greater power than the land, and doe conceale the same from the possession of the admiral. If any one be thereof indicted and convicted by twelve men, hee shall pay the value of what hee soe found.][58]

Although this passage acknowledges the sea's profound difference to land ('la mer a eut plus grant maistrie que la terre'), it asserts the King's authority at sea, though this is of course not an example of a territorial undertaking of the sea. It is clear that, at least in legal practice, the sea was frequently considered as some form of territory, although the extent of which was never precisely demarcated.[59] A similar, although land-like, treatment of the sea appears to have been in practice in 1379 when Parliament required passing ships to pay a duty 'just as one may exact payment for passage over one's field'.[60]

From a legal perspective, the *Libelle* adduces perhaps the weightiest argument for England's sovereignty over the sea by establishing a list of historical precedents of kings who have shown, asserted and enforced this claim in some form. It is no coincidence that this list corresponds to the names discussed above: Edgar, Edward III and Henry V. In fact, the listing of historical precedent creates a legal argument simulating common law practice. Having completed an enumeration of the commodities of the various

[58] Twiss, *The Black Book*, vol. 1, pp. 82–3.
[59] Albeit a speculation, it is worthwhile contemplating whether this belief did not originate in the spiritual claim of God's rule over the sea. In Chapter 2 of 'Marvellous Passages: English Nautical Piety in the Middle Ages and the Renaissance' (PhD thesis, University of California Riverside, 1999), James Conlan argues that Chaucer's *Man of Law's Tale* is an instance of offering a spiritual justification (God saving Custance at sea) for legal claims, although not necessarily maritime ones: 'the tradition of grounding extra-legal principles in divine judgements on the sea was of such long standing that as early as the fourteenth century, Geoffrey Chaucer described it as an antiquated principle of legal advocacy' (p. 56).
[60] Fulton, *The Sovereignty of the Sea*, p. 34, from N. H. Nicolas, *History of the Royal Navy*, 2 vols (London, 1847), vol. 2, p. xv. Edda Frankot informs me that England was not the only northern European kingdom with an advanced territorial notion of the sea. Denmark, for example, also levied a toll (Sound toll) from 1426 for all ships sailing through the Sound, with the effect that most of the trade between the North and Baltic Seas was taxed.

European countries and regions trading in England, Chapter 11 of the *Libelle* introduces its historically motivated plea:

> Aftere the chapitles of commoditees of dyuerse landes shewyth the conclusione of kepynge of the see environ by a storye of kynge Edgare and ij. incidentes of kynge Edwarde the iij^{de} and kynge Herry the vth.[61]

The mode in which this is presented corresponds to orthodox legal practice: following an exposition of the poem's case, the text proceeds to provide three precedents of 'kepyng of the see environ'. The first lines of this chapter again seize on the English noble, this time rendering the sea's parity with land even clearer:

> Now see well thane that in this rounde see
> To oure noble be paryformytee.
> Within the shypp is shewyd there the sayle
> And oure kynge of royall apparaylle,
> Wyth swerde drawen, bryght, sharp and extente,
> For to chastisen enmyes vyolente;
> So shulde he be lorde of the see aboute,
> To kepe enmyes fro wythine and wythoute,
> And to be holde thorowgh Cristianyte
> Master and lorde environ of the see. (lines 852–61)

There is no qualitative distinction implied here between being lord of the land and lord of the sea, rather, the phrase 'so shulde he be lorde of the see aboute' corroborates the analogous nature of the King's two realms. The text proceeds to King Edgar who built 'full thre thousande and sex hundred' (line 918) ships during the summer months to patrol the sea surrounding England, and who summoned 'viij. kynges' who were 'subdite to hym' (lines 966–7) to row with him, each holding an oar. Edgar's intimate relationship with the sea exceeds political boundaries as he is said to have sat 'in the shipp behynde / As sterisman' (lines 972–3), a position that 'hym becam of kynde' (line 973). To some extent 'sterisman' embodies the King's political qualities as sovereign of the ship of state, on the other, being 'sterisman' by natural inclination accentuates Edgar's marriage to the sea.[62] Next, Edward III is introduced as a king who balanced the land and the sea in his achievements: 'On londe, on see ye knowe his worthynesse' (line 981). This sentiment is echoed in the prose *Brut*, where Edward is 'a noble warryour, and a fortunable, bothe on lond and on the see', and in Jan van Boendale's *Deeds of the Dukes of Brabant*: 'Dat was Edewaert van Inghelant, / Die over zee vacht metter hant'

---

61 *The Libelle of Englyshe Polycye*, ed. Warner, Chapter 11, heading.
62 In Venice, the Doge's ceremonial wedding with the sea offers an exciting analogy. Cf. p. 28, n. 19.

157

[That was Edward of England who guards the sea with his person].[63] The *Libelle* concentrates on Edward's winning the Battle of Crecy and building a navy that was unmatched in his days: 'In whose tyme was no navey in the see / That myght wythstonde the power of hys mageste' (lines 1,002–3). Earlier in the poem, Edward is said to have 'felt the weyes to reule well the see' (line 188), that is, he explored ('felt') various policies to master the British seas. Finally, Henry V receives praise for having built a plethora of ships ('prince kynge Herry the vth and of his grete shippes' (line 1,009)) as well as having reached the equilibrium and, thus, perfect parity in his governance over land and sea: 'By lande and see so well he hym acquite' (line 1,046).

By the mid-1430s, the perception of the sea as territory was already advanced in England, though the legal concept of territorial waters had not been arrived at. Yet on a political, legal and, perhaps most importantly, cognitive level, the *Libelle* articulates the concept of territorial waters a century and a half before Albericus Gentilis is credited with having done so. Its overarching argument enlists a number of points made by jurists and experts elsewhere. The *Libelle*'s notion of the sea's territoriality rests on employing imperial *regalia* and authority as well as using precedent in the form of listing the 'cases' of three Kings of England. This claim is further strengthened by the need to curb piracy (corresponding to Bartolus's argument) and the constant reiteration of the political and territorial equality of land and sea.

Exactly to what extent the writer was familiar with legal treatises on the sea is difficult to determine but the argument the text constructs corresponds in its pivotal points to those made by pre-modern jurists. The composition date of the *Libelle* (1436/7) falls into the historical 'grey area' during which a notion of some form of authority over the sea had been developed although no widely held theory of territorial waters was in existence. What is important, however, is that the *Libelle* documents how far the perception of the sea had undergone modification by the early fifteenth century. This poem shows that it is possible for a late fifteenth-century writer to conceive of the sea as quantifiable, governable territory, thus sealing the land's mastery over the sea.

Although innovative, the *Libelle* is not completely isolated in its claim. Only a few years later, in 1453, John Capgrave's *Liber de illustribus Henricis* assumes a similar position on the subject of England's sea-keeping.[64] Echoing the *Libelle*'s (and Gildas's) assertion that the sea used to be a natural wall surrounding England ('Kepe than the see abought in speciall, / Whiche of

---

63 *The Brut or the Chronicles of England*, ed. F. W. D. Brie, 2 vols, EETS, o.s. 131 and 136 (London, 1906 and 1908), vol. 2, page 333, and *De Brabantsche yeesten, of Rymkronyk van Braband, door Jan de Klerk, van Antwerpen*, ed. J. F. Willems (Brussels, 1839), Chapter 11, lines 873–4. This second passage even seems to allude to the expression 'the sea of the King of England' which appends the sea to the person of the King.

64 *John Capgrave: Liber de Illustribus Henricis*, ed. Francis Charles Hingeston, Rolls Series 7 (London, 1858). Capgrave, an Augustinian friar, compiled his somewhat eccentric biography of famous Henrys (Imperial as well as English) between 1446 and 1453.

England is the rounde wall' (lines 1,092–3)), Capgrave chastises Henry VI for allowing the sea to lose its protective function as England's wall:

> Dictum est ab antiquis, quod murus Angliae mare sit; et, cum inimici nostri supra murum sint, quid putas facient accolis improvisis? Quoniam hoc negotium jam per multos annos neglectum est, idcirco hoc contigit, quod jam naves paucæ sunt, nautæ quoque rari, et ii ineruditi, quoniam non exercitati. Auferat Dominus opprobrium nostrum, et suscitet spiritum forti-tudinis in gente nostra! Falsas et fictas amicitias aliarum nationum denudat, ne subito veniant super nos dum non timemus.

> [It was said by the ancients that the sea is like England's wall; and, since the enemies are pressing at the gates, what do you think they will do with unexpected neighbours? Since then this task has already been disregarded for many years, this, therefore, comes to pass, that ships are now few and sailors, too, are rare, and what few sailors we have are unlearned because they lack the practice. May the Lord remove our disgrace and raise the spirit of strength in our people! May he reveal the false and deceiving friendships of other nations, lest they come upon us all of a sudden while we are not afraid.][65]

The keeping of the seas has been neglected for many years, says Capgrave, and he complains about the inadequate state of the navy ('naves paucæ sunt') as well as the chronic unavailability of good sailors ('rari' and 'ineruditi'). All this, continues the text, plays into the hands of England's enemies. Although the *Libelle* has not succeeded in altering England's naval and maritime poli-cies, it has sown a seed that continued to grow until it reached Selden's *Mare clausum*.

The legal understanding of the sea as territory represents only the last stage of stripping the sea of its mythical, unpredictable qualities in some of the new discourses of the fifteenth century. The gradual measuring and quan-tification of the sea – it must be noted here that jurists could not agree on the extent of the *mare adiacens* until 1648[66] – shows how profoundly the percep-tion of the sea has evolved in those spheres of human activity that can be traced in literature. At times, literary texts such as the *Libelle* even become agents of epistemological shifts. Because it is impossible, by virtue of writers' social involvement, completely to isolate mimetic and non-mimetic literature from epistemological change, representations of the sea as the realm of the unknown – the balancing item to naturalistic components in romances and other narratives – became gradually outmoded in those types of writing that were adjusted to or increasingly shaped by non-traditional tastes. The new realities of large numbers of pilgrims, soldiers and merchants crossing the sea in organised, pragmatic ways challenged outdated perceptions of the sea

---

[65] *Liber de Illustribus Henricis*, p. 136. My translation.
[66] In fact, one could argue that no agreement was reached until 1994, and even that is not binding. See n. 1.

as a powerful muscle of divine Providence. Rather than being seen again as the integrator of shores, the sea has been paved by the non-literary sea-lanes and trade-routes. To some extent, then, the mythical sea of the British Isles, that had once connected ideas and shores, could not withstand the arrival of navigators' instruments, merchants' abacuses and jurists' rulers.

And so, by the time Gonzalo suffers shipwreck in Shakespeare's *Tempest*, he is able to quantify the sea and speak of it as if it were land by applying units of land measurement – furlongs – to the sea and, simultaneously, wish for the similarity of land and sea by hinting at the yearned-for exchange-ability of the two: 'Now would I give a thousand furlongs of sea for an acre of barren ground – long heath, brown furze, anything. The wills above be done, but I would fain die a dry death.'[67]

---

[67] William Shakespeare, *The Tempest*, ed. David Lindley, The New Cambridge Shakespeare (Cambridge, 2002), Act 1, Scene 1, lines 56–8.

Epilogue

The Tempest's Many Beginnings

After all is said and done, and the Milan-bound party has left the stage, Prospero turns to the audience in one of Shakespeare's rare and perhaps last epilogues. Speaking of himself as 'confined' in 'this bare island', he asks the audience for release 'from [his] bands'

> With the help of your good hands.
> Gentle breath of yours my sails
> Must fill, or else my project fails,
> Which was to please. Now I want
> Spirits to enforce, art to enchant,
> And my ending is despair;
> Unless I be relieved by prayer
> Which pierces so, that it assaults
> Mercy itself, and frees all faults.
> As you from crimes would pardoned be,
> Let your indulgence set me free.[1]

But Prospero is free. At least according to William Falconer's late eighteenth-century syllogism:

> The inhabitants of islands … have a higher relish for liberty than those of the continents; and therefore are in general free. Thus the inhabitants of Great Britain were a free people, according to the first accounts we have of them.[2]

Falconer's passage is sometimes cited by historians as a quintessentially Insular product, but the similarity in wording with Thomas Nugent's 1750 translation of Montesquieu's *L'esprit des lois* (1748) betrays the sentiment to be an older and Continental one. In Montesquieu's work it is the sea that secures the freedom of islanders:

---

1 William Shakespeare, *The Tempest*, ed. David Lindley, The New Cambridge Shakespeare (Cambridge, 2002), Epilogue, lines 10–20. All references are to this edition.
2 William Falconer, *Remarks on the Influence of Climate etc.* (London, 1781). Quoted from Kathleen Wilson, *The Island Race: Englishness, Empire and Gender in the Eighteenth Century* (London and New York, 2003), p. 54. On eighteenth-century (and later) associations of islands with freedom, see Wilson's book, pp. 87 ff and passim.

The people of the isles have a higher relish for liberty than those of the continent. Islands are commonly of a small extent; one part of the people cannot be so easily employed to oppress the other; the sea separates them from great empires; so that they cannot be countenanced by tyranny: conquerors are stopp'd by the sea, the islanders themselves are not involved in conquests, and more easily preserve their laws.[3]

Freedom in the sense in which Montesquieu and Falconer use it (and as Churchill does when he speaks of 'our Island') is negative freedom, or negative liberty according to Isaiah Berlin's influential essay on the topic.[4] In contrast to positive freedom ('freedom to'), that is, the freedom to do what one wishes to do, negative freedom simply means the absence of restrictions, boundaries or limitations ('freedom from'). Therefore, when Montesquieu and Churchill speak of free islands they speak of the negative freedom these islands enjoy, of their independence from their neighbours whom they, strictly speaking, do not have by virtue of being islands. This independence of islands is guarded by the presence of the sea which stops conquerors, according to Montesquieu, and guards the island like a wall, the *murus Angliae* of John Capgrave and the *Libelle*. And as Thomas Jefferson's adage stresses (page 146 above), this freedom only belongs to an island if it cannot be taken away by others. In other words, Montesquieu's proposed freedom depends on an island's control over the sea.

Cardinal Richelieu's maxim, quoted at the beginning of the previous chapter (page 140), spells out the need for a ruler to exercise mastery over both land and sea to keep his realm safe. Richelieu had seventeenth-century France in mind but as the anonymous writer behind the *Libelle* has shown, this maxim carries all the more significance for fifteenth-century England. Mastery over land means conquest and colonisation; it is what Brutus did to Gogmagog and the giants of Albion, it is what the *Libelle* proposes be done to the 'wylde Iryshe',[5] and it is what Prospero does to Caliban (and, later, Robinson Crusoe to Friday). But such a reign can never be certain or free – at least from the perspective of its rulers – until the sea is also contained. The *Libelle* would like England's navy to reach this goal whilst Prospero, another island ruler, achieves this control through his magical abilities: 'I'll deliver all, / And promise you calm seas, auspicious gales' (Act 5, Scene 1, lines 311–12).

To control the sea, therefore, means much more than the ability to master uncertainty and control narratives. Sway over the elements is, as we have seen, the privilege of the divine, of God, of Neptune before him. Yet it also spells out Prospero's mastery of his island's freedom and identity. After all, islands

---

3   Charles Louis de Montesquieu, *L'esprit des lois*, trans. Thomas Nugent (1750) in *The Spirit of the Laws: A Compendium of the First English Edition*, ed. David Wallace Carrithers (Berkeley, 1977), Book 18, Chapter 5, p. 283.

4   Isaiah Berlin, 'Two Concepts of Liberty', in *Four Essays on Liberty* (Oxford, 1969), pp. 118–72. The essay was first published in 1958.

5   The Irish are branded 'wylde' at lines 687, 691, 716, 721, 725 and possibly 749.

are defined by their immediate geographic context, the sea, and acceptance of and control over the sea secures the island's independence ('freedom from'), prolonging its cultural insularity. Having 'domesticated' Caliban and subjugated the sea's will to his own, Prospero expresses an insular understanding of Englishness that integrates both land and sea. Commenting on the pantomime adaptation of *Robinson Crusoe*, first performed in 1781, Kathleen Wilson, notes that 'as in other famous English island fictions, such as *The Tempest*, mastery over both sea and land and their various inhabitants is deemed crucial for sea-girt civilisations'.[6] To some extent, then, it has been an implied ambition of this book to show that Englishness, like the freedom of islands, is an island fiction sustained by a growing physical and cultural mastery over the sea.

But to reduce *The Tempest* to a dramatic meditation on political mastery over land and sea would do the play grave injustice. It is – and has been for most of the last two decades – all too tempting to see in Caliban a metonymy for the peoples of the New World and in Prospero a 'problematised' configuration of all that is complex and multifaceted about England's newfangled colonialism. Just how thin the ice is on which such readings are still being advanced has been shown by Tristan Marshall in a provocative article some years ago.[7] Although his reading is still contested by many, Marshall has dismantled a key building brick of those theories, namely the frequent claim that Shakespeare modelled the actual storm on an incident reported in a letter written by William Strachey about the tempest which hit the *Sea Venture* on Monday 24 July 1609. The first performance of the play was in 1611 but the letter was not published until 1625, when it appeared it Samuel Purchas's *Hakluytus posthumus or Purchas his pilgrimes*.[8] Consequently it has been claimed – without a single shred of evidence – that this letter had circulated before its publication and passed through Shakespeare's hands before he penned *The Tempest*. But there is nothing particularly exciting or even characteristic about Strachey's account of the shipwreck. A good deal less far-fetched as a source would be Gower's *Confessio Amantis*, which Shakespeare and/or his collaborator had access to by 1607 or 1608 when writing *Pericles, Prince of Tyre*.[9] Two recent editors of *Pericles* go even further and claim that Shakespeare 'knew early in his career of Gower's work'.[10] Gower's *Confessio Amantis* features a number of spectacular storm passages, such as those in Book 3, lines 981 ff. and, more pertinently, the storm description in the tale of Apollonius itself, Book 8, lines 604 ff (discussed in Chapter

6 Wilson, *The Island Race*, p. 88.
7 Tristan Marshall, '*The Tempest* and the British Imperium in 1611', *Historical Journal* 41:2 (1998), 375–400.
8 Marshall, '*The Tempest* and the British Imperium', 376–7.
9 William Shakespeare, *The Comedy of Erorrs*, ed. Charles Walters Whitworth, The Oxford Shakespeare (Oxford, 2002), p. 29: 'Certainly Shakespeare and/or his collaborator (probably George Wilkins) had seen a copy of Gower's work by the time they wrote *Pericles* in 1607 or 1608.'
10 Shakespeare, *Pericles, Prince of Tyre*, ed. Doreen DelVecchio and Antony Hammond, The New Cambridge Shakespeare (Cambridge, 1998), p. 3.

4 above).[11] Storm passages are common topoi in pre-modern writings; they appear, as this book has shown, in chronicles, dream visions, biblical paraphrases and in virtually every other form of writing. In fact, Shakespeare only had to read Acts of the Apostles 27 to find an evocative storm-setting.

My reasons for ending the book with *The Tempest* and for taking this slant on the play are two-fold: first, I mean to show how heavily indebted the play is not just to the ubiquitous romance tradition but also to the many facets of the sea in pre-modern literature; second, I hope to offer an afterthought on the book that will centre the play between old and new, between established continuities of the sea in Insular writing and the beginning of other, as yet uncharted traditions. Anne Barton argues that *The Tempest* 'will lend itself to almost any interpretation, any set of meanings imposed upon it: it will even make them shine'.[12] The play's extraordinary pliancy, it would appear to me, lies in its occupying the interface between old and new.

Habitually ignored by editors of the play, Prospero's setting adrift has been studied by Helen Cooper, who has shown on at least two occasions that it is heir to the long-standing topos of rudderless boats.[13] Similarly, there is more than just an echo of the *heremum in oceano*, the desert in the ocean, when Gonzalo yearns 'for an acre of barren ground' whilst fearing to drown. All the editor of the New Cambridge Shakespeare has to say about this passage is that 'Gonzalo's desire for "an acre of barren ground" is fulfilled (in a way he does not anticipate) by the "desert" he first sees the island to be (Act 2, Scene 1, line 34)'.[14] But ocean deserts and desert islands have been a commonplace ever since Columba sought the sea desert or Brendan reached the island of the hermit Paul, who arrived there by magical boat eighty years earlier.

To this one can add many other continuities in *The Tempest*. When Miranda asks her father how they survived their setting adrift, Prospero replies that it was '[b]y providence divine' (Act 1, Scene 2, line 159). This observation, integral to the afterlife of the topos of setting adrift, is another expression of *deus gubernator*, the motif of God-as-helmsman. Celebrated in the Brendan-tradition, it also informs the description of Margery's journey to Dansk and it is a part of the many allegorical descriptions of *ecclesia*, a ship sailing over the sea of the world, steered by divine Providence.

Not all of the play's maritime aspects can be firmly embedded in a given literary tradition. Antonio's and Sebastian's cynicism notwithstanding, to

---

[11] These and other storm passages are discussed in Nicholas Jacobs, 'Alliterative Storms: A Topos in Middle English', *Speculum* 47:4 (1972), 695–719, passim.

[12] *The Tempest*, ed. Anne Barton, The New Penguin Shakespeare (Harmondsworth, 1968), p. 22.

[13] Helen Cooper, 'Prospero's Boats: Magic, Providence and Human Choice', in *Renaissance Essays for Kitty Scoular Datta*, ed. Sukarta Chaudhuri (Oxford and Calcutta, 1995), pp. 160–75, and 'Providence and the Sea: "No Tackle, Sail, nor Mast"' in *The English Romance in Time: Transforming Motifs from Geoffrey of Monmouth to the Death of Shakespeare* (Oxford, 2004) pp. 106–36.

[14] *The Tempest*, ed. Lindley, p. 7. It is actually Adrian not Gonzalo who calls the island a desert in Act 2, Scene 1, line 34.

Adrian and Gonzalo the island is a no-place, a *utopos*, with a flourishing, nigh spontaneous fecundity that recalls Columbus's description of Trinidad and the Earthly Paradise in the legend of Brendan: 'ADRIAN: "It must needs be of subtle, tender and delicate temperance"' (Act 2, Scene 1, line 41). Unimpressed by Antonio's and Sebastian's interruptions, Gonzalo then speaks of the vegetation's 'rarity' that is 'indeed almost beyond credit' (lines 56–7), before noting the effects of this otherworldly climate on his garments: 'Methinks our garments as fresh as when we put them on first in Afric' (lines 65–6).[15] Furthermore, as people are 'sea-swallowed' (line 247) and then 'belched ... up' (Act 3, Scene 3, line 56) again, *The Tempest* calls into memory not just the whale's regurgitation of Jonah but also the sea's synonymity with the Devil and Leviathan. But even beyond these observations, the sea in this play is imbued with many of the qualities that express bitterness, hostility and liminality in the texts discussed in this book: not unlike Old English compounding, Prospero speaks of 'sea-sorrow' (Act 1, Scene 2, line 170); Francisco talks of 'contentious waves' (Act 2, Scene 1, line 113) and Sebastian likens himself to 'standing water' (line 217) to verbalise his half-conscious, half-asleep state. There are mariners' superstitions (Act 5, Scene 1, lines 216–20) and, above all, there is the sea in almost everything Prospero says.

Storms, islands, deserts in the ocean, setting adrift, God as helmsman – all these are not inventions of Shakespeare; rather, he reassembles these established strands of the literary sea to open up new trajectories for thinking and writing about the sea as part of and beyond romance. *The Tempest* emerges, at least if read as a commentary on the chapters of this book, as steeped in the rich Insular traditions of the sea. But the play also taps into the developing debate about Englishness by offering a multivocal commentary on freedom, insularity, the sea and providence.

England's shock defeat of the Spanish Armada in 1588 brought insularity and independence into the centre of political and religious discourses. This was unprecedented in English history. Wellington's victory at Waterloo could never compete with 1588 because the defeat of the Armada secured the island *qua* island and established its significance for Englishness in a way that a Continental battle never could, or, as one historian puts it: 'the mythologised Armada was still serviceable in the 1940s ... [and] ... became an indispensable ingredient of "our island story"'.[16] That the impact of this victory was absorbed so quickly and lastingly was due not least to the existence of the various pre-modern traditions that explored the constantly changing approaches to the sea. Like a palimpsest holding the cultural memory of five centuries, *The Tempest* preserves the many traditions of the sea, inflected by the assertive insularity of the post-Armada years, for the new departures of

---

15 Marshall discusses the links between *The Tempest* and the Fortunate Isles, albeit in a slightly different context, in '*The Tempest* and the British Imperium', 390 ff.

16 John R. Gillis, *Commemorations: The Politics of National Identity* (Princeton, 1994), p. 64.

later English writings. The play signals the end of the long process of coming to terms with insularity. But the process that would enable this absorption and appropriation of the sea had begun much earlier, when Anglo-Norman writers first started looking at the Continent from their island homes.

Bibliography

Anthologies are listed under the name of the editor, and anonymous works are listed by their title. Medieval writers appear under their first name unless it is customary to use their surname (e.g.: Geoffrey Chaucer, John Gower).

Primary Sources

Aberdeen Bestiary, Aberdeen University Library MS 24

Adam of Bremen, *Adami Bremensis Gesta Hammaburgensis Ecclesiae Pontificum*, ed. W. Trillmich, Quellen des 9. und 11. Jahrhunderts zur Geschichte der Hamburgischen Kirche und des Reiches (Darmstadt, 2000)

—— *Adam of Bremen: History of the Archbishops of Hamburg-Bremen*, trans. Francis J. Tschan, introduction and bibliography by Timothy Reuter (New York, 2002)

Adomnán's Life of Columba, ed. A. O. Anderson and M. O. Anderson; rev. M. O. Anderson (Oxford, 1961; repr. 1991)

Albericus Gentilis, *De Iure Belli*, ed. T. E. Holland, 3 vols (Oxford, 1877)

Ambrose, *Hexaemeron*, in *Sancti Ambrosii Mediolanensis Episcopi – Opera Omnia*, ed. J.-P. Migne, *PL* 14 (Paris, 1845)

Andreas, in *The Vercelli Book*, ed. George Philip Krapp, Anglo-Saxon Poetic Records 2 (New York, 1932; repr. 1961)

Andrew, Malcolm and Ronald Waldron, eds, *The Poems of the Pearl Manuscript: Pearl, Cleanness, Patience, Sir Gawain and the Green Knight* (Exeter, 1987; fourth edn; originally published 1978)

The Anglo-Saxon Chronicle: A Collaborative Edition, ed. Janet M. Bately, vol. 3, *MS A* (Cambridge, 1986)

Arnold, Matthew, *The Poems of Matthew Arnold*, ed. Kenneth Allott (London, 1965)

Auden, W. H., *The Enchafèd Flood or the Romantic Iconography of the Sea* (London, 1951)

Augustine, *The City of God Against the Pagans*, ed. and trans. R. W. Dyson (Cambridge, 1998)

—— *De Civitate Dei*, ed. J. E. C. Welldon, 2 vols (London, 1924)

—— *Ennarationes In Psalmos*, ed. E. Dekkers and J. Fraipont, CCSL 38–40, 3 vols (Turnhout, 1956)

Bartholomaeus Anglicus, *De proprietatibus rerum*, trans. John Trevisa (1342–1402), in *On the Properties of Things, John Trevisa's Translation of Bartholomaeus Anglicus De Proprietatibus Rerum, a Critical Text*, gen. ed. M. C. Seymour, 3 vols (Oxford, 1975–1988)

Bartolus de Sassoferrato, *Gemma legalium seu Compendium aureum* (Venice, 1602)

—— *Omnium Iuris Commentaria*, ed. P. Mangrelia, 10 vols (Venice, 1602)

—— *Opera*, ed. P. C. Brederodius, 10 vols (Basle, 1589)

Bede, *The Ecclesiastical History of the English People*, ed. and trans. B. Colgrave and R. A. B. Mynors (Oxford, 1991)

—— *Venerabilis Baedae historiam ecclesiasticam gentis Anglorum*, ed. C. Plummer, 2 vols (Oxford, 1896)

Benedeit, *The Anglo-Norman Voyage of St Brendan*, ed. Brian Merrilees and Ian Short (Manchester, 1979)

—— *The Anglo-Norman Voyage of St Brendan by Benedeit*, ed. E. G. Waters (Oxford, 1928)

—— *Benedeit – Le Voyage de Saint Brandan*, ed. and trans. into German by Ernstpeter Ruhe (Munich, 1977)

—— *The Voyage of Saint Brendan: Representative Versions of the Legend in English Translation*, ed. W. R. J. Barron and Glyn S. Burgess (Exeter, 2002)

Benoît de Sainte-Maure, *Roman de Troie*, ed. Françoise Vielliard (Cologny-Geneva, 1979)

Beowulf, in *Beowulf and the Fight at Finnsburg*, ed. F. Klaeber (Boston, 1922; third edn 1950)

The Black Book of the Admiralty, ed. Travers Twiss, 4 vols (London, 1871–6)

Van Boendale, Jan, *De Brabantsche yeesten, of Rymkronyk van Braband, door Jan de Klerk, van Antwerpen*, ed. J. F. Willems (Brussels, 1839)

—— *Van den derden Edewaert, coninc van Engelant. Rymchronik geschreven omtrent het jaer 1347, door Jan de Klerk van Antwerpen*, ed. J. F. Willems (Ghent, 1840)

The Book of Margery Kempe, ed. Barry Windeatt (Cambridge, 2000; repr. 2004)

Capgrave, John, *Liber de Illustribus Henricis*, ed. Francis Charles Hingeston, Rolls Series 7 (London, 1858)

Chanson d'Antioche, ed. Suzanne Duparc-Quioc (Paris, 1977)

Chaucer, Geoffrey, *The Riverside Chaucer*, gen. ed. Larry D. Benson (Boston, 1987)

Christ, in *The Advent Lyrics of the Exeter Book*, ed. Jackson J. Campbell (Princeton, 1959)

Cicero, *Letters to Atticus*, ed. D. R. Shackleton Bailey, LCB 97 (London and Cambridge, MA, 1999)

—— *De Natura Deorum* and *Academica*, ed. and trans. H. Hackham, LCB 268 (London and Cambridge, MA, 1933)

Columbus, Christopher, *Christopher Columbus – Accounts and Letters of the Second, Third and Fourth Voyages*, ed. Paolo Taviani, Consuelo Varela, Juan Gil and Maria Conti, trans. Luciano F. Farina and Marc A. Beckwith, 2 vols (Rome, 1994)

Conrad, Joseph, *Heart of Darkness*, ed. Ross C. Murfin (New York, 1989)

Conrad of Saxony, *Conradi de Saxonia Speculum seu Salutatio Beatae Mariae Virginis ac Sermones mariani*, ed. P. de Alcántara Martínez, Bibliotheca Franciscana Ascetica Medii Aevi 11 (Grottaferrata, 1975)

Corpus antiphonalium officii, ed. Dom René-Jean Hesbert, 6 vols (Rome, 1963–79)

Dante Alighieri, *Dante – The Divine Comedy*, 3 vols, trans. Dorothy L. Sayers (Harmondsworth, 1962)

—— *The Divine Comedy*, trans. with a commentary by Charles S. Singleton, 3 vols (Princeton and London, 1970–5)

—— *The* Inferno *of Dante*, trans. Robert Pinsky (New York, 1994)

—— 'The Letter to Can Grande', in *The Literary Criticism of Dante Alighieri*, trans. and ed. Robert S. Haller (Lincoln, NE, 1973)

The Digby *Mary Magdalen*, in *Late Medieval Religious Plays of Bodleian MSS Digby 133 and E Museo 160*, ed. Donald C. Baker, John L. Murphy and Louis P. Hall, Jr., EETS o.s. 283 (Oxford, 1982)

Early South English Legendary Life of Mary Magdalen, ed. Sherry L. Reames in *Middle English Legends of Women Saints*, TEAMS (Kalamazoo, MI, 2003)

Eilhart von Oberge, *Tristrant*, in *Eilhart von Oberge*, ed. Franz Lichtenstein, Quellen und Forschungen zur Sprach- und Culturgeschichte der germanischen Völker 19 (Strasbourg, 1877)

—— *Eilhart von Oberg: Tristrant*, ed. Hadumod Bußmann, Altdeutsche Textbibliothek 70 (Tübingen, 1969)

Ephrem, *Select Works of Saint Ephrem*, ed. and trans. J. B. Morris (Oxford and London, 1847)

Fellows, Jennifer, ed., *Of Love and Chivalry: An Anthology of Middle English Romance* (London, 1993)

Foedera, ed. Thomas Rymer and Robert Sanderson, 3 vols (London, 1816–69)

La Folie Tristan d'Oxford, ed. E. Hoepffner (Paris, 1963; third edn)

Fredegar, *The Fourth Book of the Chronicle of Fredegar*, ed. and trans. J. M. Wallace-Hadrill (London, 1960)

Friar Robert, *Tristrams saga ok Ísöndar. Mit einer literaturhistorischen Einleitung*, ed. and trans. into German by Eugen Kölbing (Heilbronn, 1878)

Genesis A: A New Edition, ed. A. N. Doane (Madison, WI, 1978)

Genesis B, in *The Saxon Genesis*, ed. A. N. Doane (Madison, WI, 1991)

Geoffrey of Monmouth, *The History of the Kings of Britain*, trans. Lewis Thorpe (Harmondsworth, 1966)

—— *The* Historia Regum Britannie *of Geoffrey of Monmouth*, ed. Neil Wright, vol. 1, *Bern, Bürgerbibliothek, MS 568* (Cambridge, 1985)

The Historia Regum Britannie *of Geoffrey of Monmouth*, ed. Neil Wright, vol. 5, *Gesta Regum Britannie* (Cambridge, 1991)

Gerald of Wales, *Giraldi Cambrensis Topographia Hibernica et Expugnatio Hibernica Opera*, ed. James F. Dimock, 8 vols, Rolls Series 21 (London, 1867)

—— *History and Topography of Ireland*, trans. John J. O'Meara (Harmondsworth, 1982)

The Gest Hystoriale of the Destruction of Troy, ed. George A. Panton and David Donaldson, EETS o.s. 39, 56 (Oxford, 1869, 1874)

La Geste du Roi Arthur, ed. E. Baumgartner and I. Short (Paris, 1993)

Gildas, *De Excidio Britonum*, ed. and trans. M. Winterbottom (London, 1978)

Godfrey of Viterbo, *Pantheon*, in *Illustres veteres scriptores qui rerum a Germanis per multas aetates gestarum historias vel annales posteris reliquerent*, ed. Johann Pistorius (Frankfurt am Main, 1613)

Goswin of Mainz, *Letter to His Student Walcher*, in *Apologiae Duae: Gozechini epistola ad Walcherum; Burchardi apologia de barbis*, ed. R. B. C. Huygens and Giles Constable, CCCM 62 (Turnhout, 1985).

Gottfried of Straßburg, *Tristan*, ed. and trans. into German by Rüdiger Krohn, 2 vols (Stuttgart, 1980; third edn, 1984)

Gower, John, *The English Works of John Gower*, ed. G. C. Macaulay, 2 vols, EETS e.s. 81–2 (London, 1900–1)

—— *The Major Latin Works*, ed. and trans. Eric W. Stockton (Seattle, 1962)

Gregory the Great, *S. Gregorii Magni Moralia in Job*, ed. M. Adraien, 3 vols, CCSL 143 (Turnhout, 1979 and 1985)

—— *Homiliae in evangelia*, ed. R. Étaix, CCSL 141 (Turnhout, 1999)

Gregory of Nazianzus, *Gregor von Nazianz: Orationes et theologicae, Theologische Reden*, ed. and trans. into German by Hermann Josef Sieben (Freiburg, 1996)

—— *Orationes*, ed. James Donaldson and Alexander Roberts, in *The Ante-Nicene Fathers: Translations of the Writings of the Fathers Down to AD 325*, 10 vols (Edinburgh, 1868; repr. 1980), series 2, vol. 7

—— *Orationes*, ed. J.-P. Migne, *Patrologia Graeca* 35 (Paris, 1864)

Guy of Warwick, *The Romance of Guy of Warwick*, ed. J. Zupitza, 2 vols, EETS, e.s. 25–6 (London, 1875–6; repr. 1966)

Henry of Huntingdon, *Historia Anglorum*, in *Henry, Archdeacon of Huntingdon – Historia Anglorum, The History of the English People*, ed. and trans. Diana Greenway (Oxford, 1996)

Herodotus, *The Histories*, trans. Robin Waterfield (Oxford, 1998)

Higden, Ranulph, *Polychronicon Ranulphi Higden monachii Cestrensis*, ed. Churchill Babington and Joseph Rawson Lumby, 9 vols, Rolls series 41 (London, 1865–86)

Hilary of Poitiers, *Tractatus super psalmos*, ed. A. Zingerle, CSEL 22 (Vienna, 1891)

Hildebert of Tours, *Ven. Hildebertus/Marbodus*, ed. J.-P. Migne, *PL* 171 (Paris, 1854)

Holinshed, Raphael, *The Chronicles of England, Scotland and Ireland* (London, 1597)

Horace, *The Odes and Epodes*, ed. and trans. Niall Rudd, LCB 33N (Cambridge, MA, 2004)

—— *'Odes I' – Carpe Diem*, ed. and trans. David West (Oxford, 1995)

Hugh of St Victor, *De archa Noe morali*, ed. Patrice Secard, CCCM 176 (Turnhout, 2001)

Isidore, *The Etymologies of Isidore of Seville*, ed. and trans. Stephen A. Barney, W. J. Lewis, J. A. Beach and Oliver Berghof (Cambridge, 2006)

—— *Isidori Hispalensis episcopi etymologiarum sive originum*, ed. W. M. Lindsay, 2 vols (Oxford, 1911)

Jefferson, Thomas, *The Works of Thomas Jefferson*, ed. P. L. Ford, 10 vols (New York, 1905)

Jerome, *S. Hieronymi Presbyteri Commentariorum in Esaiam*, ed. M. Adraien, 2 vols, CCSL 73 (Turnhout, 1963)

—— *S. Hieronymi Presbyteri Opera*, ed. M. Adraien, 2 vols, CCSL 72 (Turnhout, 1959)

Justinian, *The Civil Law*, trans. S. P. Scott, 17 vols (Cincinnati, 1932)

—— *The Digest of Justinian*, ed. T. Mommsen and P. Krueger, trans. Alan Watson, 4 vols (Philadelphia, 1985)

—— *Justinian's Institutes*, ed. Peter Birks and Grant MacLeod (London, 1987)

King Horn, A Middle-English Romance, ed. Joseph Hall (Oxford, 1901)
—— *King Horn: An Edition Based on Cambridge University Library MS Gg.4.27 (2)*, ed. Rosamund Allen (New York, 1984)
—— in *Of Love and Chivalry: An Anthology of Middle English Romance*, ed. Jennifer Fellows (London, 1993)
Langland, William, *The Vision of Piers Plowman: A Critical Edition of the B-Text*, ed. A. V. C. Schmidt (London, 1995)
The Libelle of Englyshe Polycye – A Poem on the Use of Sea Power, 1436, ed. George Warner (Oxford, 1926)
Lydgate, John, *Lydgate's Troy Book*, ed. H. Bergen, 3 vols, EETS e.s. 97, 103, 106 (London, 1906–35; repr. Woodbridge, 1995, 2003)
Marbod of Rennes, *Ven. Hildebertus/Marbodus*, ed. J.-P. Migne, *PL* 171 (Paris, 1854)
Marie de France, *The Lais of Marie de France*, trans. Glyn S. Burgess and Keith Busby (London, 1986)
—— *Die Lais der Marie de France*, ed. K. Warnke (Halle, 1885; third edn 1925)
—— *Marie de France: Lais*, ed. Alfred Ewert (Oxford, 1944)
Martial, *Epigrams*, ed. and trans. D. R. Shackleton Bailey, 2 vols, LCB 94–5, (Cambridge, MA, 1993)
Martianus Capella, *De nuptiis Philologiae et Mercurii*, ed. John Willis (Leipzig, 1983)
Matthew Paris, *The Illustrated Chronicles of Matthew Paris*, ed. Richard Vaughan (Stroud, 1993)
—— *Matthaei Parisiensis, monachi Sancti Albani, chronica majora*, ed. Henry Richards Luard, 7 vols, Rolls series 57 (London, 1872–83)
The Middle English Physiologus, ed. Hanneke Wirtjes, EETS 294 (Oxford, 1991)
—— 'The Middle English *Physiologus*: A Critical Translation and Commentary', ed. and trans. Mary Allyson Armistead (unpublished MA thesis, Virginia Polytechnic Institute and State University, 2001)
The Midland Prose Psalter in *The Earliest Complete English Psalter*, ed. K. D. Bülbring, EETS 97 (London, 1891; repr. Woodbridge, 1987)
de Montesquieu, Charles Louis, *L'esprit des lois*, trans. Thomas Nugent (1750), in *The Spirit of the Laws: A Compendium of the First English Edition*, ed. David Wallace Carrithers (Berkeley, CA, 1977)
de Monstrelet, Enguerrand, *Chronique d'Enguerrand de Monstrelet*, ed. Douët D'Arcq, 6 vols (Paris, 1857–62)
von der Mülbe, Wolfheinrich, *Die Zauberlaterne* (Frankfurt am Main and Berlin, 1964)
Navigatio Sancti Brendani Abbatis, ed. Carl Selmer (South Bend, IN, 1959)
—— trans. J. F. Webb in *The Age of Bede*, ed. D. H. Farmer (Harmondsworth, 1983)
—— trans. John O'Meara and Jonathan Wooding, in *The Voyage of Saint Brendan: Representative Versions of the Legend in English Translation*, ed. W. R. J. Barron and Glyn S. Burgess (Exeter, 2002)
Nennius, *British History and the Welsh Annals*, ed. and trans. John Morris (London, 1978)

The Oak Book of Southampton, of c. AD 1300, ed. and trans. Paul Studer, 3 vols (Southampton, 1910)

The Old English Apollonius, in *The Anglo-Saxon Version of the Story of Apollonius of Tyre*, ed. and trans. Benjamin Thorpe (London, 1834)

The Old English Exodus: Text, Translation and Commentary by J. R. R. Tolkien, ed. Joan Turville-Petre (Oxford, 1981)

The Old English Orosius, ed. Janet Bately, EETS s.s. 6 (Oxford, 1980)

Origen, *Origenes Werke*, vol. 3, *Homiliae in Ieremiam, Fragmenta in Lamentationes*, ed. Erich Klosterman, rev. by Pierre Nautin, GCS 6 (second edn, Berlin, 1983)

Orosius, *The Seven Books of History Against the Pagans*, trans. Irving Woodworth Raymond (New York, 1936)

Ovid, *Heroides and Amores*, ed. and trans. Grant Showerman, LCB 41 (Cambridge, MA, 1914)

—— *Metamorphoses*, ed. and trans. Frank Justus Miller, 2 vols, LCB 43 (Cambridge, MA, 1916; third edn 1977; repr. 1984)

Partonopeu de Blois, ed. J. Gildea, 2 vols (Villanova, PA, 1967)

Patience, in *The Poems of the Pearl Manuscript: Pearl, Cleanness, Patience, Sir Gawain and the Green Knight*, ed. Malcolm Andrew and Ronald Waldron (Exeter, 1987; fourth edn; originally published 1978)

—— ed. Hartley Bateson (Manchester, 1912; second edn 1918)

The Pilgrims' Sea-Voyage (*IMEV* 2, 148), in *The Stacions of Rome and The Pilgrims' Sea-Voyage*, ed. F. J. Furnivall, EETS o.s. 25 (London, 1867; repr. Woodbridge, 2003)

Plutarch, *Moralia in Fifteen Volumes*, vol. 9, ed. and trans. Edwin L. Minar, Jr, W. C. Helmbold and F. H. Sandbach, LCB 425 (London and Cambridge, MA, 1961)

The Prose *Brut* in *The Brut or the Chronicles of England*, ed. F. W. D. Brie, 2 vols, EETS, o.s. 131 and 136 (London, 1906 and 1908)

Prudentius, *Aurelii Prudentii Clementis Carmina*, ed. M. P. Cunningham, CCSL 126 (Turnhout, 1966)

Pseudo-Tertullian, *Carmen de Jona Prophetae* in *Tertullianus*, ed. J.-P. Migne, *PL* 2 (Paris, 1844)

Pythias of Massalia, *On the Ocean: Text, Translation and Commentary*, ed. and trans. Christina Horst Roseman (Chicago, 1994)

—— *L'oceano*, ed. and trans. into Italian by Serena Bianchetti (Pisa, 1998)

Richelieu, Cardinal, *Testament politique* (Amsterdam, 1689)

Rotuli Scotiae, ed. D. Macpherson, 2 vols (London, 1814–19)

Saewulf, travels of, in *Peregrinationes tres*, ed. R. B. C. Huygens, CCCM 139 (Turnhout, 1994)

—— trans. Thomas Wright, in *Early Travels in Palestine* (London, 1848; repr. New York, 2003)

Saupe, Karen, ed., *Middle English Marian Lyrics*, TEAMS (Kalamazoo, MI, 1997)

Seneca the Elder, *The Suasoriae of Seneca the Elder*, ed. and trans. William A. Edward (Cambridge, 1928)

Seneca the Younger, *Seneca in Ten Volumes*, vol. 8, *Tragedies*, ed. and trans. F. J. Miller, LCB 62 (Cambridge, MA, and London, 1917)

Shakespeare, William, *The Comedy of Errors*, ed. Charles Walters Whitworth, The Oxford Shakespeare (Oxford, 2002)

—— *Pericles, Prince of Tyre*, ed. Doreen DelVecchio and Antony Hammond, The New Cambridge Shakespeare (Cambridge, 1998)

—— *Richard II*, ed. Andrew Gurr, The New Cambridge Shakespeare (Cambridge, 1990)

—— *The Tempest*, ed. Anne Barton, The New Penguin Shakespeare (Harmondsworth, 1968)

—— *The Tempest*, ed. David Lindley, The New Cambridge Shakespeare (Cambridge, 2002)

Sir Tristrem, ed. Alan Lupack, TEAMS (Kalamazoo, MI, 1994)

Speculum Stultorum, trans. in G. W. Regenos, *The Book of Daun Burnel the Ass* (Austin, TX, 1959)

Strabo, *The Geography of Strabo*, ed. and trans. H. L. Jones, 8 vols (London 1917–32; repr. 1966–70)

Tertullian, *De spectaculis, De idolatria, Ad nationes, De testimonio animae, Scorpiace, De oratione, De baptismo, De ieiunio, De anima, De pudicitia*, ed. A. Reifferscheid and G. Wissowa, CSEL 20 (Vienna, 1890)

Thomas (of England), *Romance of Horn*, trans. Judith Weiss, in *The Birth of Romance – An Anthology*, ed. Judith Weiss (London, 1992)

—— *The Romance of Horn by Thomas*, ed. Mildred K. Pope, 2 vols, Anglo-Norman Text Society 9–10, 12–13 (Oxford, 1955)

Thomas of Britain, *Tristan*, in *Early French Tristan Poems*, ed. Norris J. Lacy, 2 vols (Woodbridge, 1998)

—— *Le Roman de Tristan par Thomas: Poème du XIIe siècle*, ed. Joseph Bédier (Paris, 1905)

—— *Thomas of Britain: Tristan*, ed. and trans. Stewart Gregory (New York, 1991)

—— *Thomas Tristan*, ed. and trans. into German by Gesa Bonath (Munich, 1985)

—— 'Un nouveau fragment du *Tristan* de Thomas', ed. Michael Benskin, Tony Hunt, Ian Short, *Romania* 113 (1995), 289–319

Valerius Flaccus, ed. and trans. J. H. Mozley, LCB 286 (London and Cambridge, MA, 1934)

The Vercelli Book, ed. George Philip Krapp, Anglo-Saxon Poetic Records 2 (New York, 1932; repr. 1961)

Villehardouin, Geoffrey de, *Histoire de la conquête de Constantinople*, ed. Jean Longnon (Paris, 1981)

Virgil, *Eclogues, Georgics and Aeneid I–VI*, ed. and trans. H. Rushton Fairclough, rev. G. P. Goold, LCB 63 (London and Cambridge, MA, 1999)

'The Voyage of the Húi Corra', ed. and trans. Whitley Stokes, *Revue Celtique* 14 (1893), 22–69

The Voyage of Mael Duin, ed. H. P. A. Oskamp (Groningen, 1970)

—— ed. and trans. Whitley Stokes, *Revue Celtique* 9 (1888), 447–95; 10 (1889), 50–95

The Voyage of Saint Brendan: Representative Versions of the Legend in English Translation, ed. W. R. J. Barron and Glyn S. Burgess (Exeter, 2002)

'The Voyage of Snedgus and MacRiagla', ed. and trans. Whitley Stokes, *Revue Celtique* 9 (1888), 14–25

Wace, *Le Roman de Brut de Wace*, ed. Ivor Arnold, 2 vols, Société des Anciens Textes Français (Paris, 1938)

—— *Wace's Roman de Brut – A History of the British*, trans. Judith Weiss (Exeter, 1999)

William of Malmesbury, *Gesta Regum Anglorum*, ed. and trans. R. A. B. Mynors with R. M. Thomson and M. Winterbottom, 2 vols (Oxford, 1998)

Secondary Reading

Alexander, Michael, *The Poetic Achievement of Ezra Pound* (Edinburgh, 1998)

Alkire, William H., 'Technical Knowledge and the Evolution of Political Systems in the Central and Western Caroline Islands of Micronesia', *Canadian Journal of Anthropology* 1:2 (1980), 229–37

Allen, Rosamund, 'The Date and Provenance of *King Horn*: Some Interim Reassessments', in *Medieval English Studies Presented to George Kane*, ed. Edward Donald Kennedy, Ronald Waldron and Joseph S. Wittig (Cambridge, 1988), pp. 99–125

Anand, R. P., 'Non-European Sources of Law of the Sea', in *Pacem in maribus 2000*, ed. Susan Rolston (Halifax, Canada, 2002), pp. 9–20

—— *Origin and Development of the Law of the Sea* (London, 1982)

Andrea, Alfred John, 'The Relationship of Sea Travellers and Excommunicated Captains under Thirteenth-Century Canon Law', *Mariner's Mirror* 68:2 (1982), 203–9

Andrew, Malcolm, 'Jonah and Christ in *Patience*', *Modern Philology* 70:3 (1973), 230–3

—— '*Patience*: the *munster dor*', *ELN* 14:3 (1977), 164–7.

Angenendt, Arnold, 'Die irische Peregrinatio und ihre Auswirkungen auf dem Kontinent vor dem Jahre 800', in *Die Iren und Europa im früheren Mittelalter*, ed. Heinz Löwe, 2 vols (Stuttgart, 1982), vol. 1, pp. 52–79

Archibald, Elizabeth, *Apollonius of Tyre: Medieval and Renaissance Themes and Variations* (Cambridge, 1991)

Arenson, S., 'Navigation and Exploration in the Medieval World', in *The Sea and History*, ed. E. E. Rice (Stroud, 1996), pp. 97–110

Aubet, M. E., *The Phoenicians and the West: Politics, Colonies and Trade* (Cambridge, 1993)

Averkorn, Raphaela, 'The Sea as a Diplomatic, Cultural and Economic Battle-field in the Times of the Hundred Years War', in *The Sea in European History*, ed. Luc François and Ann Katherine Isaacs (Pisa, 2001), pp. 191–217

Baines, M., N. Connolly, O. Kiely, D. Lidgard and M. McKibben, *Grey Seals: Status and Monitoring in the Irish and Celtic Seas* (Dublin, 2000)

Balard, Michel, 'Coastal Shipping and Navigation in the Mediterranean', in *Cogs, Caravels and Galleons: The Sailing Ship 1000–1650*, ed. Richard W. Unger (London, 1994), pp. 131–8

—— ed., *L'Europe et l'océan au moyen age: Contribution à l'histoire de la navigation, Colloque Nantes 1987* (Paris, 1988)

Baldinger, K., *Dictionnaire étymologique de l'ancien français* (Quebec, 1974–)

Baldwin, Robert, 'The Sea, Shipwreck and Water: A Bibliography', *Bulletin of Bibliography* 48:3 (1991), 153–70

Barker, Adelem, 'Sea and Steppe Imagery in Old English and Old Russian Epic' (unpublished PhD thesis, New York University, 1976)

Barr, Helen, '"Speking for One's Sustenance": The Rhetoric of Counsel in *Mum and the Sothsegger*, Skelton's *Bowge of Court*, and Elyot's *Pasquil the Playne*', in *The Long Fifteenth Century: Essays for Douglas Gray*, ed. Kate Ward-Perkins, Helen Cooper, Sally Mapstone and Jörg O. Fichte (Oxford, 1997), pp. 249–72

Batany, Jean, 'Un *Estat* trop peu *estable*: Navigation maritime et peur de l'eau', in *L'eau au moyen âge*, Sénéfiance 15 (Aix-en-Provence, 1985), pp. 23–42

Battles, Paul, '*Genesis A* and the Anglo-Saxon "Migration Myth"', *Anglo-Saxon England* 29 (2000), 43–66

Bäuchtold-Stäubli, H., ed., *Handwörterbuch des deutschen Aberglaubens*, 10 vols (Berlin and Leipzig, 1927–42)

Baumgartner, E., *Tristan et Iseut. De la légende au récits en vers* (Paris, 1987)

Beagon, Mary, *Roman Nature: The Thought of Pliny the Elder* (Oxford, 1992)

Bennett, J. A. W., *Chaucer's Book of Fame: An Exposition of 'The House of Fame'* (Oxford, 1968)

Bennett, Josephine Waters, 'Britain among the Fortunate Isles', *Studies in Philology* 53:2 (1956), 114–40

Berlin, Isaiah, 'Two Concepts of Liberty', in *Four Essays on Liberty* (Oxford, 1969), pp. 118–72. First published 1958.

Bernier, Gildas, 'Les navires celtiques du Haut Moyen Age', *Etudes celtiques* 16 (1979), 287–91

Biggs, F. M., 'The End of the Sea: The *Old English Exodus*, Lines 466b–7a', *Notes and Queries* 32:3 (1985), 290–1

Birkholz, Daniel, *The King's Two Maps: Cartography and Culture in Thirteenth-Century England*, Studies in Medieval History and Culture 22 (London and New York, 2004)

Blamires, Alcuin, *The Case for Women in Medieval Literature* (Oxford, 1997)

Boberg, I. M., *Motif-Index of Early Icelandic Literature* (Copenhagen, 1966)

Boelens, R. G. V., and R. R. Dickson, *The Status of the Current Knowledge of the Anthropogenic Influences in the Irish Sea*, ICES Co-operative Research Report 155 (Copenhagen, 1986)

Borsje, Jacqueline, 'The Monster in the River Ness in *Vita Sancti Columbae*: A Study of a Miracle', *Peritia* 8 (1994), 30–3

—— 'Zeemonsters en de mythische dimensie van de zee', *Madoc* 13:4 (1999), 268–76

Boulton, D'Arcy Jonathan Dacre, 'The Middle French Statutes of the Monarchical Order of the Ship', *Medieval Studies* 47 (1985), 168–271

Bourke, John, *The Sea as a Symbol in English Poetry* (Eton, 1954)

Bowers, R. H., *The Legend of Jonah* (The Hague, 1972)

Bradford, Ernle, *The Mediterranean: Portrait of a Sea* (Harmondsworth, 1971)

Braudel, Fernand, *The Mediterranean and the Mediterranean World in the Age of Philip II* (*La Méditerrannée et le monde méditerrannéen à l'époque de Philippe II*, first edn 1949, second rev. edn 1966), 2 vols (New York, 1972–3; repr. Berkeley, 1995)

Brault, Gérard Joseph, 'L'Amer, l'amer, la mer: La scène des aveux dans le *Tristan* de Thomas à la lumière du fragment de Carlisle', in *Miscellanea Medievalia: Mélanges Philippe Ménard*, ed. Claude Faucon, Alain Labbé and Danielle Quéruel, 2 vols (Paris, 1998), pp. 215–226

Breeze, Andrew, 'Sir John Paston, Lydgate and the *Libelle of Englyshe Polycye*', *Notes and Queries*, n.s. 48:3 (2001), 230–1

Bridbury, A. R., *England and the Salt Trade in the Later Middle Ages* (Oxford, 1955)

von den Brincken, Anna-Dorothee, *Fines Terrae: Die Enden der Erde und der vierte Kontinent auf mittelalterlichen Weltkarten* (Hanover, 1992)

Britnell, Richard H., '*Advantagium mercatoris*: A Custom in Medieval English Trade', *Nottingham Medieval Studies* 24 (1980), 37–50

Brooks, F. W., *The English Naval Forces, 1199–1272* (London, 1932)

Brower Stahl, Ann, 'Concepts of Time and Approaches to Analogical Reasoning in Historical Perspective', *American Antiquity* 58:2 (1993), 235–60

Brown, C., and R. H. Robbins, eds, *Index of Middle English Verse* (New York, 1943); *Supplement*, ed. R. H. Robbins and J. L. Cutler (Lexington, KY, 1965)

Brown, Peter, *The Rise of Western Christendom* (Cambridge, MA, 1999)

Bullock, Amy, *The Sea in Anglo-Saxon Poetry* (PhD thesis, Boston University, 1909)

Burgess, Glyn S., and Clara Strijbosch, *The Legend of St Brendan: A Critical Bibliography* (Dublin, 2000)

Burnley, J. D., 'The *Roman de Horn*: Its Hero and Its Ethos', *French Studies* 32:4 (1978), 385–97

Burr, V., *Nostrum Mare: Ursprung und Geschichte der Namen des Mittelmeeres und seiner Teilmeere im Altertum* (Stuttgart, 1932)

Burrow, John and Ian Wei, eds, *Medieval Futures: Attitudes to the Future in the Middle Ages* (Woodbridge, 2000)

Buschinger, Danielle, *Tristan et Iseut, mythe européen et mondial. Actes du colloque des 10, 11 et 12 janvier 1986* (Göppingen, 1987)

Butel, Paul, *The Atlantic* (New York and London, 1999)

Cairns, Francis, 'Latin Sources and Analogues to ME *Patience*', *Studia Neophilologica* 59:1 (1987), 7–18

Campbell, Kimberlee A., 'En haute mer: Navire et marin dans la *chanson de geste*', in *Ce nous dist li escris ... Che est la verite. Etudes de littérature médiévale offertes à André Mosan*, ed. Miren Lacassagne, Senefiance 45 (Aix-en-Provence, 2000), pp. 35–49

Cannon, Christopher, 'Between the Old and the Middle of English', in *New Medieval Literatures VII*, ed. Wendy Scase, Rita Copeland and David Lawton (Oxford, 2005), pp. 203–21

—— *The Grounds of English Literature* (Oxford, 2004)

Carlson, Patricia Ann, *Literature and the Lore of the Sea* (Amsterdam, 1986)

Carney, J., review of C. Selmer, ed. *Navigatio Sancti Brendani Abbatis*, *Medium Aevum* 32 (1963), 37–44

Carolus-Barré, Louis, '"Aventure de mer" et naufrages en Méditerranée au mileu du XIIIe siècle', *Comptes-rendus de l'academie des inscriptions et belles lettres* (1974), 612–26

Cassard, Jean-Christophe, 'Les Bretons et la mer au Moyen Age' (Rennes, 1998)

—— 'Les saints bretons et la mer', *Mémoires de la Société d'histoire et d'archéologie de Bretagne* 64 (1987), 5–17

Chadwick, Nora K., 'Notes on Polynesian Mythology', *Journal of the Royal Anthropological Institute of Great Britain and Ireland* 60 (1930), 425–46

Chantreau, Alain, 'La mer dans la legende de "Tristan et Iseult"', *Mémoires de la Société d'histoire et d'archéologie de Bretagne* 64 (1987), 19–27

Charles-Edwards, T. M., 'The Social Background to Irish *Peregrinatio*', *Celtica* 11 (1976), 43–59

Chibnall, Marjorie, *The Debate of the Norman Conquest* (Manchester and New York, 1999)

—— *The Normans* (Oxford, 2000)

Child, C. G., 'Chaucer's *Legend of Good Women* and Boccaccio's *De Genealogia Deorum*', *MLN* 11:8 (1896), 238–45

Childs, Wendy R., 'The Perils, or Otherwise, of Maritime Pilgrimage to Santiago de Compostela in the Fifteenth Century', in *Pilgrimage Explored*, ed. J. Stopford (York, 1999), pp. 123–43

Chung, Inju, 'The *Physiologus* and "The Whale"', *Medieval English Studies* (Korea), 6 (1998), 21–57

Churchill, R. R., and A. V. Lowe, *The Law of the Sea* (Manchester, 1985; third edn 1999)

Churchill, Winston, *A History of the English-Speaking Peoples*, 4 vols (London, 1956–8)

—— *The Second World War* (London, 1985; first published 1949), 6 vols

Clancy, Tom, 'Subversion at Sea: Structure, Style and Intent in the *Immrama*', in *The Otherworld Voyage in Early Irish Literature*, ed. Jonathan Wooding (Dublin, 2000), pp. 194–225.

Classen, Albrecht, 'Storms, Sea Crossings, the Challenges of Nature and the Transformation of the Protagonist in Medieval and Renaissance Literature', *Neohelicon* 30:2 (2003), 163–82

Colin, Scott, and Monica Mulrennan, 'Land and Sea Tenure at Erub, Torres Strait: Property, Sovereignty and the Adjudication of Cultural Continuity', *Oceania* 70:2 (1999), 146–76

Colliot, Régine, 'L'eau, élément du tragique: Textes du XIIIe siècle (geste du *Doon de Mayence*, *Gui de Warewick*) au XV siècle et documents iconographiques', in *L'eau au moyen âge*, Sénéfiance 15 (Aix-en-Provence, 1985), pp. 91–110

Combarieu du Gres, Micheline de, 'L'eau et l'aventure dans le cycle du Lancelot-Graäl' in *L'eau au moyen âge*, Sénéfiance 15 (Aix-en-Provence, 1985), pp. 111–47

Conlan, James Peter, 'Marvellous Passages: English Nautical Piety in the Middle Ages and the Renaissance' (PhD thesis, University of California Riverside, 1999)

Conrad, Lawrence I., 'Islam and the Sea: Paradigms and Problematics', *Al-Qantara* 23:1 (2001), 123–54

Cook, Albert S., 'The Old English "Whale"', *MLN* 9:3 (1894), 65–8

Cooper, D. M. L., D. Guðbjartsson, B. Hallgrímsson, B. Ó Donnabháin, K. Stefánsson and G. Bragi Walters, 'Composition of the Founding Population of Iceland: Biological Distance and Morphological Variation in Early

Historic Atlantic Europe', *American Journal of Physical Anthropology* 124:3 (2003), 257–74

Cooper, Helen, *The English Romance in Time: Transforming Motifs from Geoffrey of Monmouth to the Death of Shakespeare* (Oxford, 2004)

—— 'Prospero's Boats: Magic, Providence and Human Choice', in *Renaissance Essays for Kitty Scoular Datta*, ed. Sukarta Chaudhuri (Oxford and Calcutta, 1995), pp. 160–75

Cordery, Leona F., 'The Saracens in Middle English Literature: A Definition of Otherness', *Al-Masaq* 14:2 (2002), 87–99

Cotgrave, Randle, *A dictionarie of the French and English tongues* (London, 1611)

Coulter, Cornelia Catlin, 'The "Great Fish" in Ancient and Medieval Story', *Transactions and Proceedings of the American Philological Association* 57 (1926), 32–50

Crane, Susan, *Insular Romance: Politics, Faith and Culture in Anglo-Norman and Middle English Literature* (Berkeley and Los Angeles, 1986)

Cross, T. P., *Motif-Index in Early Irish Literature* (Bloomington, IN, 1952)

Cunliffe, Barry, *Facing the Ocean: The Atlantic and Its Peoples, 8000 BC–AD 1500* (Oxford, 2001)

D'Arcy, Paul, 'Connected by the Sea: Towards a Regional History of the Western Caroline Islands', *Journal of Pacific History* 36:2 (2001), 163–82

Daston, Lorraine, and Katherine Park, *Wonders and the Order of Nature, 1150–1750* (New York, 1998)

Delitzsch, Friedrich, *Das Babylonische Weltschöpfungsepos* (Leipzig, 1896)

Dieckmann, B., *Judas als Sündenbock – Eine verhängnisvolle Geschichte von Angst und Vergeltung* (Munich, 1991)

Diekstra, F. N. M., 'Jonah and *Patience*: The Psychology of the Prophet', *English Studies* 55 (1974), 205–17

Doan, James, 'The Legend of the Sunken City in Welsh and Breton Tradition', *Folklore* 92:1 (1981)

Drewer, Lois, 'Leviathan, Behemoth and Ziz: A Christian Adaptation', *Journal of the Warburg and Courtauld Institutes* 44 (1981), 148–56

Dronke, Peter, 'Part 1', in *Growth of Literature: The Sea and the God of the Sea*, Peter and Ursula Dronke, H. M. Chadwick Memorial Lectures 8 (Cambridge, 1997), pp. 1–26

Dumville, D. '*Echtrae* and *Immram*: Some Problems of Definition', *Ériu* 27 (1976), 73–94

—— 'Two Approaches to the Dating of *Nauigatio Sancti Brendani*', *Studi medievali*, third s. 29 (1988), 87–102

Eccles, Mark, 'Halfe a yerd of rede sea', *Notes and Queries*, n.s. 31:2 (1984), 164–5

Edson, Evelyn, *Mapping Time and Space: How Medieval Mapmakers Viewed Their World* (London, 1997)

Edwards, A. S. G., 'A New Manuscript of *The Libelle of English Policy*', *Notes and Queries*, n.s. 46:4 (1999), 444–5

Eis, G., *Mittelalterliche Fachliteratur* (Stuttgart, 1962)

Ellmers, Detlev, *Frühmittelalterliche Handelsschiffahrt in Mittel- und Nordeuropa* (Neumünster, 1972)

Emerson, O. F., 'A Parallel between the Middle English Poem *Patience* and an Early Latin Poem Attributed to Tertullian', *PMLA* 10:1 (1895), 242–8

Erskine, J., S. P. Sherman, W. P. Trent, A. R. Waller, A. W. Ward and C. Van Doren, eds, *The Cambridge History of English and American Literature* (Cambridge, 1907–21)

Esposito, M., 'An Apocryphal *Book of Enoch and Elias* as a Possible Source for the *Navigatio Sancti Brendani*', *Celtica* 5 (1960), 192–206

Ewe, Herbert, 'Schiffe auf Siegeln und Karten in kulturgeschichtlicher Sicht', *Studia Maritima* 1 (1978), 39–49.

Fàj, Attila, 'Marbodean and Patristic Reminiscences in *Patience*', *Revue de littérature comparée* 49 (1975), 284–90

Farrell, A. W., 'The Use of Iconographic Material in Medieval Ship Archaeology', in *The Archaeology of Medieval Ships and Harbours in Northern Europe*, ed. Sean McGrail (Oxford, 1979), pp. 227–46

Federico, Sylvia, *New Troy: Fantasies of Empire in the Late Middle Ages* (Minneapolis, 2003)

Fenn, Jr, Percy Thomas, 'Justinian and the Freedom of the Sea', *The American Journal of International Law* 19:4 (1925), 716–27

—— 'Origins of the Theory of Territorial Waters', *American Journal of International Law* 20:3 (1926), 465–82

Fernandez-Armesto, F., *Before Columbus: Exploration and Colonisation from the Mediterranean to the Atlantic, 1229–1492* (Basingstoke and London, 1987)

Fidalgo Monge, Susana, 'The Sea in *Beowulf, The Wanderer* and *The Seafarer*: On Semantic Fields and Mediterranean Limitations', *SELIM: Revista de la Sociedad Española de Lengua y Literatura Inglesa Medieval* 9 (1999), 155–62

Finney, Ben, 'Myth, Experiment and the Reinvention of Polynesian Voyaging', *American Anthropologist* n.s. 93:2 (1991), 383–404

Fitz, Brewster, 'The Storm Episode and the Weasel Episode: Sacrificial Casuistry in Marie de France's *Eliduc*', *MLN* 89 (1974), 542–9

Fleuriot, Léon, and Auguste-Pierre Ségalen, eds, 'Les récits de navigation', in *Héritage celtique et captation française: Des origines à la fin des États*, vol. 3, *Histoire littéraire et culturelle de la Bretagne* (Paris, 1997), pp. 161–4

Ford, C. J., 'Piracy or Policy? Crisis in the Channel, 1400–1403', *Transactions of the Royal Historical Society* 29 (1979), 63–78

Frake, Charles O., 'Cognitive Maps of Time and Tide Among Medieval Seafarers', *Man*, n.s. 20 (1985), 254–70

Frank, Roberta, 'North-Sea Soundings in *Andreas*', in *Early Medieval English Texts and Interpretations*, ed. Elaine Treharne and Susan Rosser (Tempe, AZ, 2002), pp. 1–11

Friedman, John B., 'Figural Typology in the Middle English *Patience*', in *The Alliterative Tradition in the Fourteenth Century*, ed. Bernard S. Levy and Paul E. Szarmach (Kent, OH, 1981), pp. 99–129

Friel, Ian, *The Good Ship: Ships, Shipbuilding and Technology in England, 1200–1520* (London, 1995)

Frye, Northrop, *An Anatomy of Criticism: Four Essays* (Princeton, 1957)

—— *The Great Code: The Bible and Literature* (London, 1982)

Fulton, Thomas Wemyss, *The Sovereignty of the Sea: An Historical Account of the Claims of England to the Dominion of the British Seas* (Edinburgh and London, 1911)

Gaffarel, Paul, 'Les explorations maritimes des Irlandais au moyen âge', *Revue politique et littéraire* 4:2 (1875), 626–31

de Gaiffier, B., 'Un thème hagiographique: Mer ou fleuves traversés sur un manteau', *Analecta Bollandiana* 99 (1981), 5–15

Gaultier Dalché, P., 'Comment penser l'océan? Modes de connaissance des *fines orbis terrarum* du nord-ouest (de l'antiquité au XIIIe siècle)', in M. Balard *L'Europe et l'océan au moyen age: Contribution á l'histoire de la navigation, Colloque Nantes 1987*, ed. M. Balard (Paris, 1988), pp. 217–33

Gerhardt, Mia I., *Old Men of the Sea. From Neptunus to Old French Iuiton: Ancestry and Character of a Water-Spirit* (Amsterdam, 1967)

Gilles, Sealy, and Sylvia Tomasch, eds, *Text and Territory: Geographical Imagination in the European Middle Ages* (Philadelphia, 1998)

Gillis, John R., *Commemorations: The Politics of National Identity* (Princeton, 1994)

Greene, William, 'The Sea in the Greek Poets', *North American Review* 199 (1914), 427–43

Grennan, Joseph, 'Chaucer's Man of Law and the Constancy of Justice', *JEGP* 84 (1985), 498–514

Grierson, Philip, 'Muslim Coins in Thirteenth-Century England', in *Near Eastern Numismatics, Iconography, Epigraphy and History: Studies in Honour of George C. Miles*, ed. Dickran K. Kouymjian (Beirut, 1974), pp. 387–92

Guldon, Ernst, 'Das Monster-Portal am Palazzo Zuccari in Rom', *Zeitschrift für Kunstgeschichte* 32 (1969), 229–61

Gunkel, Hermann, with contributions by Heinrich Zimmern, *Schöpfung und Chaos in Urzeit und Endzeit* (Göttingen, 1896)

Hanna, Ralph, 'Alliterative Poetry', in *The Cambridge History of Medieval Literature*, ed. David Wallace (Cambridge, 1999), pp. 488–512

Hares-Stryker, Carolyn, 'Adrift on the Seven Seas: The Medieval Topos of Exile at Sea', *Florilegium* 12 (1993), 79–98

Harf-Lancner, Laurence, 'L'eau magique et la femme-fée: Le mythe fondateur du *Tristan* en prose', in *L'eau au moyen age*, Sénéfiance 15 (Aix-en-Provence, 1985), pp. 201–12

Hattendorf, John E., and Richard W. Unger, *War at Sea in the Middle Ages and Renaissance* (Woodbridge, 2003)

Haug, Walter, 'Gottfrieds von Straßburg Verhältnis zu Thomas von England im Licht des neu aufgefundenen *Tristan*-Fragments von Carlisle', *Mededelingen van de Afdeling Letterkunde*, n.s. 62:4 (1999), 5–19

—— 'Vom Imram zur Aventiure-Fahrt: Zur Frage nach der Vorgeschichte der hochhöfischen Epenstruktur', *Wolfram-Studien* 1 (1970), 264–97

—— 'Reinterpreting the Tristan Romances of Thomas and Gotfrid: Implications of a Recent Discovery', *Arthuriana* 7:3 (1997), 46–59

Hau'ofa, Epeli, 'Our Sea of Islands', *The Contemporary Pacific* 6:1 (1994), 148–61

Heijkant, Marie-José, '*Merveille est k'om la mer ne het*: De ambivalente rol van de zee in de liefdesgeschiedenis van Tristan en Isolde', *Madoc*: 13:4 (1999), 205–212

Heng, Geraldine, *Empire of Magic – Medieval Romance and the Politics of Cultural Fantasy* (New York, 2003)

Henn, Volker, '*The Libelle of Englyshe Polycye* – Politik und Wirtschaft in England in den 30er Jahren des 15. Jahrhunderts', *Hansische Geschichtsblätter* 101 (1983), 43–65

Hernández Pérez, M. B., 'Writing on the Strand: Variations of the Sea in Chaucer's Poetry', in *Variation and Variety in Middle English Language and Literature* ed. F. J. Cortés et al. (Barcelona, 2000), pp. 55–64

Heydenreich, Titus, *Tadel und Lob der Seefahrt: Das Nachleben eines antiken Themas in der romanischen Literatur* (Heidelberg, 1970)

Hiatt, Alfred, 'Blank Spaces on the Earth', *The Yale Journal of Criticism* 15:2 (2002), 223–50

Higham, N. J., 'Old Light in the Dark Age Landscape: The Description of Britain in the *De Excidio Britanniae* of Gildas', *Journal of Historical Geography* 17:4 (1991), 363–72

Higley, Sarah Lynn, 'Storm and Mind in Anglo-Saxon Poetry: A Hard Lesson', *In Geardagum* 9 (1988), 23–39.

Hilgert, Earle, *The Ship and Related Symbols in the New Testament* (Assen, The Netherlands, 1962)

Hill, Ordelle G., 'The Late-Latin *De Jona* as a Source for *Patience*', *Journal of English and Germanic Philology*, 66 (1967), 21–25

Hodnett, M. P., 'The Sea in Roman Poetry', *Classical Journal* 15 (1919–20), 67–82.

Hoepffner, E., 'Marie de France et l'*Éneas*', *Studi medievali* 5 (1932), 272–308

—— 'Pour la Chronologie des Lais de Marie de France', *Romania* 59 (1933), 351–70 and 60 (1934), 36–66

—— 'Thomas d'Angleterre et Marie de France', *Studi medievali* 7 (1934), 8–23

Holmes, G. A., 'The *Libel of English Policy*', *English Historical Review* 76 (1961), 193–216

Holton, Frederick, 'Old English Sea Imagery and the Interpretation of *The Seafarer*', *Yearbook of English Studies* 12 (1982), 208–17

Horden, Peregrine, and Nicholas Purcell, *The Corrupting Sea – A Study of Mediterranean History* (Oxford, 2000)

van Houts, Elizabeth, 'The Vocabulary of Exile and Outlawry in the North Sea Area around the First Millennium', in *Exile in the Middle Ages: Selected Proceedings from the International Medieval Congress, University of Leeds, 8–11 July 2002*, ed. Elizabeth van Houts and Laura Napran (Turnhout, 2004), pp. 13–28

Hudson, Benjamin, 'The Changing Economy of the Irish Sea Province', in *Britain and Ireland 900–1300: Insular Responses to Medieval European Change*, ed. Brendan Smith (Cambridge, 1999), pp. 39–66

Hué, Denis, 'Dérives et grenouillages: L'eau et la politique à la fin du moyen âge', in *L'eau au moyen âge*, Sénéfiance 15 (Aix-en-Provence, 1985), pp. 213–32

Hutchinson, Gillian, *Medieval Ships and Shipping* (London and Washington, DC, 1994)

Ikea, Manny, Reilly Ridgell and Isaoshy Uruo, 'The Persistence of Central Carolingian Navigation', *ISLA: A Journal of Micronesian Studies* 2 (1994), 181–206

Bibliography

Illingworth, Robin N., 'The Structure of the Anglo-Norman *Voyage of St Brendan* by Benedeit', *Medium Aevum* 55:2 (1986), 217–29

Ireland, Colin A., 'Some Analogues of the OE *Seafarer* from Hiberno-Latin Sources', *Neuphilologische Mitteilungen* 92:1 (1991), 1–14

Jacobs, Nicholas, 'Alliterative Storms: A Topos in Middle English', *Speculum* 47:4 (1972), 695–719

Jaeger, C. Stephen, *The Envy of Angels: Cathedral Schools and Social Ideals in Medieval Europe, 950–1200* (Philadelphia, 1994)

Jantzen, Ulrike and Niels Kröner, 'Zum neugefundenen *Tristan*-Fragment des Thomas d'Angleterre. Editionskritik und Vergleich mit Gottfrieds Bearbeitung', *Euphorion* 91 (1997), 291–309

Jensen, Peter, *Kosmologie der Babylonier: Studien und Materialien* (Strasbourg, 1890)

Jobbé-Duval, E., *Idées primitives dans la Bretagne contemporaine*, 2 vols (Paris, 1920)

Jones, Chris, *Strange Likeness: The Use of Old English in Twentieth-Century Poetry* (Oxford, 2006)

Jones, Robin F., 'The Mechanics of Meaning in the Anglo-Norman *Voyage of Saint Brendan*', *Romanic Review* 71:2 (1980), 105–13

Jundziłł, Juliusz, *Rzymianie a morze* (Bydgoszcz, 1991)

Jussen, Bernhard, 'The Concept of Time in the Historiography of the Eleventh and Twelfth Centuries', in *Medieval Concepts of the Past: Ritual, Memory, Historiography*, ed. Gerd Althoff, Johaness Fried and Patrick J. Geary, Publications of the German Historical Institute (Cambridge, 2002), pp. 139–65

Kahlmeyer, Johannes, *Seesturm und Schiffbruch als Bild im antiken Schrifttum* (Hildesheim, 1934)

Keen, Maurice, *England in the Later Middle Ages* (New York, 1990)

Kelly, Ellin M., 'Parallels between the Middle English *Patience* and *Hymnus Ieiunantium* of Prudentius', *ELN* 4 (1966–7), 244–7

Kelly, Henry Ansgar, 'Bishop, Prioress and Bawd in the Stews of Southwerk', *Speculum* 75: 2 (2000), 342–88

Kemna, K., 'Der Begriff 'Schiff' im Französischen' (PhD thesis, Marburg, 1901)

Kenny, Anthony, Norman Kretzman and Jan Pinborg, eds, *The Cambridge History of Later Medieval Philosophy: From the Rediscovery of Aristotle to the Disintegration of Scholasticism 1100–1600* (Cambridge, 1982)

Kircher, Timothy, 'The Sea as an Image of Temporality among Tuscan Dominicans and Humanists in the Fourteenth Century', in *Time and Eternity: The Medieval Discourse*, ed. Gerhard Jaritz and Gerson Moreno-Riaño (Turnhout, 2003), pp. 283–94

Kiser, Lisa J., '*Andreas* and the *lifes weg*: Convention and Innovation in Old English Metaphor', *Neuphilologische Mitteilungen* 85 (1984), 65–75

Kissack, Jr., Robert Ashton, 'The Sea in Anglo-Saxon and Middle English Poetry', *Washington University Studies: Humanities Series* 13 (1926), 371–89

Klein, Bernhard, *Fictions of the Sea: Critical Perspectives on the Ocean in British Literature and Culture* (Aldershot, 2002)

Kliege, Herma, *Weltbild und Darstellungspraxis hochmittelalterlicher Weltkarten* (Münster, 1991)

Kolve, V. A., *Chaucer and the Imagery of Narrative* (London, 1984)

Kötting, Bernhard, *Peregrinatio religiosa. Wallfahrten in der Antike und das Pilgerwesen in der alten Kirche*, Forschungen zur Volkskunde 33–35 (Münster, 1950; second edn 1980)

Kowaleski, Maryanne, 'The Commercialization of the Sea Fisheries in Medieval England and Wales', *International Journal of Maritime History* 15:2 (2003), 177–232

—— 'The Expansion of the South-western Fisheries in Late-Medieval England', *Economic History Review* 53:3 (2000), 429–54

Kozikowski, Stanley J., 'Allegorical Meanings in Skelton's *The Bowge of Courte*', *Philological Quarterly* 61:3 (1982), 305–15

—— 'Lydgate, Machiavelli and More and Skelton's *Bowge of Courte*', *American Notes and Queries* 15 (1977), 66–7

Krieger, Karl-Friedrich, *Ursprung und Wurzeln der Rôles d'Oléron* (Cologne, 1970)

Larmat, Jean, 'L'eau dans la *Navigation de saint Brandan de Benedeit*', in *L'eau au moyen âge*, Sénéfiance 15 (Aix-en-Provence, 1985), pp. 233–46

Latham, R. A., *Revised Medieval Latin World-List From British and Irish Sources* (Oxford, 1999; first published 1965)

Lavezzo, Kathy, *Angels on the Edge of the World: Geography, Literature and English Community, 1000–1534* (Ithaca, NY, 2006)

Lee, Brian S., 'Jonah in *Patience* and Prudentius', *Florilegium* 4 (1982), 194–209

Lee, Insung, 'The Tradition of Christian Sea Symbolism in Medieval English Poetry and Milton' (unpublished PhD thesis, University of Oklahoma, 1996)

Legge, M. D., 'Anglo-Norman Hagiography and the Romances', *Medievalia et Humanistica*, n.s. 6 (1975), 41–9

—— *Anglo-Norman Literature and Its Background* (Oxford, 1963)

Le Goff, Jacques, 'Le désert-forêt dans l'occident médiéval', in *L'Imaginaire médiéval* (Paris, 1985), pp. 59–85

Lenoir, Nicolas, 'L'eau et la mer dans la Chanson d'Aiquin (ca 1190–1200)', in *L'épopée romane, I–II*, ed. Gabriel Bianciotto, Claudio Galderisi and Bernard Guidot (Poitiers, 2002), pp. 917–25

Lerer, Seth, 'Old English and Its Afterlife', in *The Cambridge History of Medieval Literature*, ed. David Wallace (Cambridge, 1999), pp. 7–34

Lesky, Albin, *Thalatta – Der Weg der Griechen zum Meer* (Vienna, 1947)

Lester, G. A., 'The Books of a Fifteenth-Century English Gentleman: Sir John Paston', *Neuphilologische Mitteilungen* 88 (1987), 200–17

Levin, Craig, 'Seakeeping: The Effort to Maintain English Naval Superiority During the Years 1450 to 1480', available at http://www.florilegium.org/files/Travel/Seakeeping-pt1-art.html

Lewis, Archibald, *The Northern Seas, AD 300–1000* (Princeton, 1958)

—— ed., *The Sea and Medieval Civilisations* (London, 1978)

—— ed. with T. Runyan, *European Naval and Maritime History, 300–1500* (Bloomington, IN, 1985)

Lewis, Suzanne, *The Art of Matthew Paris in the Chronica Majora* (Aldershot, 1987)

—— *Reading Images: Narrative Discourse and Reception in the Thirteenth-Century Illuminated Apocalypse* (Cambridge, 1995)

Liljegren, S. B., 'Has the Poet of *Patience* Read *De Jona*?', *Englische Studien* 48 (1914), 337–41

Liszka, Thomas R., and Lorna E. M. Walker, *The North Sea World: Studies in the Cultural History of North-Western Europe in the Middle Ages* (Dublin, 2001)

Longmate, Norman, *Defending the Island from Caesar to the Armada* (London, 1989; repr. 2001)

Lorenz, Bernd, 'Apuntes para la imagen del mar en las *Confesiones* de san Augustin', *Augustinus* 31 (1986), 179–84

Lundberg, Anita, 'Being Lost at Sea: Ontology, Epistemology and a Whale Hunt', *Ethnography* 2:4 (2001), 533–56

Luttrell, Claude 'Arthurian Geography: The Islands of the Sea', *Neophilologus* 83:2 (1999), 187–96

McCobb, L. M., 'The Traditional Background of *Partonopeu de Blois*. An Additional Note', *Neophilologus* 60:4 (1976), 608–10

McCormick, Michael, *Origins of the European Economy* (Cambridge, 2001)

McCroskery, Margaret, 'Tristan and the Dionysian Sea: Passion and the Iterative Sea Motif in the Legends of Tristan and Isolde', *Midwest Quarterly* 13 (1972), 409–22

McCulloch, Florence, 'Pierre de Beauvais' *Lacovie*', *MLN* 71:2 (1956), 100–1

McEvoy, James, *The Philosophy of Robert Grosseteste* (Oxford, 1982)

McGinn, Bernard, 'Ocean and Desert as Symbols of Mystical Absorption in the Christian Tradition', *Journal of Religion* 74:2 (1994), 155–81

—— *Visions of the End – Apocalyptic Traditions in the Middle Ages* (New York, 1979)

McPherson, Clair Wade, 'The Sea as Desert: Early English Spirituality and *The Seafarer*', *American Benedictine Review* 38:2 (1987), 115–26

Manwaring, G. E., '*The Libel of English Policy*', *Times Literary Supplement* (29 June and 13 July 1922)

Marsden, R. G., *Documents Relating to Law and Custom of the Sea* (London, 1915–16)

Marshall, Tristan, '*The Tempest* and the British Imperium in 1611', *The Historical Journal* 41:2 (1998), 375–400

Martinsson-Wallin, Helene, 'Sea, Land and Sky as Structuring Principles in Easter Island Prehistory', *Rapa Nui Journal* 16:2 (2002), 74–6

Meale, C. M., '*The Libelle of Englyshe Polycye* and Mercantile Literary Culture in Late-Medieval London', in *London and Europe in the Later Middle Ages*, ed. Julia Boffey and Pamela King (London, 1995), pp. 181–228

Medas, Stefano, *De rebus nauticis: L'arte della navigazione nel mondo antico* (Rome, 2004)

Meier, Dirk, *Seafarers, Merchants and Pirates in the Middle Ages*, trans. Angus McGeoch (Woodbridge, 2006)

Mellon, James Park, '*Patience*: The Story of Jonah in a Middle English Poem' (unpublished PhD thesis, Yale University, 1972)

Metlitzki, Dorothee, *The Matter of Araby in Medieval England* (London and New Haven, CT, 1977)

Mettmann, Walter, 'Zu einigen nautischen Termini im Tristan-Roman von Thomas', in *Verba et Vocabula: Festschrift für E. Gamillscheg*, ed. Helmut Stimm and Julius Wilhelm (Munich, 1968), pp. 319–21

Meuwese, Martine, 'Uit *de zee*', *Madoc* 13:4 (1999), 256–7

Michelet, Fabienne, 'Centrality, Marginality and Distance: Britain's Changing Location on the Map of the World', in *The Space of English*, ed. David Spurr and Cornelia Tschichold, Swiss Papers in English Language and Literature 17, pp. 51–68

—— *Creation, Migration and Conquest: Imaginary Geography and Sense of Space in Old English Literature* (Oxford, 2006)

Miller, R., 'The Early Medieval Seamen and the Church: Contacts Ashore', *The Mariner's Mirror* 89:2 (2003), 132–50

Mitchell, Bruce, and Fred C. Robinson, *A Guide to Old English* (Oxford, 1982; sixth edition, 2001)

Mollat du Jourdin, Michel, *Europe and the Sea* (Oxford, 1993)

—— *Sea Charts of the Early Explorers: Thirteenth to Seventeenth Century* (New York, 1984)

Moorman, F. W., *The Interpretation of Nature in English Poetry from Beowulf to Shakespeare* (Strasbourg, 1905; repr. 1992)

Morison, Samuel Eliot, *The European Discovery of America: The Northern Voyages AD 500–1600* (New York, 1971)

—— 'The Sea in Literature', *Atlantic Monthly* 196:3 (1955), 67–77

Morris, Richard, *Time's Arrows: Scientific Attitudes Towards Time* (New York, 1984)

Morton, Lena B., *The Influence of the Sea upon English Poetry* (New York, 1976)

Mostert, Marco, 'Zoals een zeeman aan het einde van de reis', *Madoc* 13:4 (1999), 195–202

Mould, D. Pochin, 'St Brendan: Celtic Vision and Romance', in *Ireland of the Saints* (London, 1953), pp. 153–70

Murray, K. M. E., *The Constitutional History of the Cinque Ports* (Manchester, 1935)

Negriolli, Claude, 'La santé venue d'ailleurs. Simples, drogues et excipients dans un poème anglais du Moyen-Age', *Littérature, Médecine, Société* 4 (1982), 132–48

Nero, Karen, 'The End of Insularity', in *The Cambridge History of the Pacific Islanders*, ed. Donald Denoon (Cambridge, 1997), pp. 439–67

Neville, Jennifer, *Representations of the Natural World in Old English Poetry*, Cambridge Studies in Anglo-Saxon England 27 (Cambridge, 1999)

Newstead, E., 'The Traditional Background of *Partonopeu de Blois*', *PMLA* 61:4 (1946), 916–40

Nicholson, Peter, The *Man of Law's Tale*: What Chaucer Really Owed to Gower', *Chaucer Review* 26:2 (1991), 153–74

—— *Love and Ethics in Gower's* Confessio Amantis (Ann Arbor, MI, 2005)

Nicholson, R. H., '*Patience*: Reading the *Prophetia Jonae*', *Medievalia et Humanistica*, n.s. 16:8 (1998), 97–115

Nicolas, N. H., *History of the Royal Navy*, 2 vols (London, 1847)

Niitemaa, Vilho, *Das Strandrecht in Nordeuropa im Mittelalter* (Helsinki, 1955)

'Notes on the Chatham Islands', *Journal of the Anthropological Institute of Great Britain and Ireland* 28 (1898), 343–5 (correspondence from J. W. Williams)

O'Donnell, Victoria and Garth S. Jowett, *Propaganda and Persuasion* (San Francisco, 1992)

Ohler, Norbert, *Reisen im Mittelalter* (Munich, 1986)

Okken, Lambertus, 'Schiffe und Häfen in drei Episoden von Gottfrieds "Tristan"-Roman', in *Spectrum Medii Aevi: Essays in Early German Literature in Honour of George Fenwick Jones*, ed. William C. McDonald (Göppingen, 1983), pp. 429–44

O'Loughlin, Thomas, 'Living in the Ocean', in *Studies in the Cult of Saint Columba*, ed. Cormac Bourke (Dublin, 1997), pp. 11–23

Olsen, Karin, 'The Dichotomy of Land and Sea in the Old English *Andreas*', *English Studies* 79 (1998), 385–94

O'Neill, Timothy, *Merchants and Mariners in Medieval Ireland* (Dublin, 1997)

Oshitari, Kinshiro, 'The Sea in *Beowulf*', *Studies in English Literature* (1973), 3–18

Owst, G. R., *Literature and Pulpit in Medieval England – A Neglected Chapter in the History of English Letters and of the English People* (Cambridge, 1933; repr. Oxford, 1961)

Parry, J. H., *The Discovery of the Sea* (London, 1974)

Peyronnet, Georges, 'Un document capital de l'histoire du droit maritime: Les rôles d'Oléron, XII–XVII siècles', *Sources, Travaux Historiques* 8 (1986), 3–10

Piggort, Francis Taylor, *The Freedom of the Seas* (Oxford, 1919)

Plaut, Fred, 'Where is Paradise? The Mapping of a Myth', *Map Collector* 29:2 (1984), 2–7

Potter, Pitman B., *The Freedom of the Seas in History, Law and Politics* (New York, 1924; repr. Buffalo 2002)

Purcell, N., 'The Boundless Sea of Unlikeness? On Defining the Mediterranean', *Mediterranean Historical Review* 18:2 (2003), 9–29

—— with Peregrine Horden, *The Corrupting Sea – A Study of Mediterranean History* (Oxford, 2000)

Putter, Ad, *An Introduction to the Gawain-Poet* (London and New York, 1996)

—— 'Walewein in the Otherworld and the Land of Prester John', *Arthurian Literature* 17 (1999), 79–99

Raban, Jonathan, ed., *Oxford Book of the Sea* (Oxford, 1992)

Rahner, Hugo, *Symbole der Kirche* (Salzburg, 1964)

Ramras-Rauch, Gila, 'The Response of Biblical Man to the Challenge of the Sea', in *Poetics of the Elements in the Human Condition: The Sea*, ed. Anna-Teresa Tymieniecka, Annalecta Husserliana 19 (1985), pp. 139–48

Reddé, Michel, *Mare Nostrum: Les infrastructures, le dispositif et l'histoire de la marine militaire sous l'Empire romain* (Rome and Paris, 1986)

Reinhard, J. R., 'Setting Adrift in Medieval Law and Literature', *PMLA* 56 (1941), 33–68

Relaño, Francesco, 'Paradise in Africa: The History of a Geographical Myth from its Origins in Medieval Thought to its Gradual Demise in Early Modern Europe', *Terrae Incognitae* 36 (2004), 1–11

Reynolds, Susan, *Fiefs and Vassals: The Medieval Evidence Reinterpreted* (New York and Oxford, 1994)

Rhodes Peschel, Enid, 'Structural Parallels in Two Flood Myths: Noah and the Maori', *Folklore* 82:2 (1971), 116–23

Rice, E. E., *The Sea and History* (Stroud, 1996)

Richard, Jean, 'Le transport outre-mer de croisés et des pèlerins (XIIe–XVe siècles)', in *Maritime Aspects of Migration*, ed. K. Friedland, Quellen und Darstellungen zur hansischen Geschichte n.s. 34 (Cologne, 1989), pp. 3–25

Richmond, Colin, 'English Naval Power in the Fifteenth Century', *History*, n.s. 52 (1967), 1–15

—— 'The Keeping of the Seas during the Hundred Years War: 1422–1440', *History*, n.s. 49 (1964), 283–98

—— 'The War at Sea', in *The Hundred Years War*, ed. K. A. Fowler (London, 1971), pp. 96–121

Ridyard, Susan, '*Condigna Veneratio*: Post-Conquest Attitudes to the Saints of the Anglo-Saxons', in *Anglo-Norman Studies* 9, ed. R. Allen Brown (Woodbridge, 1987), pp. 180–206

Ritchie, R. L. G., 'The Date of *The Voyage of St Brendan*', *Medium Aevum* 19 (1950), 64–6

Robbins, R. H., 'Political Action Poem, 1463', *MLN* 71:4 (1956), 245–8

Roberts, Michael, 'Rhetoric and Poetic Imitation in Avitus's Account of the Crossing of the Red Sea (*De spiritalis historiae gestis* 5.371–702)', *Traditio* (1983), 29–80

Rodger, N. A. M., *The Safeguard of the Sea: A Naval History of Britain: 660–1649* (London, 1997)

Rondet, Henri, 'Le symbolism de la mer chez saint Augustin', in *Augustinus Magister: Etudes Augustiniennes*, 3 vols (Paris, 1954), pp. 691–791

Rose, John Holland, 'Chivalry and the Sea', in *The Indecisiveness of Modern War: And Other Essays* (Port Washington, NY, 1968; originally published 1927; first read as a lecture on 25 April 25 1923), pp. 180–95

Rose, Susan, *Medieval Naval Warfare, 1000–1500* (London and New York, 2001)

—— *The Navy of the Lancastrian Kings: Accounts and Inventories of William Soper, Keeper of the King's Ships, 1422–1427*, Navy Records Society Publications 132 (London, 1982)

Roth, Cecil, 'Jewish Antecedents of Christian Art', *Journal of the Warburg and Courtauld Institutes* 16:1/2 (1953), 24–44

Runyan, Timothy J., 'The Relationship of Northern and Southern Seafaring Techniques in Late Medieval Europe', in *Medieval Ships and the Birth of Technological Societies*, ed. Paul Adam, Salvino Busuttil and Christiane Villain-Gandossi, 2 vols (Valetta, 1991), vol. 2, pp. 197–209

—— 'The Rolls of Oleron and the Admiralty Courts in Fourteenth-Century England', *American Journal of Legal History* 19:2 (1975), 95–111

—— 'Ships and Mariners in Later Medieval England', *Journal of British Studies* 16 (1977), 1–17

—— ed. with Archibald Lewis, *European Naval and Maritime History, 300–1500* (Bloomington, IN, 1985)

Russell, J. Stephen, 'Skelton's *Bouge of Court*: A Nominalist Allegory', *Renaissance Papers* (1980), 1–9

de Saint-Denis, E., *La rôle de la mer dans la poesie latine* (Paris, 1935)

Saito, Isamu, 'The *Gawain*-Poet's Use of the Bible in *Patience* and *Cleanness*', *Poetica* 6 (1976), 46–63

Salmond, John W., 'Territorial Waters', *Law Quarterly Review* 34 (1918), 235–52

Sandahl, Bertil, *Middle English Sea Terms*, 3 vols (Uppsala, 1951–82)

Saunders, Corinne, *The Forest of Medieval Romance* (Cambridge, 1993)

Sayers, William, 'Chaucer's Shipman and the Law Marine', *Chaucer Review* 37:2 (2002), 145–58

—— 'Naval Architecture in Marie de France's *Guigemar*', *Germanisch-Romanische Monatsschrift* 54:4 (2004), 379–91

—— 'Sea-changes in the *Roman de Tristan* of Thomas and Dante's *bufera infernal* (*Inferno* 5)', *Romance Quarterly* 51 (2004), 67–71

—— 'Spiritual Navigation in the Western Sea: *Sturlunga saga* and Adomnán's *Hinba*', *Scripta Islandica* 44 (1993), 30–42

—— 'Twelfth-Century Norman and Irish Literary Evidence for Ship-Building and Sea-faring Techniques of Norse Origin', *Heroic Age: A Journal of Early Medieval Northwestern Europe* 8 (2005), available at http://www.heroicage.org/issues/8/sayers.html

Scafi, Alessandro, 'Mapping Eden: Cartographies of the Earthly Paradise', in *Mappings*, ed. Denis Cosgrove (London, 1999), pp. 50–70

Scafi, Alessandro, *Mapping Paradise: A History of Heaven on Earth* (London, 2006)

Scafi, Alessandro, 'The Notion of Earthly Paradise from the Patristic Era to the Fifteenth Century' (unpublished PhD thesis, Warburg Institute, University of London, 1999)

Scammell, G. V., *The World Encompassed: The First European Maritime Empires c. 800–1650* (London, 1981)

Scattergood, John, 'The *Libelle of Englyshe Polycye*: The Nation and Its Place', in *Nation, Court and Culture: New Essays on Fifteenth-Century English Poetry*, ed. Helen Cooney (Dublin, 2001), pp. 28–49

—— *Politics and Poetry in the Fifteenth Century* (London, 1971)

Schama, Simon, *Landscape and Memory* (London, 1996)

Scheidegger, J. R., 'Flux et reflux de la marée et du désir dans le Tristan et Iseut', in *L'eau au moyen age. Symboles et usages*, ed. B. Ribémont, Actes de colloque d'Orléans, May 1994, (Orléans, 1996), pp. 111–31

Schnall, Uwe, 'Practical Navigation in the Late Middle Ages – Some Remarks on the Transfer of Knowledge from the Mediterranean to the Northern Seas', in *Medieval Ships and Birth of Technological Societies*, ed. Paul Adam, Salvino Busuttil and Christiane Villain-Gandossi, 2 vols (Valetta, 1991), pp. 271–9

Schoepperle, Gertrude, *Tristan and Isolt: A Study of the Sources of the Romance*, 2 vols (Frankfurt am Main, 1913)

Schönbäck, Bengt, 'The Custom of Burial in Boats', in *Vendel Period Studies: Transactions of the Boat-Grave Symposium in Stockholm*, ed. J. P. Lamm and H.-A. Nordström (Stockholm, 1983), pp. 123–32

Semple, Ellen Churchill, 'Oceans and Enclosed Seas: A Study in Anthropo-Geography', *Bulletin of the American Geographical Society* 40:4 (1908), 193–209

Shirt, D. J., 'A Note on the Etymology of Le Morholt', *Tristania* 1 (1975), 21–8

Singer, S., *Apollonius von Tyrus: Untersuchung über das Fortleben des antiken Romans in späteren Zeiten* (Halle a. S., 1895)

Smith, Brendan, *Colonisation and Conquest in Medieval Ireland. The English in Louth, 1170–1330* (Cambridge, 1999)

—— ed., *Britain and Ireland 900–1300. Insular Responses to European Change* (Cambridge, 1999)

Smith, D. K., 'To Passe the See in Shortt Space': Mapping the World in the Digby *Mary Magdalen'*, *Medieval and Renaissance Drama in England* 18 (2005), 193–214

Smith, Roger A., 'Seafaring Imagery in Old English Poetry' (unpublished PhD thesis, Stanford University, CA, 1987)

—— 'Ships and the Dating of *Beowulf'*, *American Notes and Queries* 3:3 (1990), 99–103

Sobecki, Sebastian I., 'Bertuinus von Malonne', *Biographisch-Bibliographisches Kirchenlexikon*, vol. 26 (Hamm, 2006), columns 141–3

—— 'From the *Désert Liquide* to the Sea of Romance: Benedeit's *Le Voyage de Saint Brandan* and the Irish *Immrama'*, *Neophilologus* 87:2 (2003), 193–207

—— 'The Interpretation of *The Seafarer*: A Re-examination of the Pilgrimage Theory', *Neophilologus*, 91:4 (2007) forthcoming

—— 'Littoral Encounters:The Shore as Cultural Interface in *King Horn'*, *Al-Masaq: Islam and the Medieval Mediterranean* 18:1 (2006), 79–86

—— 'Mandeville's Thought of the Limit: The Discourse of Similarity and Difference in *The Travels of Sir John Mandeville'*, *Review of English Studies* 53:3 (2002), 329–43

—— 'Muddy Waters: *Unclæne Fisc* in Ælfric's *Colloquy'*, *Neuphilologische Mitteilungen* 107:3 (2006), 285–9

—— 'A Source for the Magical Ship in the *Partonopeu de Blois* and Marie de France's *Guigemar'*, *Notes and Queries* 48:3 (2001), 220–2

—— 'The 2,000 Saracens of *King Horn'*, *Notes and Queries* 52:4 (2005), 443–5

de Souza, Philip, *Seafaring and Civilization: Maritime Perspectives on World History* (London, 2001)

Speed, Diane, 'The Saracens of *King Horn'*, *Speculum* 65:3 (1990), 564–95

Squatriti, Paolo, 'How the Irish Sea (May Have) Saved Irish Civilisation', *Comparative Studies in Society and History* 43:3 (2001), 615–30

—— 'Offa's Dyke Between Nature and Culture', *Environmental History* 9:1 (2004), 37–56

Starr, Chester G., *The Influence of Sea Power on Ancient History* (New York, 1989)

Steel, Robert W., 'The Trade of the United Kingdom with Europe', *Geographical Journal* 87:6 (1936), 525–33

Stein, Robert M., 'Making History English: Cultural Identity and Historical Explanation in William of Malmesbury and La amon's *Brut'*, in *Text and Territory: Geographical Imagination in the European Middle Ages*, ed. Sealy Gilles and Sylvia Tomasch (Philadelphia, 1998), pp. 97–115

Stell, Geoffrey, 'By Land and Sea in Medieval and Early Modern Scotland', *Revue of Scottish Culture* 4 (1988), 24–43

Streicher, Sonnfried, *Fabelwesen des Meeres* (Rostock, 1982)

Strijbosch, Clara, *De Bronnen van De Reis van Sint Brandaan* (Hilversum, 1995)

—— 'Een reis naar inzicht. *De Reis van Sint Brandaan* tegen de achtergrond van twaalfde-eeuwse theologische opvattingen over zonde en genade', *Nieuwe taalgis* 81:6 (1988), 526–43

—— 'Himmel, Höllen und Paradiese in Sanct Brandans *Reise*', *Zeitschrift für deutsche Philologie* 118 (1999), 50–68

Strzelczyk, Jerzy, 'Społeczne aspekty iroszkockiej peregrinatio', in *Peregrinationes – pielgrzymki w kulturze dawnej Europy*, ed. Halina Manikowska and Hanna Zaremska, *Colloquia Mediaevalia Varsoviensia* 2 (Warsaw, 1995), pp. 39–50

Swan, Mary, and Elaine M. Treharne, eds, *Rewriting Old English in the Twelfth Century*, Cambridge Studies in Anglo-Saxon England 30 (Cambridge, 2000)

Szabo, Vicki Ellen, 'Whaling in Early Medieval Britain', *Haskins Society Journal* 9 (2001), 137–57

Szarmach, Paul E., 'Three Versions of the Jonah Story: An Investigation of Narrative Technique in Old English Homilies', *Anglo-Saxon England* 1 (1972), 183–92

—— '*The Vercelli Homilies*: Style and Structure', in *The Old English Homily and Its Background*, ed. Paul E. Szarmach and B. F. Huppé (Albany, NY, 1978), pp. 241–67

Szkilnik, Michelle, 'Seas, Islands and Continent in *L'Estoire del Saint Graal*', *Romance Languages Annual* 1 (1989), 322–7

Taylor, Frank, 'Some Manuscripts of the *Libelle of Englyshe Polycye*', *Bulletin of the John Rylands Library* 24 (1940), 376–418

Thompson, Stith, *Motif-Index of Folk Literature* (Copenhagen, 1955–8)

Tolan, John V., *Saracens: Islam in the Medieval European Imagination* (New York, 2000)

Torti, Anna, 'Reality of Allegory or Allegory of Reality? Skelton's Dilemma in *The Bowge of Courte* and *Speke Parott*', *Textus: English Studies in Italy* 1 (1988), 51–80

Townsend, David, 'Anglo-Latin Hagiography and the Norman Transition', *Exemplaria* 3 (1991), 385–433

Treneer, Anne, *The Sea in English Literature – From Beowulf to Donne* (Liverpool, 1926)

Trotter, David, '*Oceano* [sic] *Vox*: You Never Know Where a Ship Comes From: On Multilingualism and Language-Mixing in Medieval Britain', in *Aspects of Multilingualism in European Language History*, ed. Kurt Braunmüller and Gisella Ferraresi (Amsterdam, 2003), pp. 15–33

Tubach, F. C., *Index Exemplorum: A Handbook of Medieval Religious Tales* (Helsinki, 1969)

Tymieniecka, Anna-Teresa, *Poetics of the Elements in the Human Condition* (Dordrecht, 1985)

Tyson, Cynthia H., 'Noah's Flood, the River Jordan, the Red Sea: Staging in the Towneley Cycle', *Comparative Drama* 8 (1974), 101–11

Ullmann, Walter, 'Bartolus and English Jurisprudence', in *Bartolo da Sassoferrato: Studi e documenti per il VI centenario*, ed. D. Segolini, 2 vols (Milan, 1961), vol. 1, pp. 49–73

Unger, Richard, 'Carvel-building in Northern Europe before 1450', *Mariner's Mirror* 57:3 (1971), 331–3

—— *The Ship in the Medieval Economy 600–1600* (London, 1980)

—— ed., *Cogs, Caravels and Galleons: The Sailing Ship 1000–1650* (London, 1994)

—— with John E. Hattendorf, *War at Sea in the Middle Ages and Renaissance* (Woodbridge, 2003)

Utterback, Kristine T., 'Pirates and Pilgrims on the Late-Medieval Journey to Jerusalem', *Medieval Perspectives* 12 (1997), 123–33

Vaughan, Richard, *Matthew Paris* (Cambridge, 1959; reissued 1979)

Verdon, Jean, *Travel in the Middle Ages* (Notre Dame, IN, 2003)

Vieira, Mónica Brito, '*Mare Liberum* vs. *Mare Clausum*: Grotius, Freitas and Selden's Debate on Dominion over the Seas', *Journal of the History of Ideas* 64:3 (2003), 361–77

Wachsmuth, Dietrich, '*Pompimos o daimon* – Untersuchungen zu den antiken Sakralhandlungen bei Seereisen' (unpublished PhD thesis, FU Berlin, 1967)

Wall, Kathryn, 'Saint Gregory's *Moralia* as a Possible Source for the Middle English *Patience*', *Notes and Queries* n.s. 39:4 (1992), 436–8

Wallace, David, *Margery in Dansk: The Middle Ages Catch Us Up*, William Matthews Lecture 2005 (London, 2006)

—— '"Whan She Translated Was": A Chaucerian Critique of the Petrarchan Academy', in *Literary Practice and Social Change in Britain, 1380–1539*, ed. Lee Patterson (Berkeley, CA, 1990), pp. 156–215

Walter, Philippe, *Le gant de verre. Le mythe de Tristan et Yseut* (La Gacilly, 1990)

Ward, Robin M., 'An Elucidation of Certain Maritime Passages in English Alliterative Poetry of the Fourteenth Century' (unpublished MA thesis, University of Keele, 1991)

—— 'The Mystery of the Medieval Shipmaster – The Shipmaster at Law, in Business and at Sea' (unpublished PhD thesis, Birkbeck College, 2000)

von Wartburg, Walther, *Französisches etymologisches Wörterbuch: Eine Darstellung des galloromanischen Sprachschatzes* (Bonn, 1929)

Watts, Pauline M., 'Prophecy and Discovery: On the Spiritual Origins of Christopher Columbus's "Enterprise of the Indies"', *American Historical Review* (1985), 73–102

Webster, K. G. T., 'Two Notes on Chaucer's Sea-Fight', *Modern Philology* 25:3 (1928), 291–2

West, Delno C., 'Christopher Columbus, Lost Biblical Sites and the Last Crusade', *Catholic Historical Review* 78:4 (1992), 519–41

Whiteley, James G., 'History of the Freedom of the Seas', *The New England Magazine* 15:2 (1893), 233–40

Whitelock, Dorothy, 'The Interpretation of *The Seafarer*', in *Early Cultures of Northwest Europe*, ed. Cyril Fox and Bruce Dickins, H. M. Chadwick Memorial Studies (Cambridge, 1950), pp. 261-72

Whitfield, Peter, *The Charting of the Oceans: Ten Centuries of Maritime Maps* (London, 1996)

Wilson, Kathleen, *The Island Race: Englishness, Empire and Gender in the Eighteenth Century* (London and New York, 2003)

Windeatt, Barry, 'Introduction: Reading and Re-reading *The Book of Margery Kempe*', in *A Companion to the Book of Margery Kempe*, ed. John H. Arnold and Katherine J. Lewis (Cambridge, 2004), pp. 1–16

Wolf, Thomas, 'Massentransport zur See und die Quantifizierung für die historische Forschung', in *Der hansische Sonderweg? Beiträge zur Sozial- und Wirt-*

schaftsgeschichte der Hanse, ed. Stuart Jenks and Michael North (Cologne, 1993), pp. 225–34

Wooding, Jonathan, 'St Brendan's Boat: Dead Hides and the Living Sea in Columban and Related Hagiography', in *Studies in Irish Hagiography: Saints and Scholars*, ed. John Carey, Máire Herbert and Pádraig Ó Riain (Dublin, 2001), pp. 77–92

—— ed., *The Otherworld Voyage in Early Irish Literature* (Dublin, 2000)

Zeeman, Nicolette, *Piers Plowman and the Medieval Discourse of Desire* (Cambridge, 2006)

Ziegler, Vickie, 'Points of Law at the Point of a Sword: Tristan's Duel with Morolt in the North Sea World', in *The North Sea World in the Middle Ages: Studies in the Cultural History of North-Western Europe*, ed. Thomas R. Liszka and Lorna E. M. Walker (Dublin, 2001), pp. 33–51

Ziolkowski, Jan, 'Folklore and Learned Lore in Letaldus's Whale Poem', *Viator* 15 (1984), 107–18

Zwierlein, Otto, 'Spuren der Tragödien Senecas bei Bernardus Silvestris, Petrus Pictor und Marbod von Rennes', *Mittellateinisches Jahrbuch* 27 for 1987 (1989), 171–96

——, 'Spuren der Tragödien Senecas bei Bernardus Silvestris, Petrus Pictor, Marbod von Rennes und Hildebert von Le Mans. Mit einem Nachtrag: Seneca als Wegbereiter der *tragoediae elegiacae* des 12. Jahrhunderts', in *Otto Zwierlein, Lucubrationes Philologae*, ed. R. Jakobi, R. Junge and C. Schmitz (Berlin, 2004), vol. 1, pp. 337–84

Index

For works originally written in Latin, the English title is given unless the Latin title is more widely used. References to illustrations and their captions appear in bold type.